The Politics of Sport

Sport is an essential part of community structure, membership and identity. Whether on the field of play, in stadia, or on the streets, sport has consistently brought together disparate individuals to share culture, values and memories. Nowadays these relationships are being rewritten through the effects of global socio-economic practices, the interventions of government, the impact of cultural imperialism and, at the local level, through the actions of individuals and new constituencies that are emerging in response. Furthermore, this generates discourse on matters of regional and national identity.

This book presents a range of essays that examine the relationship between sport and society through the conceptual lenses of community, mobility and identity. Drawing upon insights from contemporary history and current political phenomena from leading academic specialists in the field, the book addresses cross-cutting themes such as loyalty and allegiance, migration and integration, identity and collective memory, and the politics of resistance and change, which will be of interest to the political scientist, the contemporary historian and sport scholar alike.

This book was previously published as a special issue of the journal *Sport in Society*.

Paul Gilchrist is Research Fellow at the Centre for Sport Research, University of Brighton. His research interests are in the cultural politics of sport and leisure, in particular people-environment relations. He is co-founder and joint convenor of the Political Studies Association's sport and politics specialist study group.

Russell Holden is the Director of In the Zone Sport and Politics Consultancy. His organisation offers an insight into the complexities of sport, whole-heartedly embracing the connection between sport and politics. He is co-founder and joint convenor of the Political Studies Association's sport and politics specialist study group and a visiting lecturer at Southampton Solent University.

The Politics of Sport

Community, Mobility, Identity

Edited by
Paul Gilchrist and Russell Holden

LONDON AND NEW YORK

First published 2012
by Routledge
2 Park Square, Milton Park, Abingdon, Oxon, OX14 4RN

Simultaneously published in the USA and Canada
by Routledge
711 Third Avenue, New York, NY 10017

Routledge is an imprint of the Taylor & Francis Group, an informa business

© 2012 Taylor & Francis

This book is a reproduction of *Sport in Society*, vol.14, issue 2. The Publisher requests to those authors who may be citing this book to state, also, the bibliographical details of the special issue on which the book was based.

British Library Cataloguing in Publication Data
A catalogue record for this book is available from the British Library

ISBN13: 978-0-415-46311-9

Typeset in Times New Roman
by Taylor & Francis Books

Disclaimer
The publisher would like to make readers aware that the chapters in this book are referred to as articles as they had been in the special issue. The publisher accepts responsibility for any inconsistencies that may have arisen in the course of preparing this volume for print.

Printed and bound in Great Britain by the MPG Books Group

Contents

SPORT IN THE GLOBAL SOCIETY – CONTEMPORARY PERSPECTIVES

Series Editor: Boria Majumdar

THE POLITICS OF SPORT

Community, Mobility, Identity

Sport in the Global Society – Contemporary Perspectives
Series Editor: Boria Majumdar

The social, cultural (including media) and political study of sport is an expanding area of scholarship and related research. While this area has been well served by the *Sport in the Global Society* series, the surge in quality scholarship over the last few years has necessitated the creation of *Sport in the Global Society: Contemporary Perspectives*. The series will publish the work of leading scholars in fields as diverse as sociology, cultural studies, media studies, gender studies, cultural geography and history, political science and political economy. If the social and cultural study of sport is to receive the scholarly attention and readership it warrants, a cross-disciplinary series dedicated to taking sport beyond the narrow confines of physical education and sport science academic domains is necessary. *Sport in the Global Society: Contemporary Perspectives* will answer this need.

Titles in the Series

Introduction: the politics of sport – community, mobility, identity

Paul Gilchrist[a] and Russell Holden[b]

[a]Chelsea School, University of Brighton, UK; [b]Director, In the Zone Sport and Politics Consultancy

The politics of sport has come of age. Sport scholars from various disciplinary backgrounds have argued that there has been a movement from an ostensibly epiphenomenal and marginal subject area to one that has produced important insights and interventions. Allen Guttmann's retrospective of sport, politics and history in the *Journal of Contemporary History* shows how historians have raised awareness of the intersections between sport and politics; so much so that the conventional liberal mantra that 'sport and politics should not mix' now appears as an isolated prescription which buckles under historical scrutiny.[1] Well-established bodies of research, he goes on, now cover sport under fascism and communism; the politics of race, ethnicity and gender discrimination; the Olympic Games as a political force; and contextual (though theory-led) analyses of sport as a mirror of socio-economic capitalist relations.

The accumulation of a body of research and scholarship known as 'sport politics' has progressed so far, argues Lincoln Allison, that one can begin to speak of an 'old politics of sport' concerned with the actions of states – seen most clearly in the 'sports diplomacy' that disrupted the international sporting calendar of the 1970s and 1980s – to a 'new politics of sport' which interrogates a wider range of political agents and institutional actors, operating at subnational, national and transnational levels.[2] This shift has been spurred on, in particular, by globalization; the multiple flows of capital, people, products and processes which are rewriting how citizens act and behave in the world and how communities are formed and cohere. Sport has not been immune from globalization, indeed it is considered by many to be constituted by and constitutive of some of these processes;[3] ensconced within a globalized culture of consumption in which media conglomerates and capitalist interests play a prominent role in the staging, representation and reception of events, and also increasingly responsive to globalized political concerns such as human rights and the environment.

The maturing of a 'sport politics' poses difficulty for the researcher as the dimensions of the political become more nebulous, moving beyond the traditional fare of the political scientist – constitutions, institutions and ideologies – to cover intellectual concerns shared by other disciplines and inter-disciplines (e.g., state-economy relations; cultural identities; the concept of power). Such is the variety with which the 'political' can be deployed to the study of sport, argues Guttmann, that the notion of the 'political' itself suffers from analytical imprecision. A 'politics of sport' could conceivably cover anything from the use of sport by the Roman Catholic Church to questions concerning the media representation of women cricketers.[4]

While there are now multiple entry points to a politics of sport, the field has also erected some barriers to entry. Writing in *Newsweek* magazine during the 2010 Vancouver Winter Olympic Games, Christopher Hitchens railed against what he saw as the denigration of serious world issues within journalistic and everyday discourse. He wrote:

> Our own political discourse, already emaciated enough, has been further degraded by the continuous importation of sports 'metaphors': lame and vapid and cheery expressions like 'bottom of the ninth,' 'goal line,' and who knows what other tripe … it also increases the deplorable tendency to look at the party system as a matter of team loyalty, which is the most trivial and parochial form that attachment can take.[5]

The examples he gave – the diplomatic fall-out between Pakistan and India over the non-selection of Pakistani players for franchises within the Indian Premier League cricket tournament; the promotion of 'thugs and mediocrities' as 'role models' – probably reveal more about the complicity of media interests in generating political significance from sport than a widespread degradation of political culture. Yet, his position has much in common with an older generation of left-wing intellectuals like George Orwell or Alfred Williams who were convinced that sports were frivolous and trivial sources of parochial attachment and 'weapons of mass distraction'.[6] But the critical interrogation of sport has evolved. Within sport studies it is no longer seen as credible to rest upon outdated political sociologies that reduce sport to a cathartic function. The idea that sport is an opiate of the masses and part of a system of social control insufficiently explains its widespread appeal; it obfuscates ways in which sport has developed deep roots within communities and how sport is embroiled in our personal and social identities and visions of the good life. Furthermore, the 'bread and circuses' thesis has been challenged by commentators for ignoring a rich history of progressive struggle in and through sport. 'Just as sports can reflect the dominant ideas of our society, they can also reflect struggle', writes the radical sport journalist Dave Zirin.[7] A core theme of Garry Whannel's recently updated reissue *Culture, Politics and Sport: Blowing the Whistle Revisited* is the degree to which sport, its cultures, institutions and practices, has been transformed by years of sustained activism from below.[8] Prominent campaigns include the anti-apartheid sporting boycotts; the impacts of the women's movement, particularly in North America, in challenging sexist and patriarchal restrictions;[9] and the anti-racism campaigns in soccer and cricket. Sport carries a rich history of political activism which has not only shaped its form and direction but also made prominent the types of values to be respected, defended and promoted across societies. For this reason Whannel concludes,

> we should never regard popular culture as epiphenomenal or marginal – it remains a central element in the political process. It constitutes a meeting ground between popular common sense and organised political discourse, and for that reason alone, it is vital that we continue subjecting it to analysis and critique.[10]

How we subject sport to analysis and critique has been matched by an increased concern with how to conduct a politics of sport as an intellectual vocation.[11] Indeed, it may even be possible to speak of a spectrum of intellectual, interventionist and activist roles that claim to be performing a 'politics of sport'. There is a strong pedigree to follow. Within the academy one can look to figures such as the American sociologist Harry Edwards, whose opposition to the marginalization of the black athlete led him beyond an oppositional politics merely practised within the confines of the conference circuit and academic journals to organize the Olympic Project for Human Rights, which led to the iconic Black Power Salute protest by Smith and Carlos at the 1968 Mexico Olympics. The desire to inform public debate and to seek social change can be found in a growing literature that professes to practise a 'politics of sport'. It can be seen, for example, in the efforts of academics to expose the global governance of international sport through highlighting corruption and unethical conduct within international sports federations and in the variety of community-oriented projects that promote and support grassroots campaigns and initiatives for sport development.[12] At the other end of the spectrum are journalists like Zirin whose writings and commentary challenge us to confront the nature of sport in late capitalist society, carving a territory where many sport journalists fear to tread.[13] Zirin calls for sport to be 'reclaimed from the corporate pirates' and sees raising awareness of the history of sport-based protests, acknowledging their effectiveness and capacity to produce powerful symbolic messages, as a necessary part of that reclamation.[14] It is a cultural politics and critical praxis that closely allies itself with Chomsky's vision of the public intellectual as a sophisticated user of the tools of academic knowledge and critique who 'seek[s] the truth behind the veil of misrepresentation, ideology and class interest'.[15]

This widening of the politics of sport as a vocational option raises questions about the role of the public intellectual within the field of sport and its wider constituencies. In a thoughtful essay on sport, intellectuals and public sociology, Alan Bairner cautions against simple celebrations of opposition and resistance within the academy.[16] There is a tendency evident in much critical interpretivist literature, he argues, toward perpetual critique at the expense of affecting social change. Bairner contends that academia is crammed with people who don't like sport and take exception to its sexist, racist, exploitative or nationalistic expressions. It is full of critique rather than critical friends. What is needed, he writes, are more critical friends who can provide critical analyses (including historical reconstructions of struggles in sport) and a more pro-sport agenda. The question is not of the political nature of sport or that sport generates discussion, debate and conflict over particular values, but about how to conduct a deeper working relationship between scholars, sport practitioners and the public in affecting social and cultural change in and through sport.[17] Thus, rather than there being a fine balance to be struck between the pursuit of a critical analysis of sport and a more activist-oriented vision of the academic,[18] a politics of sport should be practised that maintains a critical position and methodological robustness, but never loses sight of the need to influence a public who do not necessarily share the same theoretical concerns or language.

It is a position that also rings true for the teaching of sport politics. Consider the following: ask students taking an introductory module on the politics of sport about their forms of political participation and more often than not you draw a crowd of blank faces; ask them to stand up and to examine each other's attire and they slowly become aware of the nature of their own political participation through noticing their wearing of wristbands that signify opposition to racism in soccer and t-shirts emblazoned with messages about Nike's exploitative production practices. These are not just struggles for grand causes for social justice, but ones that are also subtly played out on our bodies as broader cultural struggles. Whether today's student has played an intentional part in a collective effort to transform the social order or whether they are themselves victims of contemporary consumption practices in advanced liberal economies which reduce political activism to consumer behaviours is another matter. What is apparent is the very public ways in which the nature of sport and its ideological impacts are open to challenge; and the need for a greater a reflexivity to create connections with others in pursuit of social change by problematizing the status quo.

Dialogue is important. It is within this context that this special issue emerged. We were concerned that, compared to other sub-fields within sport studies (sport economics, sport geography, sport history, sport sociology), dialogue was not occurring between the interdisciplinary field of sport politics and its parent or home discipline, in this case political studies/science. This concern is not new. Jeffrey Hill's review of sport and politics noted that there had been a 'muted emphasis' within sport studies on politics with a capital 'P' – the classic art of government, institutions, political parties and political processes.[19] Whilst Lincoln Allison has maintained that the academic study of sport is so dominated by socio-historical and sociological perspectives that a weakened discussion of what makes sport 'political' occurs. Allison frames this in terms of 'contextualisers' who offer explanation and criticism by re-describing events, and 'philosophisers' who enquire into the meanings and values inherent in sporting activity.[20] The dominance of the 'contextualisers', he argues, robs the field of a more nuanced and creative discussion of the political in which concepts like 'civil society' and 'power' could feature more strongly. A political analysis of sport is favoured that is not confined purely to materialist emphases or structuralist interpretation, but which lends greater weight to the value systems that inform certain behaviours, identities and interests within sport. Whilst some support can be found for Allison's position within politics and international studies it is a provocative challenge which, to our best knowledge, has remained unanswered.[21]

Thus, the rationale for the production of this special issue of *Sport in Society* emerged from a recognition, following Allison, that political studies/science still has a greater role to play within sport studies. Conversely, we also felt that, despite characterizations of political studies within the United Kingdom as a 'broad church' receptive to multiple theorisations, analyses and uses of the political,[22] the reality, as others have acknowledged, is of a discipline that prioritizes an ahistorical, objectivist and materialist positivism that demarcates a field of study in overly narrow terms. Political studies often stands accused of limiting the tools of research, marginalizing normative concerns as 'unscientific' and isolating politics from the broader human sciences.[23] In this regard, the essays gathered together in this volume emerged from an attempt to bridge this sense of isolation, to foster greater dialogue, and to move towards a pluralistic model of political studies in which sport is no longer, to paraphrase Whannel, epiphenomenal or 'out of place'. In all cases the papers were received from attendees of the inaugural UK Political Studies Association Sport and Politics specialist study group annual conference, held at Greynogg, Wales, in February 2007. The group is an ongoing initiative to realize further avenues for the study and practice of a politics of sport (see www.sportpolitics.net).

The substantive material for the papers in this special issue addresses the inter-linked themes of community, mobility and identity. These themes were chosen to reveal the ways in which sport is bound to ideas about property, place and nationhood; and how in a global age these rooted connections and imagined senses of belonging are challenged by the movement of people, capital and technologies. It thus shares with the 'new mobilities paradigm' a concern for understanding how the world is being reshaped through movement and flux and, most importantly, what this tells us about the nature of political power and the relative dynamics between the global and local, the nation and market, and the indigenous and transnational.[24] The new mobilities paradigm provokes us to move away from a sedentary metaphysics, which territorializes identity, to explore the differentiated dynamics of a world characterized by networks of corporeal, virtual and imaginative mobilities.[25] Some are addressed in this special issue, with authors raising questions about the movement of fans and players, the mobility of international capital and aid, and technical expertise. Their treatment of these issues invites normative and emotive assessments of the ways in which capital disrupts forms of attachment and belonging, and how it threatens the moral life and stability of a community.[26]

However, the papers avoid the seductive pull of mobility and the all-too-easy fetishization of the transitory. To use John Urry's phrase, they address 'mobilities and moorings'; the connections to place are not severed or abandoned. What is emphasized is how communities negotiate change. This theme comes out strongly in the papers that deal with citizenship, cities and fans. The section on community opens with Williams and Hopkins utilizing the ongoing financial and ownership dramas at Liverpool football club as a yardstick for assessing how a long-established sporting community can have its heart and soul undermined by the influx of new investors and owners with a diametrically different set of core values to those long held within the club and its large fan-base. In threatening the community atmosphere of a football club seeking to compete with its wealthier rivals in Manchester and London, the actions of the co-owners have also brought the established identity of the club, based on the notion of collective solidarity, into question. In the case of Liverpool FC the dilemma has been intensified by the soccer-phobia of one of its co-owners. Williams and Hopkins focus on the cultural politics of support for Liverpool FC and argue that the global ownership, production and consumption patterns that characterize other clubs, which have been the site of anti-commercialization opposition, appear peculiarly out of place at Liverpool; a club that has a deep culture of cosmopolitanism, commercialism and global outlook − a legacy of the city's seafaring past. The analysis combines the contemporary, contextual and historical to offer a nuanced and scholarly reflection on the nature of the political economy of sport whilst recording, in copious detail, the differences evident in the desires of those committed to the football club both as decision-makers and fans.

The tension between community and mobility is explored by Gilchrist and Ravenscroft in their analysis of the political claims of canoeists to rights of access to waterways in England and Wales. Mobility emerges as a form of political and ethical potential as oppositional identities (e.g., 'the roving bandit') are played out on inland waterways as a challenge to enduring forms of socio-legal relations that govern the use of water-space. This is a long-standing dispute that has generated passionate defences of property rights against perceived forces of self-interest that would challenge the long-standing settlement of water as a source of community-based values and traditional ways of life. The authors outline how deliberate acts of transgression of the social and legal codes governing watersports constitute potential events of resistance that disrupt the habitual modalities of inhabiting space, producing fissures within which new lines of flight can emerge. They caution, however, that to be successful in the pursuit of their rights claims canoeists require a greater sensitivity to spatialized power relations than has previously been displayed, particularly those that adhere to property and stewardship of the environment.

In adhering to the more traditional approach to the 'old' politics of sport, as identified by Allison,[27] Little takes the opportunity to consider how an established, yet rebel, community sought to maintain its international sporting links whilst the great majority of the United Nations membership expressed serious misgivings concerning the nature of the Rhodesian regime under the stewardship of Ian Smith. Through this examination of international protest, Little focuses attention on an episode of contemporary history that has largely faded out of the public consciousness as it never quite made the impact of the anti-apartheid struggle in South Africa. Utilizing a broad variety of records to reconsider the sport boycott against Rhodesia, Little contrasts the rationale behind the boycott movement to show how it centred on the legitimacy of Ian Smith's regime (1965–79) rather than the racial issues that characterized the anti-apartheid sport boycott against South Africa. Furthermore, he outlines the central part Britain played in the campaign and the importance of state actors rather than public protest movements in seeking to enact policy change. Little's work reminds us that sport was used as one of a number of policy instruments to encourage and effect change, yet throughout the episode, the British government feared that its policy may have intensified the siege mentality of the white community that the Smith regime sought to protect. This study has considerable value today as EU governments consider their approach to the hostile and electorally questionable credentials of the current Iranian regime.

Whilst the mobility of capital was touched on by Hopkins and Williams, Walters explores the significance of this issue in the context of the expanding sports events industry and its growing politicization. In recognizing the economic benefits that sport can bring to communities through economic regeneration and improved infrastructure, politicians have shown themselves to be keen to lend their support to the bidding process for major sporting events. However, as Walters' research shows, the role of government in this process has been marked by a remarkable sense of inconsistency. Although the United Kingdom government seeks to protect and promote the reputation of Britain as a leading sporting venue through the Department of Culture, Media and Sport operating in conjunction with sport governing bodies, it has failed to take enough practical measures that would boost the prospects of luring more events and sportspersons to compete in British sport without being financially disadvantaged. Walters charts how the government could adjust its taxation policy to help realize its clearly stated ambition, yet it appears that at present politicians lose sight of the less quantifiable benefits of support when set against the bald financial statements offered by the Treasury. However, the root of the paradox lies in the inability to address the need for a coherent approach to sport policy that involves the input of all relevant government departments in a strategic fashion as opposed to thinking in the piecemeal fashion which has convinced UEFA to take the Champions League Final to Wembley in 2011.

Carter extends the discussion of mobility to fundamental issues of labour movement with his detailed exploration of the mobility of labour in sport by focusing on those who opt to leave their country of citizenship, engaging in transnational sporting migration by means of skirting state controls, to improve their career opportunities in sport. In applying a decade of ethnographic fieldwork on Cuban sport, Carter shows how we need to take into account multiple and cross-border relations to explain patterns of migration, the reaction of totalitarian states to it, and the impacts of migration decisions upon the family and friends that remain. As such, the paper proposes a much-needed theory for understanding sports migration that incorporates and reflects both the actual experiences, routes and roots of sports migration, and all of the institutional 'players' as well as relevant individuals involved in the migration process.

Jarvie also considers the issue of transnational mobility in sport, yet his contention differs to that of Carter in that he argues that sport can play a critical role in promoting international development as it can contribute to change within national borders by boosting life chances. Although reference is made to cases of African athletes lured to several of the Gulf States through financial reward, he considers how potential migrants can be enticed to stay in their countries of origin and work as a positive force for development (as sport remains a critical device in promoting domestic as well as international reconciliation).[28] Yet this has to be mastered within a framework in which a new world order emerges in response to the 'New Depression', in which globalization has a greater element of regulation along with markets. Jarvie's tone is optimistic in a climate where budgetary pressures are increasing, but his convictions, based on the audacity of hope, provide a challenging message.

In grappling with the issues of identity and sport, especially in terms of how sport is used to project the identity of both nation-states and stateless nations, Holmes and Storey explore the complex relationships between sport and nationalism in the context of Ireland. Whilst acknowledging the work of Bairner, who asserts that sport has been one of the most valuable weapons at the disposal of nationalists, Holmes and Storey explore the shifting regulations that govern international eligibility for sportspersons seeking to represent their nation.[29] In using a diverse range of examples drawn from players classified as 'Anglos', the study explores the motivating factors of those individuals opting to play football for the Republic of Ireland. Their investigations, based upon player self-identification and the perspectives of Republic of Ireland fans, reveal the conflicting and complicated relationships that have to be negotiated by sportsmen with regard to their perspectives on career advancement and claims of cultural identity. With the broadening and increasing transnationalism of the player pool for selection both in football and in many other sports, this issue becomes more significant and has implications for the notion of imagined community and the potential of sport to generate both domestic and international harmony.

In switching attention to the sub-national level of governance, Holden assesses the role of sport in Wales through the prism of the devolution of power from Westminster to Wales as a consequence of the 1998 Government of Wales Act. In exploring how politicians in Wales have used sport as a tool for projecting and consolidating national identity, he argues that the traditional significance of sport in terms of identity has altered, via political consensus, from being driven by the notion of 'Otherness' (preoccupation with matters English that have scarred Welsh political and social history) to one driven by the impulse of neo-liberal economics. In this instance, sport is used as a vehicle to help forge a new identity based on an emerging performance culture and the fruits of commercial gain secured by promoting both Cardiff and Wales as major sporting venues. In drawing on the importance of sport to both nation-states and stateless nations he considers the impact of sport on the forging of a new, modified Welsh identity in which sport is key to a performance culture bolstered by the opening of facilities such as the Millennium Stadium, the contribution of Wales to the 2005 Ashes victory which spurred the subsequent redevelopment of Sophia Gardens and the successful hosting of the first domestic Test Match involving England on non-English soil within the United Kingdom, and the hosting of the 2010 Ryder Cup.

In summary, it is not the intention of these papers to exhaustively explore each aspect of how sport is implicated in the multiple-intersecting dimensions of community, mobility and identity. What the collection reveals are some limited empirical and conceptual insights from a selection of cases where these issues are being played out. Further dialogue, debate and research is needed to extrapolate the broader meanings of these themes and their implications for the study of a politics of sport. To reassert a point made above, we believe that this area has a bright future and there are many routes to explore, whether they be travelled out of academic disinterest, careerism, critical standpoints or committed activism. Such journeys can proceed via the routes charted by earlier pioneers and there is an important legacy to acknowledge in efforts to map the terrain and to open up terra incognita. However, topographies change along with conventional wisdoms and received orthodoxies in how to view the world. There are still roads to travel and our journeys can be made more complete and more fulfilling by understanding how we got here and occasionally taking advice from other travellers along the way.

Notes

[1] Guttmann, 'Sport, Politics'.
[2] Allison, 'The Global Politics of Sport'.

3 Maguire, *Global Sport*; Jackson and Haigh, 'Between and Beyond Politics'.
4 Guttmann, 'Sport Politics', 363.
5 C. Hitchens, 'Fool's Gold', *Newsweek*, 15 February 2010.
6 Holt, *Sport and the British*, 145–8; Peatling, 'Rethinking the History'.
7 Zirin, *What's My Name, Fool?* 21.
8 Whannel, *Culture, Politics and Sport*.
9 See Hargreaves, 2000.
10 Whannel, *Culture, Politics and Sport*, 237.
11 See McDonald, 2002.
12 Sugden and Tomlinson, *FIFA*; see Kidd, 'A New Social Movement'.
13 See Zirin, *What's My Name, Fool?; Welcome to the Terrordome; A People's History*.
14 Zirin, *Welcome to the Terrordome*, 258; see also King, 'Toward a Radical Sport Journalism'.
15 Chomsky, *American Power*, 324.
16 Bairner, 'Sport, Intellectuals'.
17 See also Jarvie, 'Sport, Social Change'.
18 See McDonald, 2002.
19 Hill, 'Introduction', 356.
20 See Allison, 'Sport and Civil Society'; *Amateurism in Sport*.
21 See, for example, Black and Van der Westhuizen, 'The Allure of Global Games'.
22 Marsh and Savigny, 'Political Science'.
23 See Grayson, Davies and Philpott, 'Pop goes IR'; Lawson, 'Political Studies'.
24 Sheller and Urry, 'New Mobilities Paradigm'.
25 Malkki, 'National Geographic'.
26 Cresswell, *On the Move*.
27 Allison, 2005.
28 Levermore and Beacom, *Sport and International Development*.
29 Bairner, 2001.

References

Allison, L. *Amateurism in Sport: An Analysis and a Defence*. London: Frank Cass, 2001.
Allison, L. 'Sport and Civil Society'. *Political Studies* 46 (1998): 709–26.
Allison, L., ed. *The Global Politics of Sport: The Role of Global Institutions in Sport*. London: Routledge, 2005.
Bairner, A. 'Sport, Intellectuals and Public Sociology: Obstacles and Opportunities'. *International Review for the Sociology of Sport* 44, nos. 2–3 (2009): 115–30.
Bairner, A. *Sport, Nationalism, and Globalization. European and North American Perspectives*. Albany, NY: SUNY Press, 2001.
Black, D.R., and J. Van der Westhuizen. 'The Allure of Global Games for "Semi-Peripheral" Polities and Spaces: A Research Agenda'. *Third World Quarterly* 25, no. 7 (2004): 1195–214.
Chomsky, N. *American Power and the New Mandarins*. New York: Pantheon Books, 1969.
Cresswell, T. *On the Move: Mobility in the Modern World*. New York: Routledge, 2006.
Grayson, K., M. Davies, and S. Philpott. 'Pop Goes IR? Researching the Popular Culture-World Politics Continuum'. *Politics* 29, no. 3 (2009): 155–63.
Guttmann, A. 'Sport, Politics and the Engaged Historian'. *Journal of Contemporary History* 38, no. 3 (2003): 363–75.
Hargreaves, J. *Heroines of Sport: The Politics of Identity and Difference*. London: Routledge, 2000.
Hill, J. 'Introduction: Sport and Politics'. *Journal of Contemporary History* 38, no. 3 (2003): 355–61.
Holt, R. *Sport and the British: A Modern History*. Oxford: Oxford University Press, 1989.
Jackson, S.J., and S. Haigh. 'Between and Beyond Politics: Sport and Foreign Policy in a Globalising World'. *Sport in Society* 11, no. 4 (2008): 349–58.
Jarvie, G. 'Sport, Social Change and the Public Intellectual'. *International Review for the Sociology of Sport* 42, no. 4 (2007): 411–24.
Kidd, B. 'A New Social Movement: Sport for Development and Peace'. *Sport in Society* 11, no. 4 (2008): 370–80.
King, C.R. 'Toward a Radical Sport Journalism: An Interview with Dave Zirin'. *Journal of Sport & Social Issues* 32, no. 4 (2008): 333–44.

Lawson, S. 'Political Studies and the Contextual Turn: A Methodological/Normative Critique'. *Political Studies* 56 (2008): 584–603.

Levermore, R., and A. Beacom, eds. *Sport and International Development*. New York: Palgrave Macmillan, 2009.

McDonald, I. 'Critical Social Research and Political Intervention: Moralistic versus Radical Approaches'. In *Power Games: A Critical Sociology of Sport*, edited by A. Tomlinson and J. Sugden, 100–116. London: Routledge, 2002.

Maguire, J. *Global Sport: Identities, Societies, Civilizations*. Cambridge: Polity Press, 1999.

Malkki, L. 'National Geographic: The Rooting of Peoples and the Territorialization of National Identity Among Scholars and Refugees'. *Cultural Anthropology* 7, no. 1 (1992): 24–44.

Marsh, D., and H. Savigny. 'Political Science as a Broad Church: The Search for a Pluralist Discipline'. *Politics* 24, no. 3 (2004): 155–68.

Peatling, G. 'Rethinking the History of Criticism of Organized Sports'. *Cultural and Social History* 2 (2005): 353–71.

Sheller, M., and J. Urry. 'The New Mobilities Paradigm'. *Environment and Planning A* 38, no. 2 (2006): 207–26.

Sugden, J., and A. Tomlinson. *FIFA and the Contest for World Football*. Cambridge: Polity Press, 1998.

Whannel, G. *Culture, Politics and Sport: Blowing the Whistle Revisited*. London: Routledge, 2008.

Zirin, D. *A People's History of Sports in the United States*. New York: The New Press, 2008.

Zirin, D. *Welcome to the Terrordome: The Pain, Politics, and Promise of Sports*. Chicago, IL: Haymarket Books, 2007.

Zirin, D. *What's My Name, Fool? Sports and Resistance in the United States*. Chicago, IL: Haymarket Books, 2005.

'Over here': 'Americanization' and the new politics of football club ownership – the case of Liverpool FC

John Williams[a] and Stephen Hopkins[b]

[a]Department of Sociology, University of Leicester, UK; [b]Department of Politics and International Relations, University of Leicester, UK

This paper focuses on arguments concerning sport and Americanization, especially in relation to English Premier League football clubs. The central case study here is of Liverpool football club in the north-west of England. The recent economic trajectory of football in England is analysed, as is the current attractiveness of the English game to foreign investors. The specific history and traditions of the Liverpool club and the city of Liverpool is offered as a means of contextualizing the initial response locally to the leveraged buyout by Tom Hicks and George Gillett Jr early in 2007. The paper considers the almost complete breakdown of relations between the new owners and Liverpool fans between autumn 2007 and spring 2008. It concludes that in attempting to maintain core aspects of the Liverpool club's organic traditions the Liverpool board, paradoxically, paved the way to the excessive commodification of the club and the alienation of many of its own supporters.

Americanization and the new economics of English football

From around the late 1960s the discourse of cultural imperialism in academic theorizing about popular culture tended to characterize the critical reception of globalization by casting the associated processes as the diffusion of specifically *American* values, consumer goods and lifestyles.[1] Later, Roland Robertson's influential work took a rather different route by seeking to establish globalization as 'the process whereby the world becomes a single place' but one characterized culturally less by American influences *per se* but by 'a general mode of discourse about the world as a whole and its variety'.[2] In the field of research on sport, recent critical theories of globalization have tended to run together the processes of commodification, homogenization and Americanization, though some accounts have stressed, instead, that we are, more accurately, witnessing an homogenization of world leisure practices and sports, rather than their Americanization.[3] Still other approaches have stressed the emerging 'glocal' character of sport, as the unity of nation states is dissolved or pluralized, thus giving way not to homogenization, but to processes of global diversity or polyculturalism.[4] Other accounts have argued, in relation to elite football in England and in Europe, that processes of *Europeanization* or of *internationalization*, rather than Americanization or free-market globalization, best define recent developments, especially in relation to the transnational flows of capital and cultural signs across national boundaries, and in the area of player recruitment.[5] Finally, and in a typically provocative and challenging thesis, the Australian sports-media theorist David Rowe has suggested that, rather than articulating processes of either globalization or Americanization, the very constitution of sport makes it a wholly inappropriate vehicle for the carriage of such a project in its fullest sense, primarily because of late-modern sport's ultimate dependence on the production of *national* cultural difference.[6]

Notwithstanding the very different positions outlined above, the recent intensive commodification and marketization of the top levels of English professional football – its emphasis, for example, on branding and merchandising; on producing highly packaged and spectacularized 'leisure experiences' aimed at sports 'customers' and 'consumers' (including advertisers); and its television-driven agendas that define sport as a digestible, dramatic *yet* pacified 'entertainment' for otherwise uncommitted armchair viewers[7] – have all been argued to correspond with some key features of the Americanization thesis. One commentator has even argued that the recently stated ambitions of the Premier League in England to stage some of its fixtures in countries around the world correspond best to the global domination of US fast food franchises: in short, 'We are witnessing the birth of the McLeague'.[8]

American-based global corporations continue to be key figures as sponsors in the staging of world sporting and football mega-events, of course, but what has been 'missing' from the English domestic football model – until fairly recently at least – has been the direct involvement of American sports entrepreneurs in the ownership structures of elite-level English football clubs. This has now begun to change. Since 2006 three top Premier League clubs (out of 20) – Manchester United, Aston Villa and Liverpool – have been purchased by American owners. How can we best interpret the new transatlantic ownership structures of elite English football clubs? One obvious narrative to explore here is the changing corporate structure and financial outlook of English football clubs in the new global markets for professional sport.

Historically, the distinctiveness of the ownership structures of UK football clubs lay in their limited liability corporate structure, a feature which dates back to the late nineteenth century. The Midlands and Northern Methodists and the local businessmen who first set up the Football League in England in 1888 also embodied in their sporting work a philosophy of 'mutual protection' in which wage restraints exercised on players, via adherence to a fixed national maximum wage, for example, and also the defence of a retain-and-transfer system which effectively tied players to their clubs, were designed to ensure that the League's better-off clubs would share common and reciprocal interests with its less wealthy members.[9] In this supportive context of mutuality and cross-subsidization, the sport's governing body in England, the Football Association (FA), introduced Rule 34 to its regulations in order to restrict the payment of dividends to football club owners and to prevent the payment of salaries to club directors. Football, it argued, should not be about generating profits for owners.

However, as neo-liberal economic and social policy began to dominate the wider political agenda in the UK in the 1980s, and with English football immersed in a series of crises around stadium provision, fan safety and hooliganism indicative of a wider crisis around the relationship between public provision and social class in Britain, these traditional 'custodian' English football club directors began to be publicly criticized.[10] A new breed of more entrepreneurial football club owners and directors rapidly began to appear in the sport in England as pressure grew inside the elite Football League clubs to 'modernize' and to change or evade the FA limits. When the London club Tottenham Hotspur became the first British football club to be listed on the Stock Exchange in 1983, it set up a holding company (Tottenham Hotspur plc) to act as a parent company for the football club in order to evade FA rules – including Rule 34. This example of 'regulatory capture' not only revealed the FA's feebleness as a regulator, but it also encouraged other clubs to adopt similar corporate structures prior to their own flotation.[11] It was in this 'marketized' climate that, in 1992, the independent FA Premier League was established in

England by a breakaway group of the sport's senior clubs, largely on the back of launch income derived from new satellite television conglomerates. Its effect was to shatter the historic mutuality of existing arrangements in the old Football League.[12] By 1998, in a public admission of its apparent impotence in the face of the aggressive new market-driven economics of the sport, Rule 34 was finally abandoned altogether by the FA.[13]

Today, the appetite of satellite television for live coverage of the Premier League shows little signs of slowing. Even in the shadow of a global economic downturn, the latest broadcasting deals involving matches of the Premier League clubs (2007–10) raised some £2.7 billion. These returns can be added to the enormous potential earnings that now exist in new sports markets which are being carefully excavated by English clubs in China, India and the Far East – and in North America too – as we have witnessed the 'accelerated expansion of transnational capital and its extension into the sport/cultural realm'.[14] With the relative absence of effective FA regulation and British government reluctance to 'politicize' football, for example by seeking to restrict foreign ownership in the English game, professional football clubs in England today have come to be regarded, less as distinctive social and cultural associations that require protection against hostile external investment and potential asset stripping, rather as 'just another business'. It is in this new febrile global business context for sport that foreign club owners have recently moved inexorably into English football including into one of the most culturally distinctive, and certainly one of the most successful, of all English football clubs, Liverpool FC.

Liverpool FC: a club 'in turmoil'

In February 2008, academic and football activist Rogan Taylor, launched the Share Liverpool FC group, a fans consortium which planned to persuade 100,000 of the club's fans worldwide to pledge to contribute £5000 each for the purchase of a single share in the club in an audacious attempt at a £500 million buyout from its new American owners. This latest example of what Wyn Grant has called the 'politics of resistance' among fans in the English game promised a new ownership structure for Liverpool, loosely based along the membership lines of Spanish clubs, including Barcelona and Real Madrid.[15] Meanwhile, in March 2008 another group of the club's supporters formed an entirely new local football club, AFC Liverpool, apparently as a protest against Liverpool FC's increasingly public and discordant ownership wrangles and rising ticket prices at Anfield.[16] Finally, at Liverpool home matches throughout the second half of the 2007/08 football season, supporters of the club regularly organized a series of angry public demonstrations, insisting its new American owners did not care either for the fans or for the club. According to the British sporting press, the traditionally stable and highly private Anfield organization was now, very publicly, a football club 'in turmoil'.

Liverpool supporters, it must be said, are no strangers to expressive forms of collective solidarity and protest in the wake of perceived external attack or threat to the club and its followers, or to the city of Liverpool.[17] But this more recent series of collective outbursts and gestures was something almost entirely new. Crucially, perhaps, it contravened a dominant rhetoric which had settled around a clutch of cultural and organizational practices popularly associated with the club locally and which is known, colloquially and affectionately among its supporters and the press, as the 'Liverpool way'. Ironically derived from a form of autocratic closure skilfully practised by the club's board of directors in the 1950s, its modern variant asserts that Liverpool fans and officials should show unity in the face of 'outsiders' and never be knowingly publicly critical of the club's staff or owners.[18] Accordingly, 'difficult' issues of the sort that actually plague *all* football clubs – supporter unrest, training ground bust-ups, financial disputes, management disagreements, boardroom rows, player indiscretions – should always be settled consensually and privately, rather than in the glare of the public eye.

This is a general approach to managing club affairs which the ex-Liverpool chief executive Rick Parry summarized recently as the 'natural conservatism' of Liverpool football club. But it also reveals an archetypical, and a much more general, suspicion on Merseyside of the national news media and what are assumed to be its nefarious agendas in relation to the city and its people.[19] It calls up, too, the very real late-modern ambivalences inside Liverpool FC concerning the value and specific meaning of the club 'brand' today and how it compares, for example, to the much more commercialized and glamorized, and more media-driven approach of fierce local rivals Manchester United. According to Rick Parry, for example:

> The great thing that Liverpool had never done was to prostitute its brand. And that is terrific. . . . The brand values that we have developed for Liverpool well the key word for us was 'respect.' In the '70s and '80s we were not loved by everybody, but there was always a respect for Liverpool, and that's a value that I think is extremely important.[20]

When the commercial bases of football in England were already beginning to change quite radically in the 1980s and early 1990s, the dominant football club *on* the field in England – Liverpool FC – soon slipped some way behind its commercial competitors off it. In fact, it might be said that the eventual (but hasty) sale of the Liverpool club to new foreign investors from the United States early in 2007 can best be read as a belated acknowledgment of the new realities and the inevitable re-ordering of the sport's financial base in the new global era. All this meant that the recent fan protests in the city about the policies and ownership of Liverpool FC were as much a reminder of the club's glorious and largely stable recent past as they were a signal of current and future tensions. It was also connected to the character of the city and some of the specifics of the American takeover; a slick piece of image management this, which, initially at least, seemed to promise considerable financial *and* emotional investment by the club's co-buyers.

Finally, this Liverpool fan unrest may have reflected a much more general concern about emerging new patterns of global investment and governance at the top levels of the English game in the twenty-first century. As Rogan Taylor had put it at the launch of Share Liverpool FC, 'The time is right to offer a different solution to the rising concerns that football fans have about the patterns of ownership developing at our major football clubs'.[21] In fact, there is relatively little evidence, beyond abstract assertions, that the proposed 'democratization' of ownership of major football clubs has popular support amongst English fans. But we would also argue that to understand fully exactly how Liverpool and its supporters came to this quite atypical pitch of agitation and discord about the ownership of the club in 2007 and 2008 we need to examine specific aspects of the cultural traditions of the city as well, briefly, as the management and ownership history of the Liverpool club. In this sense we assert, via Raymond Williams, that the local 'structure of feeling' in English cities – and the 'lived cultures' at specific English football clubs – have an important part to play in explaining local resistances and accommodations to broadly global processes.[22]

Football and local business in Liverpool: a brief history

Historically, English football clubs have always been undercapitalized, with little or no retained profit, and they have always relied on borrowing and overdrafts as a source of funding. However, Tischler has also argued that early professional football in England represented nothing less than a 'microcosm of the larger business environment' and that local Victorian and Edwardian businessmen made profits indirectly out of their role as local football club directors.[23] The early traces of the origins and forms of governance at the major Merseyside football clubs, Liverpool and Everton, would suggest that it was the *Liverpool* club, under local Tory and brewer John Houlding, which was rather more commercially driven and certainly more closely controlled by a few key shareholders, than was Everton.[24] But Liverpool FC was also, palpably, a *family* business. The Liverpool board was historically dominated by Orangemen and Freemasons, but also by fathers and sons drawn from a small cabal of wealthy local families – the Williams in the first two decades of the twentieth century; the Martindales from the 1920s to the 1940s; the Cartwrights in the 1930s and then the 1960s; and the Reakes in the 1960s and 1970s.[25] Unusually, however, in the city of Liverpool one single family was to become a very dominant feature of the funding of *both* of the major professional football clubs in the latter half of the twentieth century.

Stephen Morrow suggests that the Moores family falls firmly into the camp of those football club benefactors for whom normal business criteria have been set aside when it comes to football.[26] The Moores made their money from the Littlewoods Pools and mail-order businesses that originated between the wars and the family has, at different junctures, made investments in both the Liverpool and Everton clubs. John Moores, the co-founder of the Littlewoods Pools business, introduced his first pool in 1923 and the Littlewoods company grew to become a major and generally respected employer in Liverpool over the next 60 years. In the wake of falling attendances and perceived declining local rivalry, it was Everton Chairman John Moores who directly stimulated the Anfield club to reject its own frugal spending policies of the 1950s in a move which, ironically, spurred Liverpool, not Everton, to become the dominant football club in England, and briefly in Europe, during a period spanning the mid-1960s to 1990.[27]

When David Moores – nephew of John – eventually inherited part of the family fortune, and with it shares in Liverpool football club, he was set reluctantly on a path which he could never have envisaged for himself: he eventually became nominated as the new Liverpool football club chairman, in 1991. With the sport in England now in a period of frantic economic and cultural transformation and stalked by asset strippers and profiteers, the Liverpool club had, once again, sought comfort and stability in seeking out reliable domestic finance and by drawing on the reassuring tropes of localism and 'family'. But David Moores offered little in the way of effective leadership or political skill; in fact, he hated formality and public speaking. Notoriously thin-skinned, he confessed to having no real head for public scrutiny, conflict or high finance. At best, he acted as a bulwark against the excesses of the new market economics of the sport; at worst, he was some way out of his depth, contributing to the very real sense that Liverpool FC lacked both direction and leadership in the 1990s when the sport was rapidly diversifying, globalizing and commodifying.

It's a whole new ball game

It has been argued that globalization and the international circulation of sports capital has effectively homogenized the international ownership and investment structures of football clubs, but Morrow rightly suggests it would be a mistake to exaggerate the common features here at the expense of their local and national cultural peculiarities.[28] In Italy, for example, elite clubs are often still owned by domestic family groupings and companies (Fiat, Pirelli Parmalat, etc.) in which a small number of individuals maintain control via holding companies and cross-shareholdings and by having their voting rights concentrated at the top of a pyramidal structure. In France, the local authority is a major investor in local clubs and stadium facilities; while in Spain, season ticket and fan investors are often registered as club members who fund clubs and who vote periodically for the club president and board members, who are usually local industrialists and businessmen.

In Britain, by way of contrast, sport is the 'quintessential example' of an activity locally driven by private capital and regulated autonomously in the sphere of civil society.[29] There is little historical evidence of traditions of public investment in major English clubs; nor are there cultural or legal prohibitions today on foreign investment in clubs or, indeed, in any other British businesses and cultural institutions. Instead, the British Government (and the Premier League) has seemed, willingly, to have ceded control of its role in the world economy to a new elite of freebooting, super-rich free-market speculators and institutions that promised accountability, economic stability, transparency and thrift but, in the main, arguably delivered more volatility, chronic indebtedness, greater uncertainty and a sense of being remote from people's everyday lives.[30] In this changing governance and investment context, the market success of elite English football clubs in the twenty-first century seemed, increasingly, to demand billionaire speculative global investors, rather than rooted and committed local ones.

Since at least 2003 Liverpool FC had been urgently seeking out potential new major investors. Central here was the fact that the club had limited facilities for use on non-match days and no excess stadium capacity for league matches – customers were being turned away. Meanwhile, income streams derived from 'sweating' sports stadiums had begun to climb rapidly. But in the wake of stadium redevelopment and relocations elsewhere in England, the Liverpool club remained rooted in its historic, but by now outdated, Anfield home. Liverpool FC had actually been talking since 1999 about building a new stadium to increase the capacity from the current 45,362. The project had been closely bound up with the proposed regeneration of Anfield and Breckfield, one of the most deprived areas of the city, but by the summer of 2008 projected costs had risen four-fold to close to £400 million and preparatory work on the stadium site had barely begun. By 2010, in an economic downturn, the club still had no new stadium and no obvious way of funding one.

In seeking out new finance, Liverpool were clearly keen to conserve as much as possible of the status quo ante, in terms of the cultural heritage, the character of the administration and the 'family ethos' of the club. Ideally, in their prospectus for future development, the 'Liverpool way', built patiently over many generations of essentially conservative (and often Conservative) stewardship, would remain intact and relatively unsullied. But despite this ambition and Liverpool's complex mix of parochialism and historical 'openness' as a city – its status as a site of both economic and cultural exchange, with the port facing outward at the hub of an historic, global network of interwoven relationships[31] – the realization that investment in Liverpool football club was now being sought from all corners of the globe made some fans – especially *locally based* Liverpool fans – uneasy.[32]

But then a consortium representing Dubai International Capital (DIC), an arm of the Dubai government and ruling family, reportedly offered a total of £156 million for the purchase of all existing Liverpool shares, plus funds to cover debts and the building of a new stadium on nearby Stanley Park, a total package of around £450 million. The Liverpool board under David Moores seemed keen to accept the Dubai bid, despite human rights concerns.[33] However, just two months later, in February 2007 two American sports and property tycoons, Tom Hicks and George Gillett Jr, men who had never worked seriously together in business, raised the offer for the club to £5000 a share, or £172 million, plus promised funds for a new stadium. The DIC group had earlier sneered that the supposed 'soccer-phobic' Gillett would not know Liverpool FC from a 'hole in the ground', but it was now publicly furious at the sudden collapse in their negotiations, describing the Liverpool board as 'dishonourable' and the club as 'a shambles'.[34] Liverpool chairman David Moores eventually decided to take the plunge and agreed to sell his controlling stake to the US entrepreneurs, a decision which would raise his own cut of the club buyout by some £8 million, to a reported £89.6 million. He was also installed as honorary life president of the club in recognition of his decade-and-a-half service, and he was charged to act as something of a nominal 'boardroom delegate' for astonished Liverpool fans. But Moores may well have favoured passing on his Liverpool across the Atlantic for reasons other than mere profit. After all, these were two identifiable sports benefactors, people who seemingly understood the city of Liverpool and global sports business and who had money to invest, but who also had the club apparently at heart. These may have looked a better bet for a port with strong business and cultural links to the USA than a faceless and culturally 'alien' corporate government body from the Middle East.

But what is more significant here is that this piece of late-modern corporate sports profiteering seemed like a complete reversal of the history of the patrician and custodian local funding for Liverpool FC; indeed, it seemed like an inversion of the entire Moores family project of long-term economic investment in the two Merseyside football clubs and in the city of Liverpool itself over more than 70 years. In short, this was a business deal archetypically quarried out of the new age of global liberalization, and one that plainly traduced the core tenets of the 'Liverpool way'. It was certainly unlikely to endear David Moores to Liverpool fans in 2007, even to those who approved, initially at least, of the American investment over that offered by the men from Dubai.

Fistfuls of dollars

Two American billionaires, Tom Hicks, owner of the Texas Rangers baseball franchise and the (US) National Hockey League's Dallas Stars, and George Gillett Jr, owner of the Montreal Canadiens and formerly of the Miami Dolphins, had cobbled together in just two months an unlikely alliance to secure a reported £470 million funding package via a loan from the Royal Bank of Scotland to buy Liverpool football club and to allocate some £215 million to begin work on a new stadium. Hicks, a Texan former business partner of President George W. Bush, had precisely made his fortune from raising private equity to fund multimillion dollar corporate takeovers. Liverpool football club was suddenly in the hands of the sort of global sports capitalists who had initially made no secret of their financial motives, their ignorance of 'soccer', or of their ambitions to model this rather atypical English football club, commercially, along the lines of an NFL franchise. They openly highlighted the attractions of English football's booming TV monies, the growing internet income streams for the English game, expanding markets for the Liverpool club in South-East Asia and in South America, the prospects of stadium naming rights, and even their plans for introducing American-style 'bunker suites' into the proposed new Liverpool ground: underground 'living rooms' where corporate elites could dine in plush splendour and watch banks of TV sets before taking an elevator ride to their match seats.[35]

All this seemed like a swamping 'Americanization' writ large. And yet initial local resistance on Merseyside to this cultural, as well as corporate, takeover of one of the city's defining institutions was, for some commentators, surprisingly muted to say the least. As football business analyst David Conn later put it:

> There was remarkably little Scouse scepticism...about the men wearing scarves; the pair were presented as billionaires who would take Liverpool into their new stadium, girdled by all the banqueting required to finance competing with Manchester United, Arsenal and [Chelsea's] Roman Abramovich.[36]

This apparently benign reception for the Americans on Merseyside was mainly for four reasons, all strongly locally sourced. Firstly, as Conn implies, something of a realist resignation now existed among most Liverpool supporters that, in the age of open borders, globalization and sporting capital flows across national boundaries, international financing – and probably the additional commodification that was likely to come with it – was an almost inevitable cost for any late-modern football club in England with serious pretentions to be competitive for titles at home and in Europe. More knowledgeable (and, perhaps, more cynical) Liverpool fans could even make the appropriate historical connections here, about the origins of the club and its commercial hard-headedness. As 'Real Deep' reminded readers of *Through the Wind and Rain* in 2007:

> Haven't we been a plaything for the rich from day one, when we were formed, not for sporting reasons, but to fill a recently vacated Anfield and provide the owner, John Houlding, with a steady stream of income from both paying customers at the game and the sale of beer in the nearby hostelry? And *he* imported a whole troop of Scottish mercenaries to fill the team.[37]

Secondly, the cosmopolitan and transient 'city of the sea' of Liverpool was no stranger, of course, either to global exchange or, more specifically, to American cultural and commercial penetration. Historically, Liverpool exceptionalism had looked west, to Ireland and the United States, for guidance and inspiration on finance, culture and identity issues more than it did to England or national government. The port at Liverpool had provided direct employment for up to 60,000 people in the city, much of it in trade involving North America, and its seafront streets aped those its seafarers had experienced in America. Even before the First World War, Americans were envied in Liverpool for their supposed modernity and stylishness, and American fashions were imported by Liverpool tailors, who regularly copied clothes brought in by seamen from the eastern seaboard of the USA.[38] Later, this maritime connection – seamen on the passenger services to the USA were known locally as 'Cunard Yanks' – also fed directly into Liverpool street idioms and language, nightlife and music, with 'the most American of English cities' acting as a site of feverish transatlantic cultural exchange of a sort which allowed the city to take the lead in pop music in the world during the 1960s.[39] In short, the city of Liverpool already had deeply ingrained American sensibilities and sympathies well before Tom Hicks and George Gillett strode into Anfield early in 2007 with their 'good ole boy' homilies about 'tradition' and 'heritage'. The possibility of transatlantic investment and exchange in football was no especially alien or threatening intrusion in that sense.

Thirdly, allied to their obvious commercial savvy and despite their early carelessness with talk about profit and franchises, the new Liverpool co-owners were actually unlikely experts in what Erving Goffman has famously called 'impression management'.[40] They showed little of the alleged arrogance of the absent Glazer family, the new American owners at rivals Manchester United, for example, who seemed to believe that money was its own explanation for their actions and who had made little attempt at all to engage with Manchester United fans. 'They are very private people', said Tom Hicks of Malcolm Glazer and his family, by way of explanation. 'He [Glazer] showed us how *not* to do it'.[41] With the Merseyside press acting as unreflexive local cheerleaders, the Liverpool buyout would *not* involve the kind of leveraged deal which had loaded more than £600 million worth of Glazer debt onto the Manchester club. Indeed, in the offer document for Liverpool the Americans had made it very clear that any loans taken out to secure the deal would be personally guaranteed and that payment of any interest, 'will not depend to any significant extent on the business of Liverpool'.[42]

The new owners also cleverly played back to Liverpool's supporters some of the familiar and comforting tropes about the club's history. 'We are custodians, not owners, of the franchise' said Gillett to the press, thus uneasily blending aspects of the Victorian paternalism of John Houlding with the capitalist discourses of late-modern American sport, a combination of the reassuring and alarming. George Gillett, showing admirable restraint, told the same journalists on 6 February 2007 that the new owners were keen, but untutored, students of the club: 'Respect is the way we feel about the history and the legacy of this franchise [sic]. . . . I am still learning about the club but I will get it into my blood in every way I can'.[43]

Finally, another rhetorical device skilfully employed by the Americans and their advisors to mask some of the bleak economics of the deal was that about the Liverpool FC 'family' tradition. The patrician Moores family dynasty and its antecedents would now be seamlessly replaced inside the club by a transatlantic equivalent, made up of the Gilletts and the Hicks. It was almost as if the club had been acquired through marriage by some august royal family from a superior and distant culture. Gillett's son Foster would work inside the club on a day-to-day basis on an executive level with Rick Parry, while Tom Hicks Jr would join the club board. Symbolically this move was astute but how, exactly, it would work in practice remained a moot point because it seemed potentially full of tensions and conflict. By the end of the 2006/07 season there were already reports that Liverpool club coach Rafa Benitez had started to bypass his chief executive Rick Parry, and was talking directly to Foster Gillett in order to expedite transfers and other matters. Parry was the self-appointed guardian of continuity and the 'Liverpool way' inside the club; but he was already starting to look increasingly isolated in the new Liverpool ownership structure.

The back of love

By the spring of 2007 new tensions were clearly emerging around the administration of the club and the traditionally strong bond of trust that existed between Liverpool supporters and the club's board. By the autumn of 2007 it had become clear that the American owners would have to renegotiate a new financial package worth £350 million with RBS and the American investment bank Wachovia in order to pay off their original loans and raise cash to begin work on the Liverpool stadium. Revised plans for the new stadium insisted upon by the new owners had considerably increased its price, so proposals to raise a further £300 million for the funding of the new ground would now have to wait until 2009 at the earliest. Worse, despite their initial denials, the American owners now, reportedly, wanted to load the whole of the original acquisition debt of £298 million onto the club's balance sheet, thus replicating core aspects of the Glazer deal at Manchester United. This was reported to have been 'fiercely resisted' inside the club, presumably by Rick Parry and members of the Liverpool board.[44]

Tom Hicks seemed quite unfazed by suggestions that the Liverpool leverage deal now looked very like the Manchester United buyout. Gone, too, was much of the earlier ameliorating discourse about 'respect', 'tradition' and the 'heritage' of the Liverpool club. Instead, Hicks chose to compare the purchase of Liverpool FC to his earlier acquisition of a breakfast cereal company:

> When I was in the leverage buyout business we bought *Weetabix* and we leveraged it up to make our return. You could say that anyone who was eating *Weetabix* was paying for our purchase of *Weetabix*. It was just business. It is the same for Liverpool: revenues come in from whatever source, and if there is money left over it is profit.[45]

In the climate of an unpredicted global credit crisis initiated by the sub-prime market collapse in the USA in 2007, borrowing was now much more expensive and more difficult to secure, and a £500–600 million loan would be around 16 times Liverpool's operating profits for 2007; Manchester United's borrowings were eight times their operating profits and Arsenal's only four times.[46] Nevertheless, the first element of the refinancing package was finally agreed in January 2008, with £105 million of the debt saddled on Liverpool and £185 million secured on a holding company, Kop Investment LLC, held in the tax havens of the Cayman Islands and in the US state of Delaware. These were the routine machinations of global capitalism in full flow. The Americans increased their personal guarantees, mainly in the form of credit notes, to around a reported £55 million, but by early 2010 the reported Liverpool FC debt stood at some £237 million. This suddenly looked like very deep financial water and not the sort of deal that most Liverpool fans, or the club's guardians, had anticipated.

By January 2008 any residual debate there might have been among fans concerning the 'politics of resistance' to the *principle* of foreign ownership had effectively already been replaced by a starker pragmatism: Liverpool supporters were photographed holding up a large home-made banner reading: 'Yanks out, Dubai in: In Rafa we Love'.[47] This popular position, in favour of both DIC investment and Benitez, hardened still further when it was revealed by Hicks that he, Parry and Gillett had all secretly met with potential replacements to discuss the managerial role at Liverpool should Benitez's position at the club become 'untenable'.

Finally, as rumours began to circulate early in 2008 that DIC were considering making a new £500 million offer for the club, it was clear that Hicks and Gillett were no longer even in direct communication with each other; nor could they agree on the future of Liverpool. Gillett looked as if he might be willing to sell his share of the club, possibly to DIC, while Hicks publicly demanded the resignation of the 'failing' Rick Parry, who soon left the club. By 2010, with the business empires of Hicks and Gillett badly damaged by the global downturn, and in an increasingly uncertain global business climate, potential new investors from India were reported to be on the horizon.[48] Liverpool FC, once a model of conservative and unobtrusive (if rather autocratic) stability in the English game, suddenly seemed impossibly split; a club that appeared rudderless and constantly in the public eye.

Some conclusions

On Saturday 23 February 2008, the visiting Tom Hicks Jr was hounded out of an Anfield pub by angry Liverpool fans. Ironically, the Liverpool club had been founded by John Houlding in the same Sandon public house some 116 years before. Rarely, if ever, during that time had the club's fans been so publicly at odds with its owners. The recent Liverpool story is one that charts the complex impact of global financing and deregulation on late-modern sporting identities and attachments in a specific local setting. It maps economic change and the new business trajectories of global sport as they interpolate with local cultures and structures and shifting patterns of local adaptation and resistance, in an era in which sport is increasingly colonized by the market, transforming both its organization and production.[49]

Within this contextualizing frame, the 'condition' of Liverpool football club and its supporters in 2008 might be interpreted, by some, as simply the routine outcome of the 'normative' tensions that are likely to exist today between the profit-driven ambitions of (American) global capitalists and the 'romantic' aspirations of English football club supporters. We have tried to argue something slightly different in this account. We have suggested that, paradoxically, it was actually the clumsy attempt to *defend* and even to reproduce specific aspects of what we have called here the 'Liverpool way', the economic and cultural DNA of the Liverpool club – its distinctively modern local communalism and patrician ownership structures and cultures – that played a part in bringing the club to what (early in 2010) appeared to be a rather doomed scenario with its divided transatlantic investors.

We have also suggested that because of local historical and cultural practices which produce a highly distinctive local 'structure of feeling' in the city of Liverpool, 'Americanization' – at least as represented by transatlantic investment in the Liverpool club – was initially cautiously regarded locally as something of a positive *continuation* of Liverpool exceptionalism rather than a fracturing or dislocation of important local traditions. Sophisticated techniques of impression management around the sale of the club also contributed to this initial sense of local well-being – even pride – about the club's new American owners. This was reinforced by the public articulation of the supposed differences in the Liverpool financing strategies compared to those adopted by the Glazers at Manchester United. Street-smart Scousers had, in fact, been sold a pup; a native embarrassment. Also crucial here was the mobilization in the Liverpool case of powerful rhetorics about the emotional – as well as financial – investment supposedly in play in the buyout, including comforting tropes about the continuation of familial forms of club ownership and governance, albeit in a new global setting.

Liverpool FC had delayed its entry into the global marketplace for investors, in part precisely because of its innate conservatism, but also because of an honourable, if ultimately misconceived, attempt to try to resist some of the excesses of late-modern sporting commodification. In pursuing a politics of co-option and engagement its American owners seemed, initially at least, to share some of the Liverpool administrators' and the club's supporters' anxieties and concerns about preserving traditional and specifically *sporting* values at Anfield. But the club now seemed impaled on the horns of a familiar dilemma concerning balancing its international playing ambitions and the spread of its global brand – aspirations which many of the club's supporters still share – against more long-standing and local Liverpool traits that go right back, through the Moores' investors and the other Liverpool family owners, to the Victorian administration of John Houlding and his followers. Indeed, the early local response to the American investment in 2007 suggests to us an uneasy, and palpably unequal, tension: that between a relatively sophisticated and conditional willingness on the part of fans, in straitened times, to embrace external financing – something which is broadly in tune with the wider cultural and economic traditions of the city – *and* a determination to defend the highly specific sporting integrity and traditions of the club as a valued local sporting and cultural institution.

We cannot easily predict from these uncertain economic times (February 2010) the endgame for Liverpool FC with either Hicks or Gillett. But it seems unlikely that these Americans can easily claw back the ground now lost with the club's followers. Because the political economy of football is not conducive to an effective politics of consumerism – fans do not easily transfer their loyalty – opposition to the new owners in Liverpool thus far has been expressed via street protest and a nascent attempt at organizing a supporter buyout. But more realistic ideas about introducing, for example, a 'golden share' held by supporter trusts or national and local government in privately owned football clubs in England in order to prevent them being sold to foreign interests, obviously conflict strongly with the dominant free-market principles of the Premier League and the non-interventionist stance of British governments. The latter has undercut the possibility of an effective 'politics of resistance' at the elite levels of the sport.[50] Fan 'ownership' may ultimately also compromise the main reason why most people are involved with elite professional football in the first place – success on the field.

Conceivably, perhaps, the global financial crisis and the recent forced public invest-ment in stricken banks in the UK and the USA might yet begin to challenge conventional thinking on state intervention and regulation in the private sphere. Internationally, too, the once dominant regulatory systems of the older, modern game in Europe seem potentially newly energized in their determination to try to limit some of the economic adventurism of football's global investors, perhaps especially those recently drawn into the English game from the USA. In the summer of 2008 Michel Platini, the UEFA president submitted new regulatory plans for football to the European Union, plans which would involve a licensing system to prevent indebted clubs from competing in European competitions. Platini had previously called such clubs and their new foreign owners 'cheats' for inviting substantial debt, and asked rhetorically about American owners in England, 'You don't think they come here for the football? They don't know what football is'.[51]

A spokesperson for the British Government nervously dismissed Platini's plans as 'an unnecessary Europeanisation of sport', but in November 2008 at a meeting of sports ministers in Biarritz the French presidency put forward proposals for a new European financial commission for football, styled on the national DNCG which monitors and regulates sport in France.[52] Again, these proposals were aimed at limiting club debt and thus at making competition between European football clubs more 'fair'; though it is difficult to see, initially at least, how such regulatory practices might easily be applied equally to clubs in France – where local public subsidy for professional sport is the norm – as well as to those in England, where elite clubs are mainly privately financed. These new regulatory regimes will also be strongly opposed, of course, by the major European leagues in England, Spain and Italy and possibly by EU law.[53]

Despite these potential new interventions, we broadly agree with Wyn Grant that it seems unlikely that the British state will become more systematically engaged in the difficult task of regulating and 'politicizing' football.[54] Given this fact – and although the global economic downturn may also play its part here – Hicks and Gillett may not be the last American owners attracted into the highest reaches of the English game. And if the Liverpool story is no simple case of Americanization, nor is it – or other similar instances – easily categorized either as an example of the 'natural' cultural and economic dissonance that exists between rampant American sports capitalists and the more organic European markets for sport. In August 2006, for example, in Birmingham in the UK, the Cleveland Browns' owner and credit card billionaire Randy Lerner purchased control of the ailing Aston Villa club from its autocratic British owner Doug Ellis – and without raising a dollar of debt. Unlike Liverpool, Villa had no recent extended period of success to retrieve. Lerner then spent £4 million restoring the Holte, a Victorian public house alongside the Villa ground, whose decay had long symbolized the club's decline. In June 2008 Villa became the first Premier League club to accept loss of income by adopting the charity, the Acorns Children's Trust, as their shirt sponsor.[55] Simon Inglis, stadium historian and Villa fan, commented on Lerner that his philanthropy put most other football club chairmen to shame and that he, 'seems to have appreciated that heritage is not a luxury but an intrinsic part of football clubs'.[56]

Here, on the face of it at least, was a twenty-first century transatlantic reinvention of the English Victorian custodian club owner of exactly the type that Liverpool's Rick Parry and David Moores had searched so long – and so fruitlessly – to find.

But the rather different American ownership cases in England of Hicks and Gillett at Liverpool, the Glazers at Manchester United and Randy Lerner at Aston Villa, and the recent revival of questions about the need for increased domestic and international regulation in football, suggest that rather than focusing exclusively on the impact of processes of either globalization or Americanization, perhaps we also need to examine rather more difficult issues concerning EU law and the wider political economy of European football.[57] But we would also argue we must address questions about national and local traditions, and the 'lived cultures' and other specificities which shape patterns of football club ownership – and response to it – at the local level. In this final sense, of course, we may find that some of the fundamental questions concerning recent transatlantic football club buyouts in England might still be rather prosaic ones: *Which* city? *Which* club? And, exactly, *which* Americans?[58]

Acknowledgements

We want to thank the two anonymous reviewers for their helpful and constructive comments which have helped to improve, considerably, the earlier version of this paper.

Notes

[1] Tomlinson, *Globalisation and Culture*, 79.
[2] Robertson, *Globalisation*, 133, 135.
[3] Featherstone, *Consumer Culture and Postmodernism*, 127.
[4] Giulianotti and Robertson, 'Globalization of Football'.
[5] Martin, '"Europeanisation" of Elite Football'; McGovern, 'Globalization or Internationalization?'.
[6] Rowe, 'Sport and the Repudiation'.
[7] See Crawford, *Consuming Sport*.
[8] M. Hyde, 'Empty Seats and Dwindling Ratings? It's Time to Launch the Global McLeague', *Guardian,* 9 February 2008, 30; see also J. Williams, *Is It All Over?,* and 'Screen Grab' *Observer,* 4 November 2007.
[9] Tomlinson, 'North and South', 33; Arnold and Webb, 'Aston Villa'.
[10] See Taylor, 'English Football in the 1990s'.
[11] Morrow, *People's Game?*, 80.
[12] See J. Williams, 'Local and the Global'.
[13] Brown, 'European Football and the EU'; King, *End of the Terraces*, 128–31; Dobson and Goddard, *Economics of Football.*
[14] Schimmel, 'Sport and Political Economy', 3.
[15] See Grant, 'An Analytical Framework', for other examples.
[16] 'Liverpool Fans Form a Club in Their Price Range', *Daily Telegraph*, 18 March 2008.
[17] See J. Williams, 'Kopites, Scallies'.
[18] See J. Williams, *Red Men.*
[19] See Belchem, *Merseypride.*
[20] Quoted in J. Williams, *Liverpool Way,* 153.
[21] Quoted in Barclay, 'Super Rich Owners'.
[22] R. Williams, *Marxism and Literature*, 132.
[23] Tischler, *Footballers and Businessmen*, 69; see Taylor, *Association Game*, 70.
[24] Carter, *Football Manager*, 149; Kennedy and Collins, 'Community Politics'; Kennedy, 'Class, Ethnicity and Civic Governance'.
[25] See J. Williams, *Red Men.*
[26] Morrow, *New Business of Football*, 85.
[27] See J. Williams, *Red Men.*
[28] Morrow, *People's Game?*, 77.
[29] Moran, *British Regulatory State*, 73.
[30] Elliott and Atkinson, *Gods that Failed.*

[31] Belchem, *Liverpool 800.*

[32] See Williams and Hopkins, *Miracle of Istanbul,* 179–81.

[33] See M. Hyde, 'No Place for Grass Roots in Shifting Sands', *Guardian,* 7 December 2006.

[34] 'The Anfield Rap', *Daily Mail,* 2 February, 2007.

[35] Bond, 'Texans Vow'.

[36] D. Conn, 'Prospectors for Gold Leave Liverpool with Mountain of Debt', *Guardian,* 23 January 2008.

[37] *Through the Wind and Rain* no. 75, 2007, 14.

[38] Lane, *Liverpool,* 81.

[39] Belchem and MacRaild, 'Cosmopolitan Liverpool', 417–18.

[40] Goffman, *Presentation of Self.*

[41] Rich, 'Quiet End', S7.

[42] D. Conn, 'Prospectors for Gold Leave Liverpool with Mountain of Debt', *Guardian,* 23 January 2008.

[43] *Daily Telegraph,* 7 February 2007.

[44] *Daily Telegraph,* 21 December 2007.

[45] *Guardian,* 22 May 2007.

[46] *Daily Telegraph,* 6 September 2007.

[47] *Daily Telegraph,* 22 January 2008. On the same weekend, in January 2008, Manchester United fans daubed graffiti on the walls of the house of chief executive David Gill as a 'reminder' that a section of United's following remained 'betrayed' by the 2005 sell-out to the Glazers.

[48] Mukesh Ambani, chairman of Reliance Industries and Subroto Roy, chairman of Sahara Group were each reported to be willing to invest more than £200 million for a 51% stake in the club.

[49] Moran, *British Regulatory State,* 88.

[50] See Mitchie, 'Governance and Regulation'; also Grant, 'Analytical Framework'.

[51] BBC, *Newsnight,* 14 November 2007.

[52] Reported in the *Daily Telegraph,* 27 June 2008.

[53] M. Samuel, 'English Football at Risk from French Revolution', *The Times,* 19 November 2008.

[54] Grant, 'Analytical Framework', 88.

[55] *Guardian,* 4 June 2008. The new shirt sponsorship was reported to have cost Aston Villa £2 million per year compared to a commercial package.

[56] D. Conn, 'Guardian Profile: Randy Lerner', *Guardian,* 7 March 2008.

[57] Grant, 'Analytical Framework', has made a useful, ground-clearing, start on this project.

[58] This last point took on a special resonance when, in October 2010, Hicks and Gillett ended up in the High Court attempting to prevent the sale of Liverpool for £300 million to another group of American investors, New England Sports Ventures, led by John W Henry, and owners of the Boston Red Sox baseball franchise. As part of the refinancing of outstanding loans with the Royal Bank of Scotland Hicks and Gillett had been forced to place legal responsibility for the sale of the club to 'responsible' new owners effectively in the hands of its three British-born directors, led by chairman Martin Broughton. Hicks and Gillett claimed the club had been grossly undervalued, while Liverpool supporters attending the hearings were captured wildly celebrating the departure of its failing owners as the sale went through. The new Americans promised a winning team but also a debt-free future and their arrival was cautiously welcomed by the Spirit of Shankly group as 'Hopefully, the start of a bright future.' Time, as they say, will tell.

References

Arnold, A., and B. Webb. 'Aston Villa and Wolverhampton Wanderers 1971/2 to 1981/2: A Study of Finance Policies in the Football Industry'. *Managerial Finance* 12, no. 1 (1986): 11–19.

Barclay, P. 'Super Rich Owners Playing With Fire'. *Sunday Telegraph,* 3 February 2008.

Belchem, J., ed. *Liverpool 800: Culture, Character and History.* Liverpool: Liverpool City Council and Liverpool University Press, 2006.

Belchem, J. *Merseypride: Essays in Liverpool Exceptionalism.* Liverpool: Liverpool University Press, 2000.

Belchem, J., and D. MacRaild. 'Cosmopolitan Liverpool'. In *Liverpool 800: Culture, Character and History,* edited by J. Belchem, 311–92. Liverpool: Liverpool City Council and Liverpool University Press, 2006.

Bond, D. 'Texan Vows to Protect Spirit of Liverpool'. *Daily Telegraph,* 10 February 2007.

Brown, A. 'European Football and the EU: Governance, Participation and Social Cohesion – Towards a Policy Research Agenda'. *Soccer and Society* 1, no. 2 (2000):129–50.

Carter, N. *The Football Manager: A History*. London and New York: Routledge, 2006.

Crawford, G. *Consuming Sport: Fans, Sport and Culture*. London: Routledge, 2004.

Dobson, S., and J. Goddard. *The Economics of Football*. Cambridge: Cambridge University Press, 2001.

Elliott, L., and D. Atkinson. *The Gods That Failed: How Blind Faith in Markets Has Cost Us Our Future*. London: The Bodley Head, 2008.

Featherstone, M. *Consumer Culture and Postmodernism*. London: Sage, 2007.

Giulianotti, R., and R. Robertson. 'The Globalization of Football: A Study in the "Glocalization" of Serious Life'. *The British Journal of Sociology* 55, no. 3 (2004): 545–68.

Goffman, E. *The Presentation of Self in Everyday Life*. Harmondsworth: Penguin, 1959.

Grant, W. 'An Analytical Framework For a Political Economy of Football'. *British Politics* 2 (2007): 69–90.

Kennedy, D. 'Class, Ethnicity and Civic Governance: A Social Profile of Football Club Directors on Merseyside in the Late-Nineteenth Century'. *International Journal of the History of Sport* 22, no. 5 (2006): 840–66.

Kennedy, D., and M. Collins. 'Community Politics in Liverpool and the Governance of Professional Football in the Late Nineteenth Century'. *The Historical Journal* 49, no. 3 (2006): 761–88.

King, A. *The End of the Terraces*. London and New York: Leicester University Press, 1998.

Lane, T. *Liverpool, City of the Sea*. Liverpool: Liverpool University Press, 1997.

McGovern, P. 'Globalization or Internationalization? Foreign Footballers in the English League, 1946–95'. *Sociology* 36, no. 1 (2002): 23–42.

Martin, P. 'The 'Europeanisation' of Elite Football'. *European Societies* 7, no. 2 (2005): 349–68.

Mitchie, J. 'The Governance and Regulation of Professional Football'. *Political Quarterly* (2000): 184–91.

Moran, M. *The British Regulatory State*. Oxford: Oxford University Press, 2003.

Morrow, S. *The New Business of Football*. Basingstoke and London: Macmillan, 1999.

Morrow, S. *The People's Game: Football, Finance and Society*. Basingstoke and New York: Palgrave Macmillan, 2003.

Rich, T. 'Quiet End to the Old Order'. *The Daily Telegraph*, 7 February 2007.

Robertson, R. *Globalisation: Social Theory and Global Culture*. London: Sage, 1992.

Rowe, D. 'Sport and the Repudiation of the Global'. *International Review for the Sociology of Sport* 38, no. 2 (2003): 281–94.

Schimmel, K.S. 'Sport and Political Economy: An Introduction'. In *The Political Economy of Sport*, edited by J. Nauright and K.S. Schimmel, 1–15. Basingstoke Palgrave-Macmillan, 2005.

Taylor, I. 'English Football in the 1990s: Taking Hillsborough Seriously?'. In *British Football and Social Change: Getting into Europe*, edited by J. Williams and S. Wagg, 3–24. Leicester, London and New York: Leicester University Press, 1991.

Taylor, M. *The Association Game: A History of British Football*. Harlow: Pearson Education, 2008.

Tischler, S. *Footballers and Businessmen: The Origins of Professional Soccer in England*. New York: Holmes and Meier, 1981.

Tomlinson, A. 'North and South: The Rivalry of the Football League and the Football Association'. In *British Football and Social Change: Getting into Europe*, edited by J. Williams and S. Wagg, 25–47. Leicester, London and New York: Leicester University Press, 1991.

Tomlinson, J. *Globalisation and Culture*. Cambridge: Polity, 1999.

Williams, J. *Is It All Over? Can English Football Survive the FA Premier League?* Reading: South Street Press, 1999.

Williams, J. 'Kopites, Scallies and Liverpool Fan Cultures: Tales of Triumph and Disasters'. In *Passing Rhythms: Liverpool FC and the Transformation of Football*, edited by J. Williams, S. Hopkins, and C. Long, 99–128. Oxford: Berg, 2001.

Williams, J. *The Liverpool Way*. Edinburgh: Mainstream Press, 2003.

Williams, J. 'The Local and the Global in English Soccer and the Rise of Satellite Television'. *Sociology of Sport Journal* 11, no. 4 (1994): 376–97.

Williams, J. *Red Men! Liverpool Football Club, The Biography*. Edinburgh: Mainstream Press, 2010.

Williams, J., and S. Hopkins. *The Miracle of Istanbul*. Edinburgh: Mainstream Press, 2005.

Williams, R. *Marxism and Literature*. Harmondsworth: Penguin, 1977.

Paddling, property and piracy: the politics of canoeing in England and Wales

Paul Gilchrist[a] and Neil Ravenscroft[b]

[a]Chelsea School, University of Brighton, Eastbourne, UK; [b]School of Environment and Technology, University of Brighton, Brighton, UK

This paper situates the politics of canoeing on inland rivers in England and Wales in the context of property rights and protest repertoires. We argue that the dominance of property rights has created an asymmetrical position that has underpinned riparian rights holders' claims to exclusive use of rivers while simultaneously delegitimizing the apparently equally valid claims of paddlers and others seeking access along rivers. Utilizing a netnographic approach we interrogate the adopted cultural positions of canoeists as 'roving bandit' and 'social pirate' through a study of online discussion. By adopting identities as 'bandit' and 'pirate', paddlers seek to unsettle the hegemony over property relations exercised by anglers to win concessions for use and enjoyment of rivers. Informed by Mancur Olson's theory of property settlement by outlaws, we argue that these identities do more to substantiate the claims of anglers to possession than further the cause of paddlers to securing greater access. In order to substantiate their claims, paddlers need to shift the point of their attack from that characterized by the roving and ephemeral bandit to that of the settled ruler, in the process establishing a claim over inland waters that is as strong as that already imposed by the anglers.

Introduction

Just returned from a trip of [sic] the River Teifi (Llandysul to Cenarth Falls), during this trip we must of taken abuse from 20 + fishermen who were shouting at us from the side of the bank. They took photos of us for evidence too. This is getting out of hand now, we had some fisherman try to cast his line out at a boater – potential injury waiting to happen.[1]

I was fishing the Rheidol which was running high and had waded in to mid-stream when without warning a flash of blue shot past within inches of where I was wading. It was a canoe. It was the most frightening experience of my life. What would have happened had I stepped back and it had hit me? That could well have resulted in a fatality, as I doubt I could have found my feet and regained my balance in such strong current.[2]

These images of are a far cry from Walton's depiction in *The Compleat Angler* (1653) of angling as a form of anti-modernist escapism. Angling was supposed to be about quiet contemplation and patience, punctuated by occasional tussles with a wily freshwater foe in secluded rural idylls.[3] Instead, the therapeutic virtues of angling in early twenty-first century Britain are depicted as being under attack by other water users who are competing for shared use of a natural resource. The first, although written by a paddler (a generic term for canoeists and kayakers) to a web forum (the UK Rivers Guide Book, hereafter UKRGB), reveals a sense – on the part of the anglers – of embattlement and defence against encroachment by canoeists. The second, written by an angler, shows the sport under attack by those who use mobile waterborne ballistic missiles – canoes and kayaks – which are capable of maiming and injuring anglers, destroying the enjoyment derived from investment in a day's fishing at a favoured spot. Morgan's article in the Cardiff-based *Western Mail* highlights the angling community as a 'beleaguered "other"', a community that deliberately downplays legal and consumer privilege and adopts instead a siege mentality in order to stake a moral high ground to delegitimize alternate and competing uses of rural space – a practice, incidentally, that has recurred throughout the history of countryside recreation in Britain.[4]

The conventional rhetorical frame within which angler/paddler relations have been negotiated is informed by references to opposition (if not violence) and insider/outsider status. In particular, paddlers refer to canoeing trips that take place on waters where there are no established statutory or contractual rights as 'bandit runs'. This is both recognition of the 'extra legal' status of the activity and an evocation of the mythologizing of the participants as rebels seeking to overturn the injustice of contemporary property relations.[5] On their part, anglers have been inclined to dismiss paddlers (bandits or not) as 'other'; mere consumers seeking to put their interests ahead of those of the environment and the anglers who care for it. Morgan's depiction (in the title of the article from which the second quote was taken) of the paddler as pirate is, we believe, a recent departure designed to pathologize paddlers away from the relatively benign image of 'rogues', towards a more uncomfortable one as (after Olson), 'robbers' seeking to take by force what they have not been willing to pay for in conventional markets.[6]

Thus, while we may be some distance from Hobbes' proverbial state of nature, the contestation of claims and the delegitimization and marginalization of opposing interests (especially those which actively set out to dissent) has long been a part of the politics of securing access to natural resources.[7] In the case of paddling on non-tidal inland waters in England and Wales, actions by paddlers have kept the political debates alive, although riparian owners have, equally, been able to bound and enrol these protests in the defence of their over-arching rights of exclusivity.[8]

Yet, as 'rebel' action by the ramblers, the anti-road protesters and others has illustrated, direct and active dissent (the performance, in Parker's terms, of 'active' citizenship) can lead to political, legal and cultural outcomes that (appear to) favour the rebels and protesters.[9] However, as Parker and Ravenscroft argue, the hegemony of formal property relations is such that even 'victories', such as the statutory right to roam enacted in the Countryside and Rights of Way Act 2000, are largely pyrrhic unless the protesters are able subsequently to 'jostle' the dominant ideology sufficient to embed their claims within the mainstream political agenda.[10] The success of protest action thus rests in the ability of the protesters to capitalize on any short-term concessions that they may win. This is very much the position in which paddlers find themselves: through direct action they can – and do – paddle rivers over which others claim exclusivity; but they have not yet found a mechanism for underpinning their claim through mainstream politics.

In responding to calls made for further studies into protest in sport, therefore, we situate this paper within the long-term contest between anglers and paddlers over the recreational use of rivers in England and Wales.[11] In particular, we seek to argue that the dominance of property rights has created an asymmetrical position that has underpinned anglers' claims while simultaneously delegitimizing the apparently equally valid claims of the paddlers.[12] It is within this frame that we situate the notion of protest through 'piracy' and how it has equipped a politics of sport that is sensitive to structure and agency, space and place, mobility and moorings, and forms of individual and collective resistance. However, following Olson, we proceed to argue that this form of protest has done more to substantiate the claims of the anglers than it has to advance the claims of the paddlers.[13] This leads us to argue that, in order to substantiate their claims, paddlers need to shift the point of their attack from that characterized by the roving and ephemeral bandit (protester), to that of the settled ruler (equivalence with riparian rights holders), in the process establishing a claim over inland waters that is as strong as that already imposed by the anglers.

The problem: substantiating claims in the hegemonic context of rights

The essential problematic that frames the angler/paddler dispute is the uncertainty surrounding the extent to which the owner of the legal interest in the banks and bed of a non-tidal river has the right to determine who uses the water that flows past, and for what purposes. In the case of some – and it is only a few – rivers (and usually only some sections of these rivers), there is undisputed evidence that public rights of navigation exist. While there may be conflict between users on these sections, there is little doubt about people's rights to be there, and, pragmatically, no need to question the finer points of law, about the ability to 'own' a dynamic resource such as moving water. For the most part, however, there is no indisputable evidence about who owns what rights, nor how such rights – if they exist – can be exercised.

The position in such cases, broadly, is that ownership of and access to the banks of rivers can be established, but this does not imply 'ownership' of the water itself. Rather, it would appear – and there is no established law on this – that there are property rights pertaining to the use of the water (including fishing and navigation rights) which are, conventionally, attached to the ownership of the adjacent banks and bed of the river. This is certainly convenient for those who own the banks and bed of the river (mainly farmers and landowners), in that they can charge for access to the side of the river (over their land) and use of one or more of the possible rights of use of the river (fishing, for example). While anglers sometimes baulk at paying both charges, they have long recognized that such payment brings with it a level of exclusivity: if they have bought those rights, no-one else can use them. As a result, they have been happy to endorse claims that property rights can be attached to moving water as well as to the banks, for they need to acquire rights to both if they are going to fish on water that they cannot own, off land that they very often do not, and cannot afford to, own.[14]

In contrast, paddlers have no need of rights to gain access to the bank, other than for getting into and out of the water (and this can often be done off public land such as the highway). It is thus in their interest to argue that use of the water for a dynamic activity like navigation cannot be controlled by laws that relate to distinct – and static – real estate. And herein lies the problem: there is no legal precedent to establish which claim is superior; paddlers have long argued that their claim ought to be superior, because they do not seek to impose property rights on a resource – water – that so obviously is not real estate in the accepted sense, but instead merely require a non-exclusive licence to move along the water; anglers, in contrast, have simply imposed the exclusivity of property law, despite the fact that they do not wish to use the water for navigational purposes. For the anglers, property is by its (legal) nature exclusive; access to property is thus achieved by acquiring appropriate rights (as the anglers have done). This, they argue, is open to anyone, including paddlers. For paddlers, however, this construct of property in or over the water flowing along a river is far from axiomatic.

It is here that differential power is evident. Established customs of use alongside social and economic investment in the property allow anglers to stake a moral high ground. The custom is supported by Locke's labour-desert theory; the idea that natural rights to land are acquired through productive use or improvements to property.[15] To be rewarded is the person (or group of persons) who make the highest or best use of the land: 'the useful labourer rather than the sluggard'.[16] For anglers, best use is considered as angling and an associated stewardship role involving environmental management, sensitivity to landowners and other users, and security through surveillance. These actions help to confer a natural and hegemonic 'right' of tenure, involving partnership and shared responsibility between riparian landowner and privileged user; a confluence of interests and values that help to defend angling. It is common, for instance, for anglers to couch their enjoyment of the sport in terms of its economic contribution and environmental benefits. For example, in response to a universal right of access pursued by the British Canoe Union (BCU), Jim Glasspool, Chairman of the Fisheries and Angling Conservation Trust, said: 'The BCU's demand for unregulated, free access, without making any contribution to the maintenance or improvement of the resource is unrealistic'.[17]

In contradistinction to the responsible use maintained by anglers, canoeists are depicted as parasitic deviants, prone to selfishness, dangerous behaviour, irresponsibility and rudeness. The differential of power plays out in such cultural attitudes. Although anglers are often happy (at least, rhetorically) to share use and enjoy good relations with canoeists, for many, particularly where tensions run high or incidents occur, the negative depiction of canoeing as transgressive and harmful comes to the fore. For instance, a report written by the secretary of the Carmarthenshire Fishermen's Federation (CFF), about a canoe-related incident on the River Teifi at Cenarth, Wales, reported a confrontation between a group of canoeists and members of the Teifi Trout Association. A series of complaints were made by anglers of a group of canoeists who were aggressive and confrontational when challenged about the legal situation and their lack of a right to paddle. It was claimed the canoeists were 'itinerant' and their 'alleged demeanour exacerbated a potentially volatile situation'.[18] The report complains that the unauthorized transgression in the fishing season was fostered by misinformation propagated by local river guide books and the local access officer of the Welsh Canoe Association. As the transgression was committed in the knowledge of the law, thus with *de facto* culpability, the report defended the actions of TTA members who 'were entitled to use reasonable force to remove the trespassing canoeists'.[19] In response to the benevolence shown by the anglers, the canoeists were called upon to make public apologies.

The report concludes by moving from a tone of aggravation to warning. 'No recognised sport suffers so much interference and aggravation from another as does angling by the canoeist community'. It goes on, 'In essence, this should be regarded more as post adolescent bravado rather than criminality. Nevertheless, the tranquillity of the countryside should not be held to ransom by such a voluble minority determined to expedite their impunity through authoritative indifference'. Eye-witness reports given to the secretary of the CFF highlight a persistent use of foul language and some alleged physical and verbal intimidation. As such, the discipline shown by the anglers and reasonableness in facing confrontation was used to make a call for better self-regulation of the canoe community, to be enforced by the Welsh Assembly Government through trespass laws and anti-social behaviour orders (Asbos) under the Crime and Disorder Act 1998.[20]

This incident highlights the issue at stake. Although subsequently refuted on a canoeist web forum, it reveals how cultures of use, particularly those based around notions of 'good citizenship', provide the moral ground to maintain exclusive possession. It is in this context that we situate our paper. Although there is not scope here to relay different cultural experiences, expectations and politics of shared usage of rivers, our aim is to build upon our previous work to highlight the politicization of cultural formations of use as mobilized by canoeists in the context of asymmetrical rights to non-tidal rivers in England and Wales.[21] We are interested less in the legal efficacy of moral claims to natural resources – a subject we leave to theorists of property and justice – but, rather, with forms of political identity and agency that are being adopted by canoeists as a response to this long-standing and high-profile sporting conflict. The study is informed by insights gained from consultancy to the UK Government on the issue as well as strategic planning for water-based sport and recreation in England and Wales.[22]

The prism: 'rulers as robbers' – the role of banditry in substantiating property claims

The politics of the 'debates' over access to inland waters over which there are no established public rights of navigation are, we believe, akin to many other disputes over property. Invariably, in such disputes, the rights to property are claimed (and vigorously defended) by one party, with the other party having little option but to challenge this authority and steal the property away. In *Power and Prosperity*, Mancur Olson addresses the nature of such disputes by asking why some economies prosper while others fail. He concentrated his response on the nature of political power, and how different kinds of power promote different kinds of economic behaviour. 'We need to find out what those in power have an incentive to do and why they obtained power', he wrote.[23]

Olson memorably started his answer by utilizing a metaphor of rulers as robbers. Like Oppenheimer before him, he posed a theory of the origins of government based on conquest and confiscation.[24] The political and economic effects of two types of robber were considered: the stationary (settled) and the roving bandit. On first appearances, the position of the roving bandit seems more advantageous, both for the bandit and for the target community. Why settle down and attempt to govern when bounty can be gained from numerous sources? And surely, if considerations of fairness are to be observed, it would be better to spread theft around the land to ease the burden on a local population? However, Olson posited, the roving bandit (the paddler, in our case) is counter-productive. Returning to his previously established theory of collective action, Olson argued that if there is no action in concert, and several roving bandits exist, then a likely outcome is under-production by local populations who lack security and incentive to work.[25] The rational action for the roving bandit, therefore, would be to regulate the forms of economic extraction and settle on a system of property rights that encourages a productive use of assets. In effect, roving bandits must discipline themselves and become stationary:

> A bandit leader with sufficient strength to control and hold a territory has an incentive to settle down, to wear a crown, and to become a public good-providing autocrat....Thus governments for large groups of people have normally arisen because of the rational self-interest of those who can organize the greatest capacity for violence.[26]

Thus, if the objective of the bandit is to acquire property and prosperity it would soon become apparent, Olson argued, that greater economic benefits accrue through settled social relations in a given territory. The bandit only needs occasionally to extract the fruits of production as a form of tribute in order to meet his or her requirements. With careful stewardship, over time the stationary bandit can enjoy a monopoly of property and violence.

Analysis: the symbolic violence of the settled bandit and the (cons)piracy of opposition

Corollaries between Olson's constructs and the governance of inland water are clear: anglers realized the power of settlement many years ago and combined in angling clubs and associations to settle the best fishing grounds. And in settling these fishing grounds they have been in a position to dictate the terms upon which rights are constructed and deployed (that is, by owning the rights to the river banks and bed, the anglers have been able to restrict the use of the water, even if the actual legal status of this action is questionable). As a result, settlement has given them a strong position to ward off the claims of others, especially paddlers, by deploying their hegemonic position to resist claims that are not backed by evidence of property rights.

Paddlers, therefore, have effectively been excluded from using a resource – flowing water – by their lack of access to property rights (for which they actually have no use). Following Olson's theory, the paddler response has been two-fold: to request that riparian owners grant them access to sections of water; and to 'bandit' waters where there is no agreement. These are classic examples of the roving construct: paddlers are opportunistic in where and when they paddle, in return for which they have achieved some (often limited) agreements and some successful (undetected) bandit runs of a number of rivers (although it is likely that the number of 'bandits' is actually very small). On the other hand, as seen above, anglers have hardened their defence of areas intrinsic to their own utility. By erecting signage and fencing and verbally (sometimes physically) reprimanding transgressors, anglers have enforced their rights; leaving paddlers who have confronted this situation with a reduced enjoyment of the water, certainly not the unfettered access they hope for. As such, only those with sufficient political and (in this case) sporting capital have access to this liminal world of roving banditry, while the law-abiding others receive even less, as riparian owners – in Olson's terms – under-produce the types of facilities and services that they might otherwise expect to provide.

Thus, while enjoying some success, the current politics of settlement in effect sees paddlers attain no more than roving status: they either have to ask for access (thus underpinning extant property relations), or they have to bandit (again underpinning extant property relations). They thus make gains in canoeing where previously they did not go, but within a Hobbesian paradigm of opposition, if not terror, and without any of the facilities and support that they might reasonably expect to enjoy.

Paddlers are, thus, faced with a dilemma about the type of political tactics that they need to adopt to pursue their access and navigation claims. If they continue to rove, some may enjoy further access to inland waters that they would not otherwise enjoy. If they seek settlement, a failure to secure settlement, or conditions of settlement that limits use to particular zones and times, could undermine *de facto* gains that they have made through roving. Olson's theory of the origins of government thus sets up the core consideration of this paper: if there is a socio-spatial logic to capitalism that privileges or rewards those who opt for political and economic control over geographic entities, what becomes, culturally and politically, of the roving 'others', particularly if they fail to settle their claim?

Methodology

In studying the politics of the English and Welsh canoeing we have employed a new qualitative methodology called netnography or 'ethnography on the Internet'.[27] Carrying a similar array of methodological benefits and problems to those associated with ethnography, this technique involves the researcher using websites to observe, record and participate in the public discussions of a community gathered together by common interests and consumption activities. It is based 'primarily on the observation of textual discourse' where the aim is to gain insight into the opinions, motives, concerns and experiences of online users.[28] Netnography was pioneered in studies of consumer behaviour, particularly the relationship of offline to online consumption practices and creative processes but has been used sparingly in sport and leisure studies.[29] It offers a supplement to other research methods, can overcome problems associated with researcher interference, and is particularly useful for studying communities where participation online feeds directly into cultural practices. A strong claim to its use surrounds the monitoring of sensitive topics that raise ethical, legal and political questions (often with a relevance to the development of public policy), thus minimizing harm to the human subject, whilst offering the research a form of documentary sourcing through which can be witnessed the play of a social issue, cultural contestation and political mobilization.[30]

We have employed a netnographic approach to unobtrusively collect data to gain analytic insight into the politics of the paddler community. At no stage did we intervene in discussions. Observations were conducted virtually, recording dialogue in a public online forum that is widely used by participants in the British paddler community, the UK Rivers Guidebook.[31] The website offers an online forum to discuss paddling activity, sell and trade, highlight good areas to paddle, and engage in public discussion on issues linked to the development and practice of the sport. The rest of the site provides information on routes to paddle in England, Wales and Scotland; reports of paddling trips and expeditions around the world; information on grades of difficulty on moving water; and a bookshop profiling guidebooks for different disciplines of canoeing and kayaking.

A purposive sampling frame was adopted to search for messages relevant to the politics of paddling, using a search facility on the site for word threads (a series of posts) relating to recreational access issues (e.g. 'access', 'pirates', 'bandit', 'trespass', 'incident'). Representativeness or transferability are not offered by this method; this interpretive approach instead provides the researcher with analytic depth and insight, approximating to the 'thick description' of Geertzian ethnographic method.[32] The netnographic approach takes advantage of sites with easily accessible caches of information; in the case of the UKRGB posts to the forum are stored on the site dating back to 2002.[33] To our knowledge, the threads have not been deleted or altered in any way, thus providing comprehensive and authentic forms of discourse on a range of issues. Threads varied in length according to the nature of the issue discussed and the number of participants involved in discussions. A rudimentary analysis revealed varying levels of social ties and commitment to either the discussion, or to paddling in general, confirming Kozinets' distinction between the presence of tourists, minglers, devotees and insiders in online environments.[34]

The discussions observed showed a high presence of 'insiders': long-term paddlers with a sophisticated level of knowledge about the extra-sporting dimensions of paddling, as such providing a reliable data source. We archived messages from relevant discussions and retrieved, downloaded and printed them. Approximately 76 threads were analysed covering a period of just over two years (May 2006 – July 2008). The length of thread varied from 0 to 214 replies, although some are still active at the time of writing. The retrieved threads were coded using a constant comparative method, which involves devising categories from general and specific issues derived from the discussions after frequent (re)readings of the text to construct an accurate theoretical frame and interpretive position.[35] The authors audited these themes and made suggestions and corrections in the interpretation and writing phases, based upon understandings of the politics of the paddler community derived from nearly 10 years of consultancy and research on policy and strategic planning for water-sport in England and Wales.[36]

Netnography carries a series of ethical issues relating to informed consent, privacy, confidentiality and appropriation of individuals' life stories; not to mention unresolved intellectual property right discussions concerning copyright and fair use.[37] Whilst these issues are contested and are being resolved by social scientists using the web as a research tool,[38] we have minded Berry's call to use a non-alienating 'open source' ethical framework by being committed to maintaining a relationship of trust with the paddler community. In this endeavour, we have circulated previous web-based research to stakeholders that actively use the UKRGB,[39] in effect, returning research to the community in question to stimulate discussion on the accuracy of results, and also to expose the methodologically problematic position of 'lurking' and 'harvesting' texts (see UKRGB thread 'who else is listening and why?', April 2008).[40] Further, we have attempted to accurately and fairly record the intention of the discussions in order to broaden our understanding of the political dynamics surrounding paddling in England and Wales. It is our intention to move from netnography to other forms of research (qualitative interviews with participants, for instance) in order to confirm or reject the positions understood in this paper.

Findings: toward a politics/'piratics' of recreational access to inland waters

We have previously claimed that the construct of the 'rebel' is active within the paddling community: an individual willing to put their interests before those of others in the belief that (a) this is the only way that they can practise their sport, and (b) that their actions will have a positive long-term benefit for others, especially those less able and willing to risk conflict with landowners.[41] This is demonstrated by callwild in the following post, where he expresses surprise that fellow paddlers do not paddle where they wish when they deem it suitable:

> Where have you been living? This is exactly how a large chunk of us have been paddling for years. And I might add with very few problems. As we all know the current trespass laws do not criminalise us and as long as we behave responsibly and are well mannered when challenged, explain politely and carry on then nothing ever comes of it. I feel sorry for those that have to take organised groups as they have to stay more within the law and it is for these reasons the law mainly needs changing as the present situation doesn't really stop us paddling at all in my experience.[42]

Callwild is typical of a form of 'rebel' paddlers we have termed 'roving bandits'. Use and enjoyment of a resource comes to the fore; the water becomes a signifier of liberty and possibility for the individual. However, a rational calculating self-interest is at play which weighs decisions in light of where the greatest benefits (seen here in terms of individual satisfaction) can accrue. As such, without recourse to a collective politics or enlightened self-interest that judges the consequences of actions for a wider paddler community, roving bandits are seen to jeopardize wider social benefits that can accrue through action in concert. This criticism is levelled by both anglers (see above) who often prefer to negotiate access over shared use (even if it does impose strict limits for the canoeists) and paddlers who seek to secure safe resource and arrangements, especially to the benefit of new entrants to the sport. In responding to callwild, thus, TheKrikketWars makes the point that clubs rely on access agreements and that it would not be acceptable to put novices or those under instruction in danger on waters where there is no agreement:

> To some extent I agree .... and what he says is all fair and well for individuals; but as part of a club, if I looked up the hierarchy and said 'There's a really good river for training the intermediates how to run feature x better, it won't be at a good enough level for quite a while

after this, should we take them?' I'd be asked 'what's the access agreement say?' the reply 'there isn't one. We'll be fine if we just turn up and paddle' would receive no more than an icy glance and all the young people will think 'Access Agreement – Good; Boating When Levels Are Right – Bad'.[43]

While this may be a persuasive argument for some, 'roving bandits' tend not to see, or to respect, this broader community argument, and instead stick to a rigid individualist approach, that they will do what they wish:

'Just go paddle' is the best way to get a stupid legal situation changed or ignored. I HAVE stopped caring which one of these would be better, as long as I get to paddle. I'm sure the situation would be easier if it weren't for some paddlers doing stuff when the rivers are low/in big groups/portaging or inspecting through gardens etc'.[44]

And:

Personally I will carry on kayaking rivers until I am taken to court, prosecuted and imprisoned; other than that who cares about an opinion of access? It is redundant conversation until the law is clarified and passed.[45]

And:

for many years we were told by riparian owners that they had the right to dictate as and when we could navigate the rivers fronting their land. Unfortunately ... no one challenged them, no one stood up to them, no one asked them to point out the actual law which gave them this power.... This has been going on for nearly 50 years, to the point now that it has, in many people's minds, become a truth ... but not a truth which has a legal basis.... This basically leaves us with two choices, we accept the bully boy tactics of riparian landowners and believe their legally unsubstantiated 'truth' and only paddle when they say we can, or we accept the more paddler friendly 'truth' (admitted also legally uncertain) and enjoy our natural heritage as and when we choose. Personally, until someone can demonstrate in law that I do not have year round, unrestricted access, I will continue to believe that I do.[46]

As these posts suggest, 'roving bandits' construct themselves as vigilantes, prepared to face the law in undertaking their sport in their chosen way. Their rhetoric invokes a connection to the mythology of the 'access campaign', that paddlers have been striving for access for more than half a century, and the 'roving bandits' cannot wait any longer. Eschewing the interests of all, the 'roving bandits' claim instead an alternate solidaristic identity, a romanticized form of vanguardism, that depicts acquiescence to restriction and regulation as a form of debilitating self-sacrifice. Better to pursue self-interest than be paralysed by inaction. The post by Jules exemplifies this. Others, such as buck197 below, who would like to follow this line but do not feel able, boost the egos of these bandits and further cement their self-image as vigilantes:

I like the 'Paddle and be damned' camp and hopefully they will bring the debate into a much wider audience. I, as an old boy and with a more wussy approach, sneak in and paddle if no one spots me. Though I would happily join a demonstration of paddlers or march say.[47]

What these actions indicate is a politics associated with the roving other: that while some paddlers may have rejected formal and institutional relationships over canoe agreements, they have only been able to pursue their chosen approach (canoeing wherever and whenever they can) through opportunism. However, the response is not entirely individualistic in effect. A politicized mythology of access is evoked by these paddlers themselves through the 'bandit runs' – canoeing that takes place where there are no explicit agreements. Akin to the mass trespasses utilized by ramblers in the interwar years, the bandit run has become a signature action that establishes moral rights of access by forays into forbidden territories.[48] 'Bandit runs' are increasingly seen as a tool that can be occassionally mobilized to support an already existing culture of (individual, stealth) use.

Yet, such runs often occur as responses to specific situations, such as antagonism on the part of anglers or landowners. The following thread, from UKRGB, demonstrates the construct of the 'bandit run':

> Just returned from a trip on the River Teifi (Llandysul to Cenarth Falls). During this trip we must of taken abuse from 20 + fisherman who were shouting at us from the side if the bank.... Now as far as we are concerned, we spoke to the access officer for the area the day before. We got on the river on public land and left the river on public land – what more can we do![49]

> Sounds an ideal place for a mass trespass![50]

> The case for canoeists needs to be pressed home, open access, responsible paddling will continue to aid our cause.[51]

> Im up for that, but dont call it a mass trespass, just a mass paddling trip![52]

> No surely it will be just a coincidence that loads of people arrived the same day![53]

> I'm never one to bother with access issues. Why should we with the utter lack of respect we receive from fisherman?... If I want to run a river... I will. I have every right to enjoy myself. Sure I will stick to access agreements the WCA fight for and certainly won't go looking for troublesome stand offs.[54]

While this approach has certainly provided opportunities to canoe for some people in some places and at some times, it has effectively deflected the politics away from the legal/moral stance of the riparian owners. The politics of 'roving banditry' is instead a form of countercultural romanticized mythologization of outsiders in need of status as marginal and thus 'Other'. This, of course, is Moc Morgan's project in inscribing ideas of terror on an activity normally associated with quiet enjoyment. As Olson has described, this roving banditry has led, on the part of many land and riparian owners, to a general condemnation of all paddlers as outlaws seeking to take for themselves what they are unable (or unwilling) to acquire legally, through the market.[55] Rather than opening the way for others, therefore, the actions of bandits have had the opposite effect: to catalyse and legitimize opposition to all forms of paddling, under all circumstances.

In beginning to recognize the unintended consequences of the 'roving bandit', the paddler community is faced with a stark choice: to press ahead with their roving culture (in the knowledge that this is both exclusive and increasingly threatening to those who do not want to assume the pirate identity); or to seek ways of settling that allow them to assume a stronger 'ruler' identity, much as anglers have done for the last century or more. The problem is that 'settling' suggests accepting territorial and temporal constraints to their activity that are the antithesis of the freedoms that they have sought to paddle wherever they want, subject only to environmental considerations. Therefore, paddlers must be careful what to wish for, as settlement may actually diminish enjoyment. Perhaps even harder to accept is that this construct inevitably means that paddlers will have to behave more like anglers, even to the point of joining their clubs and forming associations with them. While, rhetorically at least, many anglers would welcome this outcome, it would be largely because this would give them the power to determine when and where paddling can take place, safe in the knowledge that this is now governed by a club culture that they understand and can manipulate and administer.

Faced with these untenable options, an increasing number of paddlers are now seeking a new 'settled' construct of, effectively, 'social' pirate. This complicates our previous model of a 'rebel' identity and the types of politics that are and can be pursued.[56] While the 'roving bandit' carries a gloss of a romanticized outsider identity, in effect, the agency is a fairly conventional individualized, consumer-based politics of use, akin to tactics employed by squatters, among others.[57] The 'social' pirate instead evokes a form of political agency that is drawn from the mythology of the struggle for canoe access, but repositioned such that the current legal presumptions in favour of landowner and riparian rights are rejected in favour of mass rights that are available to all. The actions of the social pirate thus seek to replace the settled nature of the current legal and social order with a new settlement based on mass rights of access to all inland waters:

> Unfortunately for those fishermen who want exclusivity on the rivers, we **are** going to go paddling without prior permission. This is because it is not wrong or unlawful to do so – if it was, you would surely be able to point us to the law in question, wouldn't you?[58]

> Paddle when and where the water is – treat other river users with courtesy, and respect any genuine environmental concerns, and remember that you have a right to your natural heritage. There is no need to restrict yourself to the fishermen's close season – the river is no more theirs than yours.[59]

> I think the general attitude of individual paddlers is now in line with the WCA – paddle when there is water with respect to the countryside and other river users. I can only hope that more clubs can start to see the light too! Obviously if there's a fishing competition going on it will be better to choose a different river! But single fishermen on the bank can either be portaged or can direct you to which side of the river you can best pass on.[60]

> Yes, it is. It's our's. We need to collectively get off our arses, and go and paddle.[61]

This is very much the antithesis of the roving mentality of the 'bandit run', with its implication of an accepted illegality. Rather, it is an attempt at settlement, at reworking the hegemony of the land and riparian owners in favour of a new orthodoxy in which all people have access rights. Social pirates thus favour a form of settlement and possession, where the claim and act are no longer subversive, but reflect a new-found confidence in the ability to access and use inland waters, and the concomitant need to develop governance procedures to ensure that user conduct reflects this new paradigm. This point is made by StoneWeasel:

> I for one bandit rivers on a fairly regular basis over the winter months, welcoming the fact that a landowner may well take it upon them to take me to court for trespass and I know I am not alone in doing so. The reason? Simple, trespass is traditionally hard to prove and rarely holds big penalties and if a paddler was to win a court case against the riparian land owner then precedent shall be set and hopefully the rivers shall become a free for all. Viva la revolution.[62]

> Mr Weasel, < Stern voice > We have been through all this before. We do not use terms like 'bandit' here (definitely non-pc). I think you meant 'exercise my ancient right of navigation' (pc version).[63]

And:

> Until such time as we can agree sensible sharing of scarce river resources with other users, as they certainly do in France (fishing dawn to about 9 am, paddling 9 am to 6pm then fishing till dawn or something similar) then we should just paddle when conditions are suitable. . . . There cannot be bandit runs if you act as if you have the right to be there.[64]

It is apparent that, for many paddlers, the identity of 'pirate' is complex and, at times, contradictory. Many of those who see themselves as pirates (and belong to clubs such as the Paddle Pirates) construct their identity as free thinking, independent and socially responsible. As the Paddle Pirates Club website claims, many of its members are 'dedicated' members of their own canoe clubs, but belong to the Paddle Pirates as a way of expressing their dissatisfaction with the current access situation and their wish to challenge the status quo.[65] Yet, there is also a more 'light-hearted' message, that even pirates prepared to risk everything in the pursuit of access are still 'of' the people, as the following section of posts – responding to angler Moc Morgan's claims in the *Western Mail* – illustrate:

> On the Glaslyn a pilot scheme was fully approved by the owners but then to the dismay of the angling club ... 'pirate' canoeists used the entire river – totally disregarding the agreement. 'Pirate' canoeists have to be controlled somehow, as it is they who destroy the good relationships that have been established at local level.[66]

> Oh yes, tell us more about those good local relations.[67]

> Oh that is it! From now on I'm wearing an eye patch when out on the water. Now if I can just find a way to get a parrot to sit on my shoulder.[68]

> Personally I prefer the term 'Bandit', but on this occasion I shall let it slide.[69]

> The Government do not think canoeing is illegal, the Police do not think it is illegal, the Environment Agency have run out of options to enforce any legality and the fisheries know they are on a dodgy wicket. So accept that open access is here to stay and enjoy the rivers, sooner or later all river users will be getting along just fine.[70]

> After much faffing I now have an appropriate avatar, Look out for a 58 year old teenager (hooligan ?) in a yellow burn sporting the jolly roger. Pm me if you want to become a pirate, I have a few stickers spare, £5 each, to go towards sponsoring a GB UK freestyle team paddler.[71]

This led to an intervention on UKRGB site by a well-known Welsh angler representative who sought to restore order, but with little effect:

> We go to a lot of trouble to look after our little country and its rivers. Indeed we are so proud of them that we welcome people from across the border to share our interests. In fact they come from afar to especially to enjoy the rivers and fisheries. ..... should you wish to join our ranks and take an active part in, and contribute towards looking after our rivers, then we would be delighted to welcome you.[72]

> Welcomed by you or not, I'm still gonna paddle.[73]

> Garth, we weren't waiting to be welcomed. I don't need your permission to paddle a river.[74]

Thus, the contemporary politics/piratics of the canoe lobby in England and Wales is to assert a status that, while different to the anglers, is no less settled. This new politics is based on a challenge to the dominant ideology of property, certainly in terms of who can gain access to, and use of, private property, but more fundamentally in terms of limiting the ability of individual property rights owners to exclude particular people from undertaking specific activities on their property. The attempt to embed this settled status necessarily involves displacing those who were previously settled; to this extent it is violent, although not necessarily in the way described by Hobbes. Rather, the violence that supports the challenge is both legal and moral: put up (a legal case against paddlers), or shut up.

Concluding discussion: the effectiveness of banditry as a political strategy

Olson understood that the legitimization of a system of stationary property rights depended upon a demonstration of social benefits, or public goods.[75] The moral claim exercised by settled bandits (in our model, the 'social pirate') would be stronger as settlement confers positive externalities for members, seen in terms of positive rights (e.g. the right to enjoy greater or exclusive use of a property) and negative rights (e.g. freedom from external interference – or sovereignty). In effect, Olson claims, property settlement upholds a Lockean proviso of rights conferred by the productive benefits accrued.[76]

However, appeals to an aggregate notion of social benefit or public good do not aid the 'roving bandit'. The landowner response is relatively straightforward. Why satisfy a consumer-based claim to a natural resource based around notions of self-development and individual satisfaction when the present incumbents (anglers) can successfully convert a consumer need into economic revenue? For this strategy to be successful, the bandit either has to effectively disturb the existing incumbents sufficient enough that only marginal returns are forthcoming as they seek more exclusive and better controlled waters elsewhere. This would require the paddler to frequently bandit run a river or to do so in concert – similar to the 'sustained mass trespass' tactics exercised by the Ramblers Association in the 1990s.[77] However, political scientists have shown that this is likely to fail unless individual satisfaction can also be derived from a strong common interest based around securing a common good, in this case, 'access for all'. The incentive to act collectively will be constantly undermined if there is factionalism and competition between groups, leaving routes to individual satisfaction open and an easier option.[78] These problems of collective action are present in the paddler community. Mass protest is infrequent and posts to the web forums highlight clandestine, short-lived trips that evade the disciplinary gaze of the landowner are preferred.[79] Akin to the charge levelled by Hobsbawm of the social bandit, the promise of political opposition and resistance a bandit identity brings rarely materializes. It is better to view the bandit as a symptom of dispossession and victim of capitalist property relations; a 'primitive rebel' who delights in 'jurisdictional ambiguity'.[80] In the final instance, bandits are 'not ideologists or prophets'; they lack a programmatic ideological agenda and the agentive capacity for social change.[81]

However, this is not to deny any political effect or form of settlement. The pleasures of 'jurisdictional ambiguity' are potentially part of a micropolitical performance of resistance where agents carefully negotiate spatialized power relations to elide regimes of governance and discipline.[82] They erect what Hakim Bey has termed a 'temporary autonomous zone' (TAZ), a form of post-structural standpoint where externally imposed constraints are set aside and forms of individual enjoyment come to the fore.[83] The TAZ is present in the calls made by roving bandits for permanent mobility that selectively ignores engagement with the political and economic interests governing access. The message is clear: get out and paddle. As a strategy it is successful in part because other interests (anglers, landowners) – although settled – cannot secure, patrol, police and regulate space all the time – at least not without high levels of presence or sophisticated surveillance technologies. As Bey writes, 'hidden enfolded immensities escape the measuring rod'.[84] Consequently, symbolic and physical space is left for individuals and communities to appropriate. Knowledge of the ownership of a property is put to one side as the moral claim is toward *use*, based loosely around the satisfaction of individual needs. As with Hegel's theory of property ownership, therefore, unused or unsupervised property thus creates objective moral claims based around the development of the person.[85] As a political strategy, roving banditry as an exercise of the TAZ thus makes explicit how an individual can project his or her will onto a space as a form of possessive act. Akin to Deleuze and Guattari's 'nomadology' it ascribes a condition of reflexive and practical agency to momentarily evade the bureaucratic rules of discipline set by territorial forms of governance. Strategic resistance can thus be encountered through temporary action by those who understand that public space cannot be dominated.[86]

Yet, such a strategy calls for settlement on a different level. To be successful, bandits require high levels of spatial knowledge in order to exploit the gaps left by territorial governance. Furthermore, rather than using centralized organizations to deliver better access (such as the national governing bodies of canoeing), the bandit requires instead that sophisticated histories and memories are developed to support claim-making and demands where challenged. As we have shown above, the websites sustained by the paddler community are key. They not only provide mechanisms for socialization, recall and mobilization for a broader bandit movement,[87] but also act as a repository for spatialized knowledge of inland waterways, highlighting examples of constraint, abuse and moral claim based upon individual accounts of damaged personhood and impaired satisfaction. Such information is regularly posted to the UKRGB and is an explicit part of sites maintained by the Welsh Canoe Association and the River Access Campaign through access-incident reporting sections.[88] As Bey states:

> If the TAZ is a nomad camp, then the Web helps provide the epics, songs, genealogies, and legends of the tribe; it provides the secret caravan routes and raiding trails which make up the flowlines of tribal economy; it even contains some of the very roads they will follow, some of the very dreams they will experience as signs and portents.[89]

For the political strategy of the bandits to work, therefore, it requires a process of informational settlement itself predicated on continuing material and physical practices. As Crouch and Parker's work on 'digging' (alternate uses of land that challenge existing ownership and use) has shown, alternative uses of land can successfully utilize the tools of heritage and history but require material and physical practice to be effective.[90] For the paddler, therefore, a reflexive process is called for that involves practice (paddling), embodied semiotics (textual embellishment of the cultural meanings of canoeing and kayaking in light of the spatial and political constraints encountered) and active citizenship (a claim of a social or cultural right to float with a concomitant demonstration that the exercise of the right can be limited to ensure contesting users of water space can exercise their own – in this case, asymmetrical – rights of use).

In a sense, 'social pirates' require 'roving bandits' in order to make a distinction between their noble intent, capability to self-regulate, modest claims and responsible attitude, next to the 'ignoble' or disrespectful actions of the bandit. However, whereas the threat of banditry serves the creation of an outsider status that can garner media interest, the distinction helps to reinforce property-based elements of a civil citizenship; marginalizing the 'roving bandit' and a universal right to float on inland rivers in England and Wales where no statutory right of access exists, in favour of a process of settlement that ultimately positions the 'social pirate' closer to that of the settled angler.[91] The upshot is not a diversification of repertoires of protest in pursuit of a common goal (a universal right of access) but increasing marginalization of the bandit next to dominant constructions of legitimate use. The case therefore speaks to the presence of a factionalized post-subcultural protest formation alongside a still to be played out *realpolitik* on the rivers, akin to the political and spatial dynamics that shaped the history of the institutionalization of piracy during the seventeenth and eighteenth centuries.[92] Further qualitative research into the political life-world of the paddler will help us to confirm or modify these positions. Yet, it would be premature to suggest that there is an immovable dynamic toward settlement. For, as Foucault warned, political power can be nebulous and further 'conditions of possibility' are generated when spaces for resistance are curtailed.[93] As Parker has noted with respect to British environmental protest at the turn of the millennium (and contrary to Olson), when legal and moral passages are closed for the pursuit of rights claims, new escape channels open – discipline provokes resistance and new bands of 'outlaws' spring into being.[94] The waterways of England and Wales may yet be our best example to illuminate Foucault's cycle of discipline, regulatory control and escape; highlighting the deep interconnections between political and sporting mobilities.

Notes

[1] Posted by madocks on 29 July 2007, UK Rivers Guide Book web forum, www.ukriversguidebook.co.uk.

[2] Moc Morgan, '"Pirates" Threaten Peace and Safety of Our Rivers', *Western Mail*, 5 February 2008.

[3] Franklin, 'Naturalizing Sports'.

[4] Cox and Winter, 'The Beleaguered "Other"'; Darby, *Landscape and Identity*.

[5] See Church, Gilchrist and Ravenscroft, 'Negotiating Recreational Access'; Gilchrist and Ravenscroft, 'Power to the Paddlers?'.

[6] Olson, *Power and Prosperity*; see also Parker and Wragg, 'Networks, Agency and (De)stabilization'.

[7] Darby, *Landscape and Identity*; Parker, *Citizenship*.

[8] See Gilchrist and Ravenscroft, 'Power to the Paddlers?', with respect to paddling on the River Dee, for example; Parker, *Citizenship*, 107

[9] Parker, *Citizenship*.

[10] Parker and Ravenscroft, 'Land, Rights and the Gift'.

[11] Wilson and White, 'Revive the Pride'; Davis-Delano and Crosset , 'Using Social Movement Theory'.

[12] Church, Gilchrist and Ravenscroft, 'Negotiating Recreational Access'.

[13] Olson, *Power and Prosperity*.

[14] Coalter, 'Angling and Canoeing'; Telling and Smith, *Public Right of Navigation*.

[15] Locke, *Second Treatise on Government*.

[16] Ibid., 336.

[17] http://www.talkangling.co.uk/upload/other_angling_chat/5771-anglers_call_canoe_union_get_real.html/, accessed 5 July 2008.

[18] Roberts, 'A Canoe-Related Incident'.

[19] Ibid.

[20] Ibid.

[21] Church, Gilchrist and Ravenscroft, 'Negotiating Recreational Access'; Gilchrist and Ravenscroft, 'Power to the Paddlers?'.

[22] See University of Brighton Consortium, *Water-Based Sport;* University of Brighton Consortium, *A Strategic Plan for Water Related Recreation in the South West Region;* University of Brighton Consortium, *A Strategic Plan for Water Related Recreation in the East of England Region.*

[23] Olson, *Power and Prosperity*, 1.

[24] Oppenheimer, *The State.*

[25] Olson, *Logic of Collective Action.*

[26] Olson, *Power and Prosperity*, 10–11.

[27] Kozinets, 'Field Behind the Scene'.

[28] Ibid., 64; Langer and Beckman, 'Sensitive Research Topics'.

[29] For some exceptions see Millward, 'We've All Got the Bug'; Millward, 'Rebirth of the Football Fanzine'; Morgan, 'Making Space for Experiences'.

[30] See Langer and Beckman, 'Sensitive Research Topics'; Millward, 'Rebirth of the Football Fanzine'.

[31] http://www.ukriversguidebook.co.uk

[32] Geertz, *Interpretation of Cultures.*

[33] Sharf, 'Beyond Netiquette', 244.

[34] Kozinets, 'Field Behind the Scene'.

[35] Glaser and Strauss, *Discovery of Grounded Theory.*

[36] Ravenscroft et al., *Improving Access for Canoeing;* University of Brighton Consortium, *Water-Based Sport*; University of Brighton Consortium, *A Strategic Plan for Water Related Recreation in the South West Region*; University of Brighton Consortium, *A Strategic Plan for Water Related Recreation in the East of England Region.*

[37] See Berry, 'Internet Research'; Brownlow and O'Dell, 'Ethical Issues'; Lawson, 'Blurring the Boundaries'.

[38] Sharf, 'Beyond Netiquette'.

[39] Gilchrist and Ravenscroft, 'Power to the Paddlers?'.

[40] Bakardjieva and Feenberg , 'Involving the Virtual Subject'; Markham, *Life Online.*

[41] Gilchrist and Ravenscroft, 'Power to the Paddlers?'.

[42] Posted by callwild on 16 July 2007 to UKRGB.

[43] Posted by TheKrikketWars on 16 July 2007 to UKRGB.

[44] Posted by richard e on 18 July 2007 to UKRGB.

[45] Posted by Slaphappy on 7 February 2008 to UKRGB.

[46] Posted by Jules on 13 February 2008 to UKRGB.

[47] Posted by buck 197 on 16 July 2007 to UKRGB.

[48] See Shoard, *This Land is Ours*, for example.

[49] Posted by Madocks on 28 July 2007 to UKRGB.

[50] Posted by buck197 on 29 July 2007 to UKRGB.

[51] Posted by morsey on 29 July 2007 to UKRGB.

[52] Posted by bala boater on 29 July 2007 to UKRGB.

[53] Posted by Dave Manby on 29 July 2007 to UKRGB.

[54] Posted by ERU on 29 July 2007 to UKRGB.

[55] Olson, *Power and Prosperity*.

[56] Gilchrist and Ravenscroft, 'Power to the Paddlers?'.

[57] Cobb and Fox, 'Living Outside the System?'.

[58] Posted by Pete the kayaker on 26 February 2008 to UKRGB.

[59] Posted by clarky999 on 10 March 2008 to UKRGB.

[60] Posted by Jim Pullen on 10 March 2008 to UKRGB.

[61] Posted by Tom_Laws on 15 July 2007 to UKRGB.

[62] Posted by StoneWeasel on 20 October 2005 to UKRGB.

[63] Posted by Pete the kayaker on 20 October 2005 to UKRGB.

[64] Posted by Frank B on 14 December 2006 to UKRGB.

[65] www.paddlepirates.co.uk

[66] Moc Morgan, '"Pirates" Threaten Peace and Safety of Our Rivers, *Western Mail*, 5 February 2008.

[67] Posted by Adrian Cooper on 5 February 2008 to UKRGB.

[68] Posted by Unstabler on 5 February 2008 to UKRGB.

[69] Posted by Matt R on 5 February 2008 to UKRGB.

[70] Posted by morsey on 6 February 2008 to UKRGB.

[71] Posted by Frank B on 8 March 2008 to UKRGB.

[72] Posted by Garth on 11 March 2008 to UKRGB.

[73] Posted by Gupster on 11 March 2008 to UKRGB.

[74] Posted by Unstabler on 11 March 2008 to UKRGB.

[75] Olson, *Power and Prosperity*.

[76] This argument has been exercised in the defence of other forms of banditry and piracy. Graffiti artists have been considered less a sign of urban decay than an indicator of the presence of a 'creative class' central to the economic regeneration of urban areas. Concerns over anti-social behaviour are set aside as authorities highlight the visual merit and cultural value of the artform. Other 'deviants' have been discussed in terms of their ability to create public goods. Rojek argues, for instance, that forms of 'net banditry', in particular peer-to-peer electronic file sharing, can contribute to wider outcomes of social inclusion, empowerment and distributive justice. While their practices raise important political and ethical questions about the justness of international regimes of property, Mason argues that 'punk capitalists' – from hackers, to hip-hop artists, to open-source publishers – should be embraced for their ability to fashion identities, create new products and concomitant forms of consumption. See Rojek, 'P2P Leisure Exchange'; Mason, *Pirate's Dilemma*; also, Leadbeater, *We-Think*.

[77] Doherty, Paterson and Seel, *Direct Action*.

[78] See Jones, 'Logic of Expressive Collective Action'.

[79] See also Gilchrist and Ravenscroft, 'Power to the Paddlers?'.

[80] Gallant, 'Brigandage', 40.

[81] Hobsbawm, *Bandits*, 19.

[82] Parker, 'Rights'.

[83] Bey, 'Temporary Autonomous Zone'.

[84] Ibid., 406.

[85] Hegel, *Elements of the Philosophy*, 73–102.

[86] Deleuze and Guattari, *A Thousand Plateaus*.

[87] Gilchrist and Ravenscroft, 'Power to the Paddlers?'.

88 www.welsh-canoeing.org.uk; www.riveraccess.org.
89 Bey, 'Temporary Autonomous Zone', 412.
90 Crouch and Parker, '"Digging-Up" Utopia?'.
91 See Parker, 'Rights'; Wheaton, 'From the Pavement'.
92 Land, 'Flying the Black Flag'; Mackie, 'Welcome the Outlaw'.
93 Foucault, 'Powers and Strategies'.
94 Parker, 'Rights'.

References

Bakardjieva, M., and A. Feenberg. 'Involving the Virtual Subject'. *Ethics and Information Technology* 2, no. 4 (2001): 233–40.

Berry, D.M. 'Internet Research: Privacy, Ethics and Alienation: An Open Source Approach'. *Internet Research* 14, no. 4 (2004): 323–32.

Bey, H. 'The Temporary Autonomous Zone'. In *Crypto Anarchy, Cyberstates and Pirate Utopias*, edited by P. Ludlow, 401–34. Cambridge, MA: MIT Press, 2001.

Brownlow, C., and L. O'Dell. 'Ethical Issues for Qualitative Research in Online Communities'. *Disability & Society* 17, no. 6 (2002): 685–94.

Church, A., P. Gilchrist, and N. Ravenscroft. 'Negotiating Recreational Access under Asymmetrical Power Relations: The Case of Inland Waterways in England'. *Society & Natural Resources* 20, no. 3 (2007): 213–27.

Coalter, F. 'Angling and Canoeing: Value Conflicts and Administrative Solutions'. In *New Approaches to Access in the Countryside for Recreation*, edited by H. Talbot-Ponsonby, 7. Bristol: Countryside Recreation Research Advisory Group, 1986.

Cobb, N., and L. Fox. 'Living Outside the System? The (Im)morality of Urban Squatting After the Land Registration Act 2002'. *Legal Studies* 27, no. 2 (2007): 236–60.

Cox, G., and M. Winter. 'The Beleaguered "Other": Hunt Followers in the Countryside'. In *Revealing Rural 'Others': Representation, Power and Identity in the British Countryside*, edited by P. Milbourne, 75–89. Cheltenham: Countryside and Community Foundation, 1997.

Crouch, D., and G. Parker. '"Digging-Up" Utopia? Space, Practice and Land Use Heritage'. *Geoforum* 34 (2003): 395–408.

Darby, W.J. *Landscape and Identity: Geographies of Nation and Class in England*. Oxford: Berg, 2000.

Davis-Delano, L.R., and T. Crosset. 'Using Social Movement Theory to Study Outcomes in Sport-Related Social Movements'. *International Review for the Sociology of Sport* 43, no. 2 (2008): 115–34.

Deleuze, G., and F. Guattari. *A Thousand Plateaus: Capitalism and Schizophrenia*. Minneapolis: University of Minnesota Press, 1986.

Doherty, B., Paterson, M., and B. Seel, eds. *Direct Action in British Environmentalism*. London: Routledge, 2000.

Foucault, M. 'Powers and Strategies'. In *Power/Knowledge*, edited by C. Gordon, 134–45. Brighton: Harvester Press, 1980.

Franklin, A. 'Naturalizing Sports: Hunting and Angling in Modern Environments'. *International Review for the Sociology of Sport* 33, no. 4 (1998): 355–66.

Gallant, T.W. 'Brigandage, Piracy, Capitalism, and State-Formation: Transnational Crime from a Historical World-Systems Perspective'. In *States and Illegal Practices*, edited by J. Heyman and A. Smart, 23–61. Oxford: Berg, 1999.

Geertz, C. *The Interpretation of Cultures*. New York: Basic Books, 1973.

Gilchrist, P., and N. Ravenscroft. '"Power to the Paddlers?" The Internet, Governance and Discipline'. *Leisure Studies* 27, no. 2 (2008): 129–48.

Glaser, B., and A. Strauss. *The Discovery of Grounded Theory*. London: Weidenfeld & Nicholson, 1967.

Hegel, G.W.F. *Elements of the Philosophy of Right*. Cambridge: Cambridge University Press, 1991.

Hobsbawm, E. *Bandits*. London: E. Baylis & Son, 1969.

Jones, P. 'The Logic of Expressive Collective Action: When Will Individuals "Nail Their Colours to the Mast"?'. *The British Journal of Politics and International Relations* 9, no. 4 (2007): 564–81.

Kozinets, R. 'The Field Behind the Scene: Using Netnography for Marketing Research in Online Communities'. *Journal of Marketing Research* 39, no. 1 (2002): 61–72.

Land, C. 'Flying the Black Flag: Revolt, Revolution and the Social Organization of Piracy in the "Golden Age"'. *Management & Organizational History* 2, no. 2 (2007): 169–92.

Langer, R., and S.C. Beckman. 'Sensitive Research Topics: Netnography Revisited'. *Qualitative Market Research* 8, no. 2 (2005): 189–203.

Lawson, D. 'Blurring the Boundaries: Ethical Considerations for Online Research Using Synchronous CMC Forums'. In *Readings in Virtual Research Ethics: Issues and Controversies*, edited by E.A. Buchanan, 80–100. Hersey, PA: Idea Group, 2004.

Leadbeater, C. *We-Think: The Power of Mass Creativity*. London: Profile, 2008.

Locke, J. *Second Treatise on Government*. Oxford: Blackwell, 1966.

Mackie, E. 'Welcome the Outlaw: Pirates, Maroons, and Caribbean Countercultures'. *Cultural Critique* 59 (2005): 24–62.

Markham, A. *Life Online: Researching the Real Experience in Virtual Space*. London: AltaMira Press, 1998.

Mason, M. *The Pirate's Dilemma*. London: Penguin, 2008.

Millward, P. 'The Rebirth of the Football Fanzine: Using E-Zines as Data Source'. *Journal of Sport and Social Issues* 32, no. 2 (2008): 299–310.

Millward, P. '"We've All Got the Bug for Euro Aways": What Fans Say About European Football Club Competition'. *International Review for the Sociology of Sport* 41, nos. 3–4 (2006): 375–93.

Morgan, M. 'Making Space for Experiences'. *Journal of Retail and Leisure Property* 5, no. 4 (2006): 305–13.

Olson, M. *The Logic of Collective Action*. Cambridge: Harvard University Press, 1965.

Olson, M. *Power and Prosperity*. New York: Basic Books, 2000.

Oppenheimer, F. *The State*. New York: Free Life Editions, 1975 [1914].

Parker, G. *Citizenship, Contingency and the Countryside*. London: Routledge, 2002.

Parker, G. 'Rights, the Environment and Part V of the Criminal Justice and Public Order Act 1994'. *Area* 31, no. 1 (1999): 75–80.

Parker, G., and N. Ravenscroft. 'Land, Rights and the Gift: The Countryside and Rights of Way Act 2000 and the Negotiation of Citizenship'. *Sociologia Ruralis* 41, no. 4 (2001): 381–98.

Parker, G., and A. Wragg. 'Networks, Agency and (De)stabilization: The Issue of Navigation on the River Wye, UK'. *Journal of Environmental Planning and Management* 42, no. 4 (1999): 471–87.

Ravenscroft, N., A. Church, P. Gilchrist, R. Hickey, and B. Hammond. *Improving Access for Canoeing to Inland Waterways in England. Countryside Research Note 79*. Cheltenham: Countryside Agency, 2004.

Roberts, G. 'A Canoe-Related Incident on the River Tiefi at Cenarth'. Unpublished Report Prepared for the Carmarthenshire Fishermens Federation 2007.

Rojek, C. 'P2P Leisure Exchange: Net Banditry and the Policing of Intellectual Property'. *Leisure Studies* 24, no. 4 (2005): 357–69.

Sharf, B. 'Beyond Netiquette: The Ethics of Doing Naturalistic Discourse Research on the Internet'. In *Doing Internet Research: Critical Issues and Methods for Examining the Net*, edited by S. Jones, 243–56. Newbury Park, CA: Sage Publications, 1999.

Shoard, M. *This Land is Ours*. London: Paladin Grafton, 1980.

Telling, A.E., and R. Smith. *The Public Right of Navigation*. A Report to the Sports Council and the Water Space Amenity Commission. Study 27. London: Sports Council, 1985.

University of Brighton Consortium. *A Strategic Plan for Water Related Recreation in the East of England Region*. Report to the Environment Agency 2008.

University of Brighton Consortium. *A Strategic Plan for Water Related Recreation in the South West Region*. Report to the Environment Agency 2008.

University of Brighton Consortium. *Water-Based Sport and Recreation: The Facts*. Bristol: DEFRA, 2001.

Walton, I. *The Compleat Angler*. London: Hamlyn, 1971 [1653].

Wheaton, B. 'From the Pavement to the Beach: Politics and Identity in "Surfers Against Sewage"'. In *Tribal Play: Subcultural Journeys Through Sport*, edited by K. Young and M. Atkinson, 113–34. Oxford: Elsevier, 2008.

Wilson, B., and P. White. '"Revive the Pride": Social Process, Political Economy and a Fan-Based Grassroots Movement'. *Sociology of Sport Journal* 19, no. 2 (2002): 119–48.

The sports boycott against Rhodesia reconsidered

Charles Little

London Metropolitan University, London, UK

Lost amongst the contemporary debate over Zimbabwe's place in world sport (and especially international cricket) is an awareness that its predecessor state, Rhodesia, had itself been the target of an international sporting boycott during its period of Unilateral Declaration of Independence from Britain (1965–79). This paper reconsiders that campaign and analyses its broader significance. Two key elements of the campaign against Rhodesian sport are highlighted that are particularly worthy of wider attention. The first was the fundamental rationale behind the boycott movement. Unlike the initial campaign against apartheid sport in South Africa, the boycott against Rhodesia was always centred on the nature and legitimacy of Ian Smith's regime rather than on racial issues within Rhodesian sport itself. Sport became a tool of the wider campaign to deny the legitimacy of Rhodesian independence and nationhood. Secondly, the depth of involvement of the British Government in the boycott campaign is revealed. Indeed, it was the British Government that first instigated the sporting boycott of Rhodesia, and a significant feature of the overall campaign was that it was almost exclusively led by state actors rather than public protest movements. The paper thus examines the motivations and behaviour of successive British governments in using sport as a tool of their overall policy towards Rhodesia.

Introduction

The question of sporting contacts with Robert Mugabe's Zimbabwe has been one of the most prominent issues concerning sport, diplomacy and foreign policy in the early twenty-first century. In particular, the question of whether the English cricket team should have boycotted matches in Harare and Bulawayo during the 2003 Cricket World Cup occupied a great deal of attention, as both the England Cricket Board and the Blair Government prevaricated and displayed great reluctance to take a definitive stance over the issue, and the issue has remained an ongoing cause of crisis within cricket.

One point that was overlooked amongst all of the debate surrounding the issue was that there was a direct precedent of the England cricket team refusing to play in Zimbabwe, and doing so because of opposition to the ruling regime in that country. In that case, however, the regime in question belonged not to Robert Mugabe, but instead to Ian Smith, who led what was then Rhodesia during its period of 'independence' from Britain between 1965 and 1979. This earlier cricketing boycott had occurred in 1969 when the MCC, under the leadership of former Conservative Prime Minister Alec Douglas-Home, acceded to a request from Howard Wilson's Labour government to forgo its traditional visit to Rhodesia as a part of its proposed tour of South Africa.

The cancellation of the MCC's planned 1969 visit to Rhodesia was just one part of a long-running international diplomatic campaign against the white minority government of

Ian Smith. Between 1965 and 1979 Rhodesia existed as an international pariah state, with Britain, the Commonwealth, most African states, and the United Nations amongst those ranged against it. This paper aims to examine and analyse the ways in which sport became one of the elements in this campaign.

Although this paper is titled 'The sports boycott against Rhodesia reconsidered', in actuality the entire issue has barely been considered in the first instance. Not only have media accounts of the contemporary controversy ignored its antecedent, but the entire question of the sports boycott against Rhodesia has been almost totally ignored by academics. At best, the issue has been treated as little more than a footnote to the much more widely covered issue of South African involvement in international sport, earning only the occasional paragraph in studies of sporting politics.[1]

The Rhodesian issue has been even more neglected in studies of modern British sport. Holt and Mason's *Sport in Britain 1945–2000* mentions the Unilateral Declaration of Independence (UDI) in Rhodesia in terms of the broader racial context surrounding the D'Oliveira Affair, but makes no mention of the debate surrounding continuing Rhodesian participation in international sport. Neither do Polley's *Moving the Goalposts* or Hill's *Sport, Leisure & Culture in Twentieth Century Britain*. Even Coughlan and Webb's study of *Sport and British Politics since 1960* devotes less than one sentence to the issue, and that is only in passing. The issue is briefly highlighted in Beacom's article on sport and international relations, but only in the context as a topic worthy of future analysis rather than as a substantial part of the work itself. The issue has finally began to receive some attention in recent years, with two journal articles examining Rhodesia's exclusion from the 1968 and 1972 Olympic Games, but the issue remains largely unexplored.[2]

In spite of this paucity of academic attention, there are a number of significant reasons why the sports boycott against Rhodesia is deserving of greater attention. Most obviously, it provides additional context to the contemporary debates surrounding sporting relations with Mugabe's Zimbabwe, allowing us to examine the actions of today's sportsmen, administrators and politicians from a different perspective.

Another reason is the light that it sheds on the British Government's willingness to use sport as a tool for its wider political objectives. British governments are usually perceived to have been relatively reluctant to mix foreign policy and sport. Polley has noted that in the early twentieth century the Foreign Office pursued an ideology of non-involvement in sporting matters, exemplified by its discouragement of any attempts to boycott the 1936 Olympics.[3] In the case of Rhodesia, however, not only was Britain extremely heavily involved in unilateral action against Rhodesian participation, but it also took the lead in instigating international sanctions against Rhodesian sport. As such, it can be seen as an important catalyst for a more assertive engagement in sporting diplomacy.

Thirdly, a crucial issue surrounding sporting sanctions against Rhodesia, and its key difference from the campaign against apartheid-sport in South Africa in the 1960s, was the essential reason for the boycott. Unlike the case of South Africa at this time, the campaign against Rhodesian participation in international sport was focused almost solely on the nature of the Rhodesian government, and not on racial issues in Rhodesian sport itself. The focus was thus purely in the realm of broader foreign policy, aiming to isolate a racially discriminatory regime, rather than in sport. In fact, the campaign against Rhodesia foreshadowed the shift in focus of the South African campaign in the mid to late 1970s.

And this, in turn, provides a final reason for devoting attention to the issue. As perhaps the first comprehensive attempt to use enforced sporting isolation as a tool against a rogue state, what can this case study reveal to us about the effectiveness of sports boycotts as a diplomatic tool? Houlihan has stated that historical research into past examples of sporting boycotts 'would provide valuable insights into the utility (and limitations) of sport as a diplomatic resource'.[4] Thus, this article seeks to understand the impact (if any) that sporting sanctions had on the overall politics of UDI.

Sporting sanctions in context

Before analysing the specific case study of international sporting contacts with Rhodesia, it is necessary to place the issue of sanctions, and particularly sporting boycotts, within their broader context. The sports boycott of Rhodesia was but one of a number of such examples throughout the later part of the twentieth century. The most notable of these were the long-running campaign to isolate apartheid-era South Africa and the tit-for-tat American–Soviet boycotts of the 1980 and 1984 Summer Olympic Games, but other boycott campaigns targeted Israel, Taiwan and Serbia amongst others.[5] Boycotts also remain a ongoing part of the contemporary global sporting landscape, with current campaigns including New Zealand's ban on sporting contacts with Fiji, a variety of reciprocal boycotts involving India and Pakistan, and calls for a boycott of Israel over the issue of the Palestinian territories.

The preceding examples show that sports boycotts can be driven by a range of actors, including both governmental and non-state organizations. One defining characteristic of the sports boycott against Rhodesia is that it was driven almost exclusively by state actors (a point that will be returned to later in the paper). Sports boycotts are one of the range of non-violent measures available to governments to exert pressure on targeted states, with others including economic, political and cultural measures. Each boycott campaign will obviously have its own aims and objectives, but Doxey has identified eight theoretical goals for diplomatic sanctions: deterrence, compliance, punishment, destabilization, limitation of conflict, solidarity, symbolism and signalling.[6]

In the specific case of sports boycotts, the most relevant of these are compliance, punishment, destabilization, solidarity and symbolism. The sports boycott against South Africa, for instance, was initially focused on forcing South Africa to comply with demands for the removal of racial discrimination within its domestic sports system (compliance), although from the 1970s onwards these goals changed to using sporting isolation as a tool to isolate white South African from the rest of the international community (destabilization). By contrast, the US boycott of the 1980 Olympics was intended to signal American disapproval of the Soviet invasion of Afghanistan (punishment and symbolism).[7]

Picking up on Doxey's last goal of sanctions, signalling, any consideration of sanctions as a diplomatic tool needs to acknowledge that they are often designed to send messages to a broad range of different constituencies. Thus, as well as being obviously directed at the targeted state, they may also be intended to send messages to a broad range of domestic and international audiences.[8] This was a crucial consideration surrounding British sanctions against Rhodesia, as the Government was forced to balance domestic political considerations (including widespread public support for the Rhodesian cause) against demands from the Commonwealth to take decisive action against Rhodesia.

Rhodesia, Britain and UDI

The sports boycott of Rhodesia emerged in response to its Unilateral Declaration of Independence, which had been the outcome of the longstanding controversy over the future status of the British Colony of Southern Rhodesia (known from 1964 onwards simply as Rhodesia) in post-colonial Africa. Rhodesia had a substantial white minority (around 8–10% of the total population) who already enjoyed a substantial degree of self-government and sought to maintain their privileged position into independence. Granting independence to a white minority government was unacceptable for the British in the international political situation of the 1960s, and they sought to negotiate a solution. These efforts failed and, fearful of losing their privileged position, the Rhodesian Government of Ian Smith declared its independence from Britain on the 11th of November 1965.[9]

The British Government, led by Prime Minister Harold Wilson, declared UDI an illegal act of rebellion and claimed that Britain retained legal authority over Rhodesia. The British Parliament backed this up with a vigorous campaign to deny any international recognition to the Smith regime, but stood short of taking any direct action to replace the Rhodesian Government. These actions, and particularly the failure to take military action, were heavily criticized by the newly independent African members of the Commonwealth, and the ensuing crisis threatened to undermine the future of the Commonwealth itself.[10]

Although unwilling for the United Nations to take a lead on the issue, the British sponsored a number of resolutions to the United Nations Security Council to further its aims. These included trade sanctions, an arms embargo, and restrictions on the transfer of currency.[11] As a consequence of these sanctions, and the almost total diplomatic non-recognition of the Smith regime, Geldenhuys argues that Rhodesia became 'the most ostracised country this century has witnessed in peacetime' and that 'in meting out severe collective punishment to Rhodesia, the international community acted with a unity of purpose and action rarely demonstrated on political issues'.[12]

The sports boycott against Rhodesia

Efforts to deny international legitimacy to the Smith regime soon extended into the realm of sport, and from 1967 onwards the British government argued that sporting contacts were a form of 'comfort to the illegal regime in Rhodesia'. These initial efforts succeeded, amongst others, in preventing international tours by the Rhodesian hockey team and in dissuading British football and cricket teams from touring Rhodesia. Not all efforts were successful, with Oldham Athletic football club and the French and British Lions rugby union teams ignoring requests to cancel visits to Salisbury. Rhodesia was also successful in gaining admission to tennis' Davis Cup competition in 1968, although its away tie against Sweden was forced to be abandoned after anti-racism protestors staged an invasion of the match venue.[13]

Such endeavours did not find universal favour within Britain, particularly from the right-wing press. After the government had succeeded in dissuading the Yorkshire County Cricket Club from touring Rhodesia in 1967 the *Daily Telegraph* launched a stinging editorial which claimed that:

> For a Commonwealth Office spokesman to suggest now that, in playing cricket with a Rhodesian team, Yorkshire would be offering 'aid and comfort to an illegal regime' is ludicrous.... The next step in this decision will be postal censorship of Christmas cards in case Mr Smith is getting some goodwill message across. Fascist Italy and Germany used to align their athletics closely to their foreign policies, and Britain is in danger of making the same pernicious mistake.[14]

Given the direction of British policy towards Rhodesia and its participation in sport, it is not surprising that the 1968 Olympic Games emerged as a major test of resolve between the two countries. The significance attached to the Olympic Games has ensured that they have been surrounded by political considerations since the very establishment of the modern movement in the 1890s. In particular, participation in the Games has been a popular platform for states seeking international recognition of their independence and legitimacy.

Rhodesia had competed in the 1960 and 1964 Games prior to UDI, and the International Olympic Committee (IOC) viewed the change in regime as irrelevant to its continuing participation. The British Government, on the other hand, felt that Olympic participation would be a PR coup for the Smith regime and sought to prevent their participation in the games. After failing to persuade the IOC to revoke its invitation, the British Government changed tack and instead put increasing pressure on the Mexican hosts to refuse entry to any Rhodesian competitors.[15]

What followed was a concerted diplomatic effort to pressure the Mexicans into acting against Rhodesia. Significantly, the British did not just place bilateral pressure, but instead actively campaigned to bring multilateral pressure against the Mexicans. In particular, the British sought to involve the nations of the Commonwealth, and particularly the newly independent members from Africa and the Caribbean, in pressurizing the Mexicans. Indeed, the extent of British involvement in this went as far as actively instigating these nations to threaten a boycott of the Games unless the Mexicans took action against the Rhodesians.[16]

Staging the 1968 Games was a major political project for the Mexican Government, and they were intended to both stimulate and publicize the development of the nation. Joseph Arbena notes that 'the objective was to show Mexico at its best, both to enhance image and pride as an end in itself, but clearly also to open channels for more trade, investment and tourism'. Naturally, any events that threatened the success of the Games were bad news for the Mexican organizers.[17]

Such a threat had only narrowly been avoided over the South African issue. At least 40 African and Asian nations had threatened to boycott the Games if South Africa participated, and there were strong suggestions that the Soviet Union, and by extension its allies in Eastern Europe, were considering following suite. This would have been a disaster for the Mexicans and the Games would have been thrown into disarray. Having narrowly survived the South African issue, the Mexicans had little desire for any similar problems associated with Rhodesia's participation. In the face of this pressure the Mexicans finally buckled to British pressure and ensured that the Rhodesians were excluded from the Games. Faced with the counter-threat of the IOC revoking their right to stage the games if they banned any competing nation, the Mexicans creatively managed to 'lose' Rhodesia's entry forms, thus securing their exclusion.[18]

A change in leadership

Following the election of the Edward Heath's Conservative Government in 1970 Britain slightly eased its role as leader of the boycott movement, although it still opposed Rhodesian participation in most international events, and tours to Rhodesia by British national teams. Leadership of the boycott movement was taken up by African governments and sporting administrators, whose efforts would culminate in the forced exclusion of Rhodesia from the 1972 Munich Olympics.

Even shortly prior to UDI, however, African sports administrators had deliberately excluded Rhodesia (along with South Africa and the Portuguese colonies of southern Africa) from the first All-African games in Brazzaville, arguing that her then colonial status rendered her ineligible (a decision that led some IOC members to demand that the Games be denied the title 'All-Africa').[19] In the immediate aftermath of UDI, Rhodesia had hoped to still be able to compete in the 1966 Commonwealth Games in Jamaica, but the threat of a boycott by most African and Asian countries muddied the waters and the Rhodesians agreed to withdraw (given that UDI was legally an act of rebellion against the British Crown, the Rhodesians had been left with little choice in this matter).[20]

It would be with the 1972 Olympic Games, however, that African opposition to Rhodesian participation in international sport would reach its zenith. The IOC had initially engineered a compromise solution to allow Rhodesia's involvement in the Games, with the Rhodesian team agreeing to compete under the Union Jack (in essence, under the same conditions as at the 1960 and 1964 Games). On the eve of the Games, and with the Rhodesian team already in the Games village, almost all African states threatened to withdraw from the event unless the Rhodesians were excluded. This last minute boycott threat forced the IOC to revoke Rhodesia's invitation to the Games.[21]

The events of Munich meant that Rhodesia found itself excluded from almost all international multi-sport events. Aside from the already mentioned examples of the All-African and Commonwealth Games, Rhodesia had also been excluded from the World University Games in 1969. The Jewish Maccabiah Games provided one last outpost of Rhodesian participation but, following UN condemnation for allowing Rhodesian participation in the 1973 edition of the Games, Israel was pushed into excluding them from later tournaments.[22]

The Paralympic Games initially proved to be an interesting exception to this trend. The British Government had deliberately held-off from opposing Rhodesian participation in the 1968 and 1972 events on PR grounds. Commonwealth Office officials decided that being seen to ban wheelchair users from a sporting event would paint Britain in a negative light and might stimulate support for Rhodesia, even declaring that 'it would be wrong to bring cripples into the political arena'. The Canadian Government had no such qualms about intervening in disabled sport, however, and refused visas for the Rhodesia team to attend the 1976 Games in Toronto.[23]

Rhodesia also faced exclusion from a number of international sporting federations. After only having become a member in 1965, and having been a controversial presence in the qualifying rounds for the 1970 World Cup, Rhodesia were suspended from FIFA in 1970. It was later suspended from international boxing for competing in a tournament in South Africa whilst the latter country was under suspension, and expelled from swimming's governing body after a FINA commission of enquiry. A number of other Rhodesian sports were also rebuffed in their attempts to join their international federations.[24]

Aside from the boycott threats, Rhodesia's opponents also had the benefit of United Nations sanctions to support their aims. And it is these UN resolutions that make the Rhodesia story one of greater significance. Although UN resolutions were used from the late 1970s onwards in the campaign against sporting links with South Africa they had limited overall impact. The Rhodesian sanctions were different, however, in that they were imposed by the Security Council of the United Nations, which gave them an enforceability that was lacking from the General Assembly's resolutions against South Africa.

The Security Council resolutions against Rhodesia had been imposed in 1968, at the instigation of the British Government. Although sporting contacts were not specifically included amongst the targets of the resolutions, the breadth of their coverage ensured that they could be utilized for this purpose. Prohibitions on the transfer of funds into and out of Rhodesia, for instance, placed economic impediments on sporting contacts.[25]

The most significant elements of these sanctions from a sporting perspective, were the non-recognition of Rhodesian passports and travel bans imposed on those deemed to be representative of the Smith regime. The non-recognition of passports issued by the Smith regime had an obvious impact on the ability of sportspeople to travel to international competitions. Rhodesia's Springbok cricketer Colin Bland was, for example, denied entry into Britain in 1968 on these grounds.[26]

This element was not enough, however, to prevent any Rhodesians travelling internationally, as the resolution only applied to Rhodesian passports, whereas the vast majority of white Rhodesians had some form of dual citizenship, usually either British or South African, and were able to travel freely under the passport of these other nations. This meant that individual Rhodesian athletes were able to travel internationally and compete in events like golf and tennis. It also opened the way for club teams from Rhodesia to tour internationally.

Nationally representative sporting teams were less able to exploit this loophole, as they were increasingly defined to be representatives of the Smith regime and thus in contravention of the travel ban. Because it was backed by the power of the Security Council, this resolution ought to have been enforced even by governments that normally opposed 'political interference' in sport, Thus, even the National Party-led New Zealand government, which was probably the most determined defender of sporting contacts with apartheid-era South Africa, was reluctantly forced to ban Rhodesian teams from entering New Zealand.[27]

Despite the apparent comprehensiveness of the UN sanctions, however, a number of countries remained willing to accept tours by Rhodesian teams, including national representative tours in a number of sports. In 1975 alone, for instance, the Rhodesian men's hockey team played matches in Belgium, France, Austria, Spain and West Germany. Switzerland (which was not a member of the UN, and thus technically not required to adhere to UN resolutions) allowed Rhodesian teams into the country to compete in world championships in archery and combat pistol shooting, the Rhodesian team contested (and won) the World Pairs golf championship in Colombia, Rhodesian Boy Scouts attended an international jamboree in Norway, while France allowed the entry of Rhodesian teams for the world Fireball Class yachting championships and tennis' Federation Cup. In the later case, intensive diplomatic lobbying by the United Kingdom saw a last-minute reversal of the decision, with the Rhodesians being officially expelled from the tournament just 10 minutes before their opening match (although they were allowed to play out their scheduled matches).[28]

Many sporting organizations also gave their support to Rhodesia and sought to circumvent any political sanctions against it. The World Amateur Golf Council, for instance, insisted that any nation wishing to stage the Eisenhower Trophy tournament must agree to accept Rhodesian's participation in the event. This stance prevented Malaysia and New Zealand from staging the tournament, although the Dominican Republic and Portugal were happy to sidestep the UN sanctions to host the event. The International Lawn Tennis Federation, whose voting system was heavily weighted in favour of white nations, was another firm advocate of Rhodesia and accepted her entry to the Davis Cup on a number of occasions (although the refusal of individual federations and governments to compete against the Rhodesians effectively stymied any Rhodesian involvement in the competition).[29]

In another example, the World Ploughing Organisation was, largely by dint of the obstinacy and bloody-minded persistence of its Cumbrian president, able to convince the British Government that the Rhodesian ploughing team was not, in fact, technically a team at all (because even though selected by a national federation and representing that body in competition, the ploughmen competed as two individuals in the competition), and thus not covered by these sanctions. Using this ruse, Rhodesia gained entry to world championship events hosted by England, the Republic of Ireland, Canada, the United States and West Germany (although the governments of Finland, Sweden and the Netherlands refused to be swayed by this argument).[30]

In all of the above cases, Rhodesia retained its membership of the relevant International Sporting Federations. Even by the late 1970s, Rhodesia remained in good standing on the international federations of six Olympic sports, plus tennis and golf, and a host of more minor sports like body-building, parachuting and ploughing. Furthermore, although not an official member of the governing bodies of cricket, rugby union and polo, Rhodesia retained a friendly relationship with them for many years.[31]

In rugby union, for instance, both national and club teams repeatedly rejected government requests and undertook tours; the British Lions visited Rhodesia on their tours of South Africa in 1968 (to the considerable embarrassment of the British Government, who were at that very time campaigning for the exclusion of Rhodesia from the Mexico City Olympic Games) and 1974, as did national sides from France (1967), Australia (1969), New Zealand (1970) and Italy (1973); while there were numerous tours by British club sides.[32]

This reveals one of the problems with sanctions in general – too often there are those who are only too willing to circumvent them for their own ends. In the case of the broader UN sanctions against Rhodesia, both South Africa and Portugal (which had solidarity with Rhodesia due to its colonial possessions in southern Africa) had political motivations for supporting the Smith regime, and this support proved critical in maintaining Rhodesia's ability to survive the economic effect of sanctions. Many organizations and individuals from the rest of the world were also willing, for either financial or ideological reasons, to ignore sanctions and to maintain links.[33] As has been shown, many sporting organizations were equally willing to overlook and ignore sanctions in order to maintain sporting contacts with Rhodesia.

Reasons for the boycott

Having accounted for the outcome of international efforts to exclude Rhodesia from international sport we must now turn to the reasons for these actions. It is in this area that the distinctions between the sporting boycotts of Rhodesia and South Africa are most important. Whereas the sports campaign against South Africa in the 1960s and 1970s focused on segregation and racism within South African sport itself, in the case of Rhodesia it was from the outset firmly aimed at opposing the existence and policies of the Smith regime.

Thus, the arguments regularly employed to oppose sporting contacts with Rhodesia included the lack of recognition for the Smith regime and Rhodesia's existence as a rogue state without international legitimacy; the fact that the African majority were effectively excluded from the electoral process; and the racist policies adopted by the Smith Government. Concerns that the Rhodesian Government would exploit sporting contacts for propaganda purposes were also frequently cited; while, in some cases, the justification given for opposing Rhodesian involvement in international sport was simply the existence of the UN resolutions in themselves, without giving recourse to the reasons behind them in the first place.[34]

It is important to consider here exactly what Britain's goals were in instigating sporting sanctions against Rhodesia. As was noted earlier, the whole issue of how to respond to UDI had posed a huge problem for the Wilson Government, which was caught between significant domestic support for the Rhodesian cause, British economic interests in southern Africa, and an increasingly assertive Commonwealth clamouring for decisive action against Smith and his regime. Its response to this was to devise a strategy that sought to contain the crisis. Although there were initial hopes that economic sanctions would force the Rhodesian Government to surrender, this optimism quickly evaporated. Thereafter, the extension of sanctions can be seen as a means of prolonging the stalemate and of ensuring that Britain would be seen to be taking a strong hand.[35]

For the most part, the inclusion of sport within this wider boycott was a largely defensive action, aiming to support Britain's wider policy objectives. Diplomats had little expectation that isolating Rhodesia from international sport would have any significant influence on the policies of the Smith regime. Instead, they sought to ensure that their wider goals of isolating the regime were maintained (see for instance the discussions surrounding the 1968 Olympics[36]), and ensuring that Rhodesian involvement in international sport never emerged as a source of embarrassment or criticism of Britain's overall Rhodesia policy. Novak notes, for instance, that Britain's key goal surrounding the 1972 Munich Olympics was to 'prevent a public relations disaster that would aggravate growing criticism of British Rhodesian policy'.[37] The actions of the diplomats working to enforce sporting sanctions can therefore be seen as a form of pre-emptive 'firefighting'. Thus, whereas utilizing the typologies devised by Doxey, we find that most sporting boycotts have had either punishment, compliance or destabilization as their goals, in the case of Rhodesia it can be argued that signalling (especially towards the Commonwealth) was the key objective.

This is not to say that there was no racism within Rhodesian sport. Indeed, a strong case could have be made for opposing sporting contacts with Rhodesia on the grounds of racial discrimination, although the situation was rather complicated. One the one hand, there were no legal barriers to multiracial sport, as least at open-age level, within Rhodesia. Much Rhodesian sport had, by 1965, moved towards multiracialism. In football, Giulianotti notes that the first multiracial fixture took place in 1948, between an African and an Asian team, although integrated football teams and leagues remained uncommon. By the early 1960s, however, a 'multiracial' national league was founded, and, in January 1965, intervention by FIFA led to the reformation of the national governing body, the Football Association of Rhodesia, as a multiracial organization. The first multiracial athletics meeting had taken place in 1958, and multiracial track and field teams were selected for the 1960, 1964 and 1968 Olympic Games.[38]

On the other hand, in 1968 the Smith regime barred mixed sport from taking place within state-funded schools. And, although other public sporting facilities were integrated, the government had introduced segregation in public swimming pools.[39] Furthermore, the integration of football and athletics was not matched in all other sports. In 1973, an IOC investigatory committee found that many sports within Rhodesia, including field hockey, tennis, golf and boxing, were either confined exclusively to the white population or had little racial integration. Rhodesian sport, as an institution, could therefore not claim to be fully multiracial, and indeed in some cases remained deeply rooted in racist practices. Moreover, school sport and swimming apart, the racial discrimination that existed within Rhodesian sport was the consequence of the attitudes and actions of the nation's sporting clubs and bodies themselves, and could not be attempted to be explained away as the consequence of government action.[40]

It is one of the ironies of the Rhodesian boycott that the majority of the sports in which it retained international contact were the least integrated and had made the least progress towards multiracialism. The IOC commission of enquiry, for instance, reported that yachting, shooting, archery, equestrian, golf and tennis were almost exclusively white, whilst cricket, hockey and rugby union were effectively segregated at club level. On the other hand, it was the most integrated of Rhodesian sports that often found themselves facing international isolation. The first sport to be expelled from its international federation was football, which was, alongside athletics, the most integrated of all sports, and also the most popular sport amongst Rhodesia's black population. Cycling, judo and weightlifting were also relatively non-racial, yet were amongst the sports that faced the greatest isolation.[41]

There was also the irony that African athletes were the most likely to be impacted by the boycott, especially with regards to passports. As has been noted, most white Rhodesians had entitlements to either British or South African passports, which allowed them to circumvent the UN travel ban. This loophole was not available to the vast majority of Africans, meaning African sportsmen and women were particular disadvantaged. Prior to the 1968 Olympics, for instance, British government officials suggested that possibly the only athletes unable to circumvent the ban on Rhodesian passports would have been the two black Rhodesian members of the team, Mathias Kanda and Bernard Dzoma, which had the potential to draw ridicule on any efforts to enforce this ban.[42]

It was the in the attitudes of private sports clubs that the most serious cases of racism within Rhodesian sport could be found. These private sports clubs provided the foundation of many sports in Rhodesia, amongst them cricket, tennis and golf, and a large number of them maintained racially exclusionary policies. Thus, non-white athletes were denied both the opportunity to join some of the country's leading sports teams, and also faced being denied access to clubhouses, changing rooms and even toilets on those occasions when racially mixed sport was practised on their facilities.[43]

However, and this is a very important however, this case against Rhodesian sport was never made (except in the unique case of swimming).[44] Aside from a few isolated occasions, the justifications given for the boycott of Rhodesia were solely related to the nature of its government and its policies.[45]

The boycott forgotten

It was one of the features of the sporting boycott against Rhodesia that almost all of the impetus was from national governments, and some sporting administrators, rather than public protest movements. In particular, Rhodesian sport does not appear to have been a major issue for the anti-apartheid movement, which was so active in opposing sporting links with South Africa. Activists in New Zealand and the United States occasionally raised the issue of Rhodesia, but usually only in the context of broader campaigns targeting South African sport (for instance, the 1968 Olympics and the 1970 All Blacks tour of southern Africa). In these cases these groups gave no strong independent rationale for opposing contacts with Rhodesia. Only the Irish anti-apartheid movement appears to have seized upon this as a separate and significant issue, launching a number of specific campaigns against Irish sporting links with Rhodesia.[46]

This may provide one of the reasons why the sports boycott against Rhodesia has faded from popular consciousness. There was no equivalent of the public controversies surrounding Springbok sporting tours to Britain in 1969 and 1970, Australia in 1971, and New Zealand in 1981, which helped to sear the campaign against sporting contacts with South Africa into popular and political memory.

This focus on diplomatic manoeuvring rather than public protest may also help to explain why the Rhodesia issue has been overlooked by historians. Whereas the campaign against South African participation in sport was characterized by high-profile public campaigns and the glare of publicity, most of the efforts against Rhodesia took place outside of the spotlight. The exclusion of Rhodesia from high-profile events like the 1968 Olympics and the 1976 Paralympic Games was exclusively the result of behind-the-scenes diplomatic activity, and the reasons for Rhodesia's absence were often overlooked by the media. Apart from a few incidents, most notably the 1972 Olympics, records of these events scarcely exist outside of official files, and there is often little evidence to indicate that anything took place at all.

Indeed, the British government in particular was at pains to keep the issue of Rhodesian participation in international sport, and their own efforts to prevent it, out of the limelight. This was partly prompted by domestic considerations, mindful of both public support for the white Rhodesian cause and fearful of accusations of bringing politics unnecessarily into sport, as had happened when it lobbied Yorkshire CCC from touring Rhodesia in 1967. The sentiment that sport and politics should not mix still held much popular sway.

The main reason for this discretion, however, stemmed from a concern that the failure of high-profile campaigns against Rhodesian participation would hand an even-bigger propaganda victory to the Smith regime. Participating in, say, the Olympic Games would be one thing, but doing so in the face of strong British Government opposition would be far more significant, leading one Commonwealth Office official to warn in 1968 that 'we must too be careful not to engage our prestige too heavily and too obviously against Rhodesian participation: the Olympics is not a good ground to pick for a public trial of strength with the regime'. Another official noted,

> that [if] Rhodesia should be seen to win it after all our influence has been thrown into a lobbying exercise with governments would seem to represent a much greater victory politically for Rhodesia than if we were to take a relaxed line from the start.[47]

The boycott reconsidered

On reflection then, what are some of the broader issues that can be derived from an analysis of these events? Firstly, this analysis has demonstrated that the Rhodesian issue was not merely a footnote to the campaign against South Africa. It was a wholly separate action, waged by separate actors with a separate range of objectives.[48] It was also distinct in that it was targeted against the policies and actions of the Rhodesian Government, rather than focusing on racial issues within sport. As such, it certainly provides a direct precedent to contemporary issues surrounding Zimbabwe, with the then British Government and at least some sporting bodies being willing to use sporting boycotts as a means of dealing with rogue political regimes.

But did sporting sanctions against Rhodesia actually have any impact? In terms of isolating Rhodesian sport they were relatively successful, arguably more so than the efforts against South Africa during the same period. As such, they highlight the effectiveness of locating any future sports sanctions within the broader confines of UN Security Council resolutions.

More important, however, is whether these efforts had any impact on the Rhodesian state. Such questions can be difficult to answer; for instance, academics are divided in their conclusions as to whether sporting sanctions against South Africa had any impact on altering or ending the broader apartheid system. Some, like Black and Nauright, argue that cultural and sporting sanctions played a key role in undermining support for apartheid amongst white South Africans, with Doxey also supporting this viewpoint. On the other hand, Booth cautions that any evidence to support such an argument 'remains highly circumstantial' and Houlihan claims that 'the application of the boycott was, in itself, an irritation rather than a major threat to apartheid' (although he acknowledges that it had a greater impact in raising public consciousness about apartheid). In many ways these divergent views mirror Doxey's analysis of the impacts of sanctions against South Africa in general, which suggests that 'those who thought sanctions would achieve the goal of ending apartheid claim that they played a dominant role in forcing change. On the other hand, those who were sceptical about sanctions lay greater emphasis on other factors'.[49]

In the case of Rhodesia the answer appears equally complex. Although evidence is again largely circumstantial (especially in the absence of access to Rhodesian Government records), there are no indications that sporting sanctions changed the policies of the state in any way. Perhaps the strongest evidence to support this viewpoint can be seen in the election campaign leading up to the 1969 referendum on the adoption of a new constitution and declaration of a republic. The (white) opposition highlighted the impact of the sports boycott as one of their reasons for urging a no vote (which would have served as a *de facto* vote of no confidence in Smith's Rhodesia Front government and UDI), but despite this the constitution was endorsed by a sweeping majority of the electorate.[50] If anything, sporting sanctions may even have contributed to the 'siege mentality' prevalent amongst the bulk of the white Rhodesian population, whilst also earning them some degree of international sympathy.

However, it is doubtful if the instigators of sporting sanctions, particularly within the British Government, ever really expected such an outcome. There was never any significant expectation that sporting isolation would lead to political change. Nor were sanctions implemented with any intention of challenging racism within Rhodesian sport. Sporting sanctions were implemented with the goal of complementing and upholding wider British policy objectives, and to ensure that any possible sporting links would not embarrass the British Government. For the most part this goal was met, and in this light the sanctions can be considered a success.

Notes

1. A full overview of the (limited) literature surrounding the topic is located in Little, 'Preventing a Wonderful Break-Through'.
2. See Beacom, 'Sport in International Relations'; Little, 'Preventing a Wonderful Break-Through'; Novak, 'Rhodesia's "Rebel and Racist"'.
3. Polley, 'Amateur Ideal'.
4. Houlihan, 'Politics and Sport', 218.
5. Ibid.; see also, Booth, *Race Game*, 85–122; Hill, *Olympic Politics*, 118–60; Macintosh and Hawes, *Sport and Canadian Diplomacy*, 37–58; Doxey, *International Sanctions*, 40.
6. Doxey, *International Sanctions*, 11, 54–8.
7. Houlihan, 'Politics and Sport', 217–20.
8. Doxey, *International Sanctions*, 57–8.
9. Clarke, *Hope and Glory*, 266, 296–8.
10. Mansergh, *Commonwealth Experience*, 163–201; Lloyd, *British Empire 1558–1995*, 357–80.
11. Strack, *Sanctions*, 16–21.
12. Geldenhuys, *Isolated States*, 59.
13. Little, 'Rebellion, Race and Rhodesia'; Little, 'No Politics, Mucho Rugby'.
14. *Daily Telegraph*, 13 September 1967.
15. Little, 'Preventing a Wonderful Break-Through'.
16. Ibid.
17. Arbena, 'Sport, Development', 359–60; Burke, 'Mexico City 1968'.
18. *Rhodesia Herald*, 31 August 1968.

[19] Minutes of the 63rd Meeting of the International Olympic Committee, Madrid, 6–9 October 1965 (IOC Documentation Centre, Lausanne); Minutes of the Meetings of the IOC Executive Board, 18 August – 11 September 1972 (IOC Documentation Centre, Lausanne).

[20] *Rhodesia Herald*, 21 January 1966, 26; 22 January 1966, 13–14; 17 January 1966, 1; 28 March 1966, 1; 29 March 1966, 8.

[21] Novak, 'Rhodesia's "Rebel and Racist"'.

[22] Although the official Rhodesian team was excluded from the 1977 Maccabiah Games, four lawn bowlers and tennis players did compete as individual athletes. United Nations, *Sixth Report*, 91–6; *Jerusalem Post*, 1 July 1977, 2; 15 July 1977, 3.

[23] British Embassy Tel Aviv to Foreign Office, 1 March 1968 (Public Records Office (hereafter PRO) FCO 36/317); Young to Faber, 5 March 1968 (PRO FCO 36/317); Mansfield to Fingland, 30 March 1972 (PRO FCO 36/1295); Little, 'Pierre Trudeau's U-Turn'.

[24] In addition to the examples mentioned above, Rhodesia was also expelled from the international federations of chess (1974), weightlifting (1977) and basketball (1978). FINA, 'Resolution Reference the Membership of Rhodesia and South Africa', 30 August 1073 (IOC Documentation Centre, Lausanne); *The Times*, 16 June 1970; Letter from Association International de Boxe Amateur to IOC, 12 December 1972 (IOC Documentation Centre, Lausanne); Schodl, *The Lost Past*, 196–7; *Rhodesia Herald*, 9 October 1978, 16.

[25] Strack, *Sanctions*, 16–21.

[26] *Rhodesia Herald*, 19 August 1968; 3 September 1968.

[27] Cabinet Minute, 'United Nations Sanctions on Southern Rhodesia', 20 January 1976 (National Archives of New Zealand, 139/400/3 part 2).

[28] *Rhodesia Herald*, 14 January 1975, 3; 12 April 1975, 16; 7 May 1975, 1; 10 May 1975, 15; 21 June 1975, 16; 24 June 1975, 20; 23 July 1975, 3; 19 August 1975, 14; 30 August 1975, 7.

[29] *Otago Daily Times*, 14 January 1976, 14; *Rhodesia Herald*, 26 February 1976, 14; 20 July 1978, 20.

[30] Hall, *Ploughing, Politics and Fellowship*; Little, 'Pierre Trudeau's U-Turn'.

[31] These Olympic sports were archery, athletics, equestrian, shooting and yachting. Circular from Lord Killanin to International Sports Federations, 23 January 1975 (Zimbabwe Correspondence 1975–76, IOC Documentation Centre, Lausanne).

[32] Little, 'No Politics, Mucho Rugby'.

[33] Geldenhuys, *Isolated States*, 61.

[34] See, for example, *Morning Star*, September 22, 1970; *Bulawayo Chronicle*, July 13, 1973; Herbert (Foreign and Commonwealth Office) to Offen (Department of the Environment), 18 January 1977 (PRO AT60/120); A. MacEachen (Minister of External Affairs) to Exeter (IAAF), 26 April 1976 (National Archives of Canada 55-26-OLYMP-3-RH).

[35] Coggins, 'Wilson and Rhodesia'.

[36] Little, 'Preventing a Wonderful Break-Through'.

[37] Novak, 'Rhodesia's "Rebel and Racist"', 1380.

[38] Giulianotti, 'Between Colonialism'; *Rhodesia Herald*, 8 December 1968, 11; *Rhodesia Herald*, 1 January 1966, 9; Little, 'Preventing a Wonderful Break-Through'.

[39] Davies, *Race Relations in Rhodesia*, 342–4.

[40] International Olympic Committee, *Report for the Commission of Enquiry for Rhodesia*, 23 October 1974 (IOC Documentation Centre, Lausanne).

[41] Ibid.

[42] This issue also arose surrounding the 1971 World Ploughing Championships in England and the 1977 Stoke Mandeville Games. Palliser to Williams, 31 July 1968 (PRO FCO 25/549); Cypher from Salisbury to Commonwealth Office, 23 July 1968 (PRO FOC 25/549); Harrison to Rowlands, 6 July 1977 (PRO FCO 36/2114).

[43] For examples of this discrimination see Little, 'Rebellion, Race and Rhodesia'; Little, 'No Politics, Mucho Rugby'.

[44] Swimming was unique in that it was the only sport in which racial discrimination in adult sport was the result of specific Government policy. Thus, FINA was the only international sporting federation to expel Rhodesia on the specific grounds that the sport was not integrated within the country. FINA, 'Resolution Reference the membership of Rhodesia and South Africa', 30 August 1073 (IOC Documentation Centre, Lausanne).

[45] The findings of the IOC Commission of Enquiry into Rhodesian sport, which it ought to be noted proved to be a very fair and balanced analysis of the situation, could perhaps be argued as having

provided a case to exclude Rhodesia on solely sporting grounds, but there is no evidence to prove what impact, if any, it had on the decisions of the IOC members who voted to expel Rhodesia from the IOC in 1975. Given the similarity of the margin of this vote to that of the one to exclude Rhodesia from the Munich Games, it would appear that most had already made up their minds on the issue.

46 Pamphlet by Irish Anti-Apartheid Movement, May 1968 (National Archives of Ireland, 305/94/1); *Irish Independent*, 16 September 1968; *Irish Times*, 2 February 1974; *Amandla* (Ireland), September 1975, 5.

47 Barker to Diggines, 11 January 1968 (PRO FCO 25/549); Faber to Bottomly, 28 November 1967 (PRO FCO 36-316); Bottomley to Secretary of State, 29 November 1967 (PRO FCO 36/316).

48 In some ways, it could be argued that the most appropriate sporting parallel to the Rhodesian issue was not the boycott of South Africa, but rather the contests for national legitimacy and recognition that fuelled the debates over German and Chinese representation within the Olympic movement. Ironically, it was at the 1968 Games that East Germany (the German Democratic Republic) made its independent Olympic debut, an important step in showcasing the legitimacy of that regime and the division of Germany. Both the British and Rhodesian governments saw the likelihood of Rhodesian participation having the same potential impact on the perception of the international legitimacy of the Smith government and UDI.

49 Black and Nauright, *Rugby*, 93; Doxey, *International*, 25–6; Booth, 'Hitting Apartheid for Six?'; Houlihan, 'Politics and Sport', 218.

50 *Rhodesia Herald*, 16 June 1969, 12; 21 June 1969, 1.

References

Arbena, J. 'Sport, Development and Mexican Nationalism, 1920-1970'. *Journal of Sport History* 18, no. 3 (1991): 359–60.

Beacom, A. 'Sport in International Relations: A Case for Cross-Disciplinary Investigation'. *The Sports Historian* 20, no. 2 (2000): 1–23.

Black, D., and J. Nauright. *Rugby and the South African Nation*. Manchester: Manchester University Press, 1998.

Booth, D. 'Hitting Apartheid for Six? The Politics of the South African Sports Boycott'. *Journal of Contemporary History* 38, no. 3 (2003): 477–93.

Booth, D. *The Race Game: Sport and Politics in South Africa*. London: Frank Cass, 1998.

Burke, M. 'Mexico City 1968'. In *Olympic Cities: City Agendas, Planning and the World's Games*, 1896–2012, edited by J. Gold and M. Gold, 183–8. London: Routledge, 2007.

Clarke, P. *Hope and Glory: Britain 1900–1990*. London: Penguin, 1996.

Coggins, R. 'Wilson and Rhodesia: UDI and British Policy Towards Africa'. *Contemporary British History* 20, no. 3 (2006): 363–81.

Coughlan, J., and I. Webb. *Sport and British Politics since 1960*. London: Falmer, 1990.

Davies, D. *Race Relations in Rhodesia: A Survey for 1972–73*. London: Rex Collings, 1975.

Doxey, M. *International Sanctions in Comparative Perspective*. Basingstoke: Macmillan, 1996.

Geldenhuys, D. *Isolated States: A Comparative Analysis*. Cambridge: Cambridge University Press, 1990.

Giulianotti, R. 'Between Colonialism, Independence and Globalization: Football in Zimbabwe'. In *Football in Africa: Conflict, Conciliation and Community*, edited by G. Armstrong and R. Giulianotti. Basingstoke: Palgrave, 2004.

Hall, A. *Ploughing, Politics and Fellowship*. Cumbria: The Author, 2000.

Hill, C. *Olympic Politics: Athens to Atlanta 1896–1996*. Manchester: Manchester University Press, 1996.

Hill, J. *Sport, Leisure & Culture in Twentieth Century Britain*. Basingstoke: Palgrave, 2002.

Holt, R., and T. Mason. *Sport in Britain 1945–2000*. Oxford: Blackwell, 2000.

Houlihan, B. 'Politics and Sport'. In *Handbook of Sports Studies*, edited by J. Coakley and E. Dunning, 213–27. London: Sage, 2002.

Little, C. '"No Politics, Mucho Rugby": International Rugby Contacts with Rhodesia during the UDI Period'. Paper presented at 'Le rugby du village au global' Conference, Paris October 2007.

Little, C. 'Pierre Trudeau's U-Turn: The Canadian Government and Sporting Contacts with Rhodesia in the UDI Period'. Paper presented at the 'To Remember is to Resist: 40 Years of Sport and Social Change' Conference, Toronto 2008.

Little, C. 'Preventing "A Wonderful Break-Through for Rhodesia": The British Government and the Exclusion of Rhodesia from the 1968 Mexico Olympics'. *Olympika (The International Journal of Olympic Studies)* 14 (2005): 47–68.

Little, C. 'Rebellion, Race and Rhodesia: International Cricketing Relations with Rhodesia During UDI'. *Sport in Society* 12, nos. 4–5 (2009): 523–36.

Lloyd, T. *The British Empire 1558–1995*. Oxford: Oxford University Press, 1996.

Macintosh, D., and M. Hawes. *Sport and Canadian Diplomacy*. Kingston: McGill-Queens University Press, 1994.

Mansergh, N. *The Commonwealth Experience*. Vol. 2. *From British to Multiracial Commonwealth*. London: Macmillan, 1982.

Novak, A. 'Rhodesia's "Rebel and Racist" Olympic Team: Athletic Glory, National Legitimacy and the Clash of Politics'. *International Journal of the History of Sport* 23, no. 8 (2006): 1369–88.

Polley, M. 'The Amateur Ideal and British Sports Diplomacy, 1900–1945'. *Sport in History* 26, no. 3 (2006): 450–67.

Polley, M. *Moving the Goalposts: A History of Sport and Society since 1945*. London: Routledge, 1998.

Schodl, G. *The Lost Past: A Story of the International Weightlifting Federation*. Budapest: The Federation, 1992.

Strack, H. *Sanctions: The Case of Rhodesia*. Syracuse: Syracuse University Press, 1978.

United Nations. *Sixth Report of the Security Council Committee Established in Pursuance of Resolution 253 (1968) Concerning the Question of Southern Rhodesia*, 9 January 1974.

Bidding for international sport events: how government supports and undermines national governing bodies of sport

Geoff Walters

Department of Management, Birkbeck, University of London, UK

Over the last 20 years bidding for the rights to host sport events has become increasingly competitive. While a range of factors underpin successful bids, political support, particularly in the context of bidding for mega sport events such as the Olympics or the FIFA World Cup, is essential. This has resulted in an increasingly politicized bidding process. The role of government policy and the impact on sport-event bidding therefore plays a key role in determining whether a national governing body of sport (NGB) is competitive during the bid process. Two central issues are considered within this article. First, it considers the ways in which the UK government is supportive of NGBs during the bidding process. Second, it focuses specifically on government taxation policy and discusses how the tax environment in the UK has the potential to undermine the competitiveness of UK NGBs when bidding to host sport events. Drawing on semi-structured interview data from 10 individuals representing nine national governing bodies of sport and six other stakeholders involved in the bidding process, the article illustrates that NGBs receive bid support from central government through the Department for Culture, Media and Sport, from local government, in addition to non-departmental public bodies including regional development agencies and UK Sport. The interview analysis also illustrates that this support is offset by the adverse impact of income tax and VAT policy of HM Treasury. The article concludes with the identification of four key issues which require further research. First, should HM Treasury introduce legislation to relinquish the right to tax a percentage of worldwide endorsement income from overseas sports people? Second, when bidding for one-off sport events, should HM Treasury provide exemptions from player tax and HMRC guarantee that they will not pursue the tax liability? Third, is there a need for HM Treasury to create a specialist sports events unit, and fourth, should a reduced VAT rate of 5% on spectator entry fees be introduced.

Introduction

Over the last 20 years increasing commercialization within the sport industry has been particularly evident in the context of sport events. Mega sport events, specifically the Olympic Games and the World Cup, in addition to major sport events and annual sport events generate significant spectator, media and commercial interest, and demonstrate that the sport-event industry is a key sector within the sport industry. The increased importance of sport events has resulted in the bid process assuming greater significance for those stakeholder organizations involved. One of the key stakeholders is government at both national and regional level. Political support is a key success factor during the bidding stage.[1] Subsequently the bidding process has become increasingly politicized on three levels. Firstly, the size and scale of mega events such as a World Cup or an Olympic

Games requires national government support and coordination, particularly where 'mega-events have tended to be the creation of political and economic elites'.[2] Second, sport events have been perceived as an opportunity by governments to showcase a country or region and to deliver a range of benefits, thereby increasing political involvement during the bid process. Third, it has also become more common for international sports federations to require political support during the bid process. For example, the International Olympic Committee requires government support for an Olympic bid in order for a city to be accepted as a candidate city.[3]

In the UK political support and involvement in the bidding process has increased in recent years. During 2001 and 2002 a series of reports published by the Department for Culture, Media and Sport (DCMS) demonstrated a cautious approach towards bidding and hosting sport events, stating that sport events should be a means and not an end; that a bid could only be justified if there were both sporting and non-sporting benefits to the UK; that historically there had been instances of poor investment appraisal, poor management and coordination; and that there was a need for earlier government intervention, engagement and support for mega events.[4] These reports followed the decision by Government not to develop an athletics stadium at Picketts Lock in north London due to inflated costs, with the UK subsequently losing the rights to host the 2005 IAAF World Athletics Championship. Nevertheless these reports were instrumental in determining the approach and the support provided by DCMS during the Olympic bid from 2003, with the Government committing £30 million during the bid phase and putting in place a more strategic planning process. The successful bid ensures that the UK will host many 'test' events for Olympic sports prior to the 2012 Games. In addition, the UK is set to host the 2014 Commonwealth Games, the 2015 Rugby World Cup, the 2013 Rugby League World Cup and the 2019 Cricket World Cup, while the Football Association recently bid (unsuccessfully) for the 2018 FIFA World Cup.

Political support, however, is complex. While particular aspects of government policy can strengthen a bid, a lack of strategic thinking between government departments can result in broader policy developments that have a negative impact on the bid process. One particular area is government taxation policy. When bidding for the rights to host an international sport event, UK national governing bodies of sport (NGBs) have to consider the implications of legislation on corporation tax, income tax and value-added tax (VAT) during the bid process. The present UK situation is that NGBs are subject to corporation tax on any profit they make from hosting a sport event; a non-UK resident sports person is subject to income tax on earnings made in the UK during an event; and event receipts are liable to VAT of 15%. The significance of this income tax policy was made clear in 2008 following the failure of the Football Association to secure the right to hold the 2010 Champions League final at Wembley. The reason underpinning the decision by UEFA was that the UK Government would not provide a guarantee that they would not pursue the players for tax on income earned in the UK. This was despite DCMS supporting the bid by the Football Association and appealing to Treasury. The Government has since given this guarantee to UEFA and Wembley has been chosen as the venue for the 2011 Champions League final. However, this decision does not represent a change in taxation policy and instead represents a one-off decision that does not extend to other sport events.

This article is based on research that was undertaken with the objective to identify key challenges that NGBs face when bidding to host an international sport event. Two central issues are considered within this article. First, it seeks to illustrate the ways in which the UK Government is supportive of NGBs during the bidding process. Second, it will focus specifically on government taxation policy and discuss how the tax environment in the UK has the potential to undermine the competitiveness of UK NGBs during the bidding process. The article begins with a brief review of literature that discusses the perceived benefits of hosting sport events that have resulted in increasing political involvement during the bid process. Critical literature that questions the validity of these benefits is also presented. The following section sets out the methodology, which details the way in which the empirical interview data was collected. The analysis of the interview data is used to examine the two key objectives. This includes firstly, the identification of four key governmental agencies that are supportive of NGBs during the bid process, and second, an analysis of how income tax and VAT policy can counteract government support and have an adverse effect on the ability of UK NGBs when bidding for sport events. The article concludes by considering the extent to which government support for sport-event bidding conflicts with, and is undermined by, taxation policy. Four key issues are identified and presented as areas that require further research.

Reasons for political involvement during the sport-event bid process

The predominant reason commonly used by governments to justify public support for sport-event bids is that an event has the potential to deliver positive economic benefits within a city or a region due to the additional direct, indirect and induced expenditure within an economy.[5] However, as recently as the 1970s the hosting of a mega sport event was seen to be a financial burden, owing to the £692 million loss sustained by the Montreal Olympics in 1976 and the £178 million loss at the Munich Olympics four years previous.[6] The commercial success of the 1984 summer Olympic Games in Los Angeles altered the perception that hosting mega sport events inevitably resulted in financial loss and provided the stimulus for the development and commercialization of the sport-event industry.[7] Drawing on multiplier analysis to forecast the economic impact, *ex ante* economic impact studies have often predicted that sport events will contribute a positive economic impact. For example, Blake has predicted that the London 2012 Olympics will result in an increase in GDP between 2005 and 2016 of £1.936 billion and create an additional 8164 full-time equivalent jobs.[8]

There have been concerns over the reliability of *ex ante* economic impact studies[9] with *ex post* studies illustrating that the economic impact of a sport event is often substantially less than forecast.[10] For example, an *ex post* analysis of the economic impact of the 1994 World Cup held in the US showed that the event resulted in an overall negative impact on each host city and the US economy in contrast to the *ex ante* estimates of a $4 billion positive impact.[11] Moreover, the 1992 Winter Olympics in Albertville incurred debts of £20 million, despite estimates during the bid stage that the event would break-even.[12] It has been suggested that many studies are over optimistic about the number of spectators and their spending habits at a sport event; they do not take into account the decreased spending by local residents; and they fail to consider the substitution effect where the gains achieved in the host city may be at the expense of a reduced level of tourism in another.[13]

Governments have also increasingly seen sports events as a means to regenerate urban areas.[14] The 1992 Barcelona Olympics are widely regarded as regenerating the urban environment and infrastructure in the city,[15] while in the UK in the 1980s and 1990s, sport events were used to promote urban regeneration and create leisure, retail and tourism facilities in former industrial cities.[16] The Olympic bids made by Birmingham and Manchester in the 1980s and 1990s and the total investment of £670 million in sporting facilities, transport and infrastructure in Manchester for the 2002 Commonwealth Games underpinned the belief that sport could be used as a means to promote urban regeneration, a better image and new employment opportunities.[17] Moreover, one of the five key legacy promises from the DCMS for the London 2012 Olympics is to transform the urban environment within East London.[18] However, there have been concerns raised in regard to sport events and the impact on urban regeneration. For instance, the Olympic stadium that was built for the 1976 Montreal Olympics far exceeded its original budget; it was not completed until 1987; and the Quebec government had to introduce national lotteries, tobacco taxes and property taxes to offset the cost.[19] Moreover, it has been questioned whether the income spent on urban regeneration projects to accompany the staging of a sport event could not be better spent elsewhere and that there is the potential to neglect education, training, affordable housing and the needs of social services.[20]

Many local governments have also integrated sport-event bidding into their strategic policy to raise the tourism profile of a region or city.[21] Developments in broadcasting technology and the rise in corporate sponsorship of sport events have provided key opportunities for local authorities to market their city.[22] Mega events such as the Olympic Games in particular attract significant publicity and provide global marketing opportunities and a chance for governments to improve the brand identity and image of a city and promote cultural and economic activity.[23] For example, the hosting of the 2002 Commonwealth Games was a key factor in Manchester moving from 19th to 13th in the European Cities Monitor, which is used to identify the best cities to locate a business.[24] The bidding process itself can also increase the level of exposure to tourist markets and result in an enhanced image of the bidding nation, a point that is particularly important for developing nations and highlighted by the Cape Town bid for the 2004 Olympic Games.[25]

Additional reasons underpinning government support for sport events include the development of sporting infrastructure and the hope that this will lead to legacy benefits including improved participation levels, social and cultural benefits such as building civic pride, community identity, and social inclusion benefits through community volunteer programmes.[26] For instance, the 2002 Commonwealth Games in Manchester resulted in £200 million investment in a range of new sporting facilities including a new velodrome for cycling, a national squash centre and an aquatics centre. These facilities have been used to stage additional UK and international championships; by 2003 a total of 250,000 new and existing visitors had used the facilities.[27] However, the extent to which sport events actually deliver social and cultural benefits to the majority of people in a city has been questioned.[28] If sport events are to contribute towards sport development and social benefits, appropriate strategies are needed. For example, Manchester had a Commonwealth Games Opportunities and Legacy Partnership Board while the Sydney Olympic Park was converted into a 'sports town' following the games in 2000 with an extensive range of sporting facilities and Vision 2025, a long-term strategic plan.

Methodology

This article is based on a research project that focused on identifying the key challenges that NGBs face when bidding to host a sport event. The issue of taxation was one of the key issues identified early in the project and further considered during a series of qualitative semi-structured interviews. The data was collected through recorded interviews with a sample of 16 senior representatives from NGBs and organizations that support NGBs during the bidding process. Senior representatives were selected on the basis that they would be able to provide information relevant to the research, therefore reflecting a purposive or judgemental sampling technique.[29] The Central Council of Physical Recreation, the organization that represents the interests of 270 national governing bodies and representative bodies of sport in the UK acted as facilitator during the research project and helped to arrange a number of interviews.[30]

An initial interview was undertaken with two tax consultants at a major accountancy firm in the UK. This interview provided background information into taxation issues and was useful in the development of further interview schedules. This was followed up with interviews with 10 individuals from nine NGBs. A senior representative from each NGB was interviewed including chief executives, a competition manager, chairmen and a director of operations. The sample included two major sport NGBs, five Olympic NGBs and two non-Olympic development sports. These organizations were chosen for two reasons. Firstly they represent a range of different sports, the reasoning being to gain an understanding of issues that exist around the bid process from a broader range of NGB perspectives. Second, these organizations also conformed to one of three criteria; they had recently been successful in a bid for a sport event, unsuccessful in a bid, or were currently in the process of bidding. A further four interviews were undertaken with senior representatives from three organizations that work with NGBs and provide support during the bidding process. These included a representative from a government department; two representatives from a non-departmental governing body; and a senior executive at an additional London-based accountancy firm. Whilst different sized NGBs were chosen in order to be more representative of the broad range of UK NGBs, the small sample size means that it is not possible to generalize conclusions. However what this does allow is the identification of key issues which require further research.

Each interview lasted between one hour and one and a half hours with an interview schedule used to structure the direction of questioning. Questions focused on a number of areas including the previous and current experiences of the bid process; issues and challenges during the bid process; the role of government and government policy; and the impact of tax policy on bidding and hosting events. The majority of interviews were tape-recorded after permission was granted, allowing each interview to be transcribed. The first stage of interview analysis began with reading the interview transcriptions in full to provide a general understanding of the responses. The interview transcripts were then imported into NVivo which allowed for more in-depth analysis and involved the identification of basic descriptive coding themes that were developed in relation to topics drawn out from the interview schedules. Further reading of the interview transcripts enabled the identification of different sub-themes. The coding scheme aided the interpretation of the data and helped to identify key issues in relation to the two key objectives of this article. The interviews were triangulated with secondary sources including official government reports and documents related to tax legislation, EU documents, newspaper material and information from websites. Secondary data, in particular, was useful in providing historical insights into taxation policy. The qualitative findings and analysis are presented below.

Government support for sport-event bidding

The first part of the analysis of the interview data revealed that there are four key government agencies that can provide support to NGBs when bidding to host sport events. They are DCMS, local authorities, regional development agencies and UK Sport. Each of these is looked at in turn.

Department for Culture, Media and Sport

DCMS is the government department responsible for sport policy. Given the size and scale of the forthcoming London 2012 Olympic Games the responsibilities of DCMS are firmly focused on delivering the Olympics. For instance, between 2008 and 2011, the Government has 30 Public Service Agreements (PSA) that outline strategic priorities. DCMS is the lead department on PSA 22 that focuses on the delivery of the Olympic Games and is responsible for financing the Olympics and for providing long-term legacy benefits. DCMS has overseen the implementation of the London Olympic Games and Paralympic Games Act, which was passed in the House of Commons in 2006 to provide a legal framework for the organization of the 2012 Games, with legislation on street trading, advertising and ticket touting.

To coordinate the government approach to the Olympics, DCMS also set up a cross-departmental network of individuals from within government to inform strategic thinking between government departments. This structure is important as the second key role of DCMS in the context of sport events is their support for the 2018 World Cup bid. In 2006, DCMS and HM Treasury commissioned a feasibility study into hosting the World Cup in 2018 and the chance for success should a bid take place.[31] While the decision to put forward a bid was ultimately taken by the Football Association (FA), the purpose of the feasibility study was to provide evidence to support the FA's decision. The study made a number of positive conclusions including the solid foundation of public support for England pursuing a bid and that the UK is well placed to handle the large number of expected overseas visitors whilst also recognizing key issues such as the costs associated with hosting an event of the scale of the World Cup and the importance to assess accurately the costs and the financing options to inform a bid.[32]

Local authorities

While DCMS is a central government department, local authorities are responsible for the provision of a range of services within the regions in which they govern. While sport is not central to the role of local authorities, there are many examples where sport events have become integrated within local government strategic policy as they are seen to deliver a range of benefits to a region. For example, during the 1980s and 1990s, the strategy of using sport events to promote urban regeneration and create leisure, retail and tourism facilities in former industrial cities was popular.[33] With many local authorities actively supporting the hosting of sport events there are opportunities for financial support. For example, Manchester City Council is very supportive of sport events, and through a partnership involving the Northwest Regional Development Agency (NWDA) and UK Sport achieved a SportBusiness Sports City Gold Award for its commitment to hosting sport events. The type of support also extends further than simply financial contributions. As one interviewee from a non-Olympic governing body due to host a World Championship event in Manchester stated:

> We have been fortunate enough to get some money from Manchester City Council. Now they will contribute a lot more in kind. They will help us with advertising and their staff time ... they are extremely helpful, they are very supportive to us.[34]

However, it is clear that funding support from local councils can vary. While Manchester City Council governs a large urban area, other sport events that are restricted by geography find that the availability of funding from smaller local authorities is less forthcoming:

> A lot of the councils that we deal with are quite small, because they are seaside towns. The amount of money Manchester have just put into the short-course swimming was just mind-blowing, and they underwrote the whole event, whereas councils that we operate with can't do that. They are just small towns.[35]

Regional development agencies

Regional development agencies (RDAs) are non-departmental public bodies that were created in the UK in 1999 to further economic development and regeneration and promote investment and employment. The RDA total budget of £2.3 billion in 2007–8 was funded by six government departments including DCMS. There are a total of nine RDAs in the UK. Each RDA has a regional economic strategy (RES) and funding support is provided to projects that meet the objectives set out in the RES. Sport events have the potential to contribute towards the RES, stimulating regional economic development and consolidating the link between sport events and urban regeneration.[36] In this context, many RDAs have developed major event strategies that can provide funding support to NGBs. For instance, the NWDA produced a strategy document in 2004 outlining support for major events.[37] As noted above, the partnership involving the NWDA, Manchester City Council and UK Sport has been instrumental in Manchester's success in the sport-event field. A further example is the partnership between the South East England Development Agency, Sport England, Tourism South East and the South East Cultural Consortium that resulted in the creation of the Sports Events South East partnership in 2005 with the aim to provide support to NGBs and encourage sport events to the region.[38] Since then, the 2007 the Archery World Championships, the 2008 Junior World Beach Volleyball event and stage one of the Tour de France have all been held in the south-east region, while funding has been allocated for future events such as the 2011 European Eventing Championships at Blenheim. For an NGB, one of the benefits of RDA funding is that it reduces the dependence on individual funders:

> The dependency on UK Sport as a percentage is decreasing and it is spread across more partners now. We are already working with the Welsh Assembly in Wales and SEEDA should come on board – the South-East Economic Development Agency – so I think that side is working. Some of those are government agencies and that all seems quite positive.[39]

UK Sport and the World Class Events Programme

UK Sport is a non-departmental public body funded through DCMS and lottery income. The objective of UK Sport is to distribute DCMS and lottery funding to support elite athletes and promote world-class performance. This objective is supported by the World Class Events Programme (WCEP), a key distributor of funds to support NGBs when bidding for and hosting major events in the UK. The WCEP was created in 1999 after it was recognized that there was a need to implement a more strategic process in relation to bidding and staging major sport events. The key role of the WCEP is to provide funding to Olympic sport NGBs to bid for and to host sport events. Bidding for mega events including the World Cup or the Olympics are therefore outside the remit of UK Sport; these are events in which DCMS and the Government has responsibility. Securing funding support from UK Sport is critical for many NGBs during the bid stage, as two interviewees emphasized:

> The fact that it [the bid] was supported by UK Sport made it do-able. Frankly they are not that commercially viable without the funding support.[40]

> That combined with the knowledge of the venue and being underwritten in advance of the bid, underwritten by UK Sport, which is very important, is what helped us win it.[41]

Between 1999 and 2008, approximately 120 events have received funding from UK Sport. Between 1999 and 2005 the WCEP funded on average four to six events a year on an annual budget of £1.6 million. However, since winning the bid for the 2012 Olympics in

2005, there has been a significant increase in funding to the WCEP to £3.3 million per year. This has enabled UK Sport to increase significantly the number of events to which it provides financial support. Nineteen events were supported in 2007, while 17 events received funding in 2008, including six world championship events, such as the UCI World Track Cycling Championships, the IAAF World Cross Country Championships and the FINA World Short Course Swimming Championships. In 2009, UK Sport will provide funding support to host a large number of events including the Modern Pentathlon World Championships, the World Netball Championships, World Triathlon Championships, and the European Jumping and Dressage Championships. Despite the increase in funding the chair of one governing body still felt that the government should provide further funding to the WCEP: 'as far as we are concerned UK Sport have been fantastic but on the other hand I don't think that government has supported UK Sport enough with their budget for major events'.[42]

The role of the WCEP extends further than providing financial support. Additional support is provided to Olympic event NGBs through the Event Management Forum that enables event managers to come together to share knowledge and best practice. Specialist support and training is also provided on issues such as business planning and securing commercial sponsorship, while the Cities and Regions Group brings together local authorities, regional partners and NGBs to develop strategies to facilitate partnership working. As one interviewee confirmed: 'Its not just the financial support, I think it is the actual physical support you get. The events division there, in fact the whole of UK Sport are quite impressive really. If you ask a question you get an answer'.[43]

Government taxation policy and bidding for sport events

The second part of the analysis focuses specifically on government taxation policy. It identifies four key areas of concern. These are the taxation of endorsement and sponsorship income, pursuing athletes for tax liabilities, underwriting tax liabilities and VAT on sport events.

Taxation of endorsement and sponsorship income

At present, the UK has double-tax treaties with over 120 countries. These treaties are put in place to ensure that foreign nationals resident and subject to income tax within these countries do not incur a tax liability on any income that they earn within the UK during a short period of stay. In the context of sport events, employees of international federations, overseas NGBs and non-playing officials are therefore not subject to tax in the UK provided they are from a country with which the UK has a double-tax treaty. However with regard to international athletes, the 1986 Finance Act introduced a special tax regime for non-resident entertainers and sportspeople. Under this legislation overseas entertainers and sportspeople are subject to UK taxation on income earned in the UK, for which they may receive a tax credit in their country of residence under the terms of the double-tax treaty. This means exemption from UK income tax under a double-tax treaty is not available to a non-UK resident sportsperson and they are subject to income tax on earnings made in the UK.

A key issue is in relation to endorsement and sponsorship income earned by individual sportspeople from contracts with non-UK companies. This was the subject of the case between HMRC and Andre Agassi. HMRC sought to tax a percentage of the annual endorsement income received by Agassi's image rights company (a US resident) from two US companies (Nike Inc. and Head Sport AG). Where previously HMRC allowed a deduction of between 25% and 65% from endorsement income in recognition of the image rights of an athlete, a change made in 1997 meant that HMRC insisted that endorsement income was subject to UK tax in relation to the time spent participating in competitions within the UK. This meant an increase in the tax liability on player endorsements in the UK. This ruling withstood a legal challenge from Agassi in the House of Lords in 2006, who disputed the legality of HMRC in assessing income tax on endorsement payments made between three non-UK resident corporate entities. HMRC's success in this case established a precedent, and leaves any overseas entertainer or sportsperson exposed to the risk that HMRC may seek to tax a percentage of global endorsement contracts by reference to the time the individual spends competing in the UK in a given tax year. Currently the UK and the US are the only two major nations that levy tax on an overseas athletes' endorsement income.

Taxing endorsement and sponsorship income acts as a disincentive to the top athletes to come to the UK to compete in sporting events and could undermine the UK NGBs ability to compete during the bid process. As the interview with one of the tax consultants revealed:

> The International Federations will say if I have got a bid on the table from this country who has agreed not to tax, you just come and go as you please when it comes to player taxation and we are going to give you this big incentive, then that country is going to have a competitive advantage.[44]

However the interview analysis revealed that sponsorship and endorsement income is not a critical issue for many NGBs where the athletes do not have lucrative endorsement contracts. Where it is an issue is in major sports and particularly individual sports where athletes have lucrative endorsement deals such as tennis and golf. While it is unlikely that a major event with a strong sporting heritage, such as the British Open or Wimbledon, will have an issue attracting top athletes, taxation on player endorsements may ultimately impact upon smaller events where an athlete could end up paying more in tax in the UK on their endorsement income than they actually earn in prize money. For example, there have been concerns that many tennis players will be unwilling to enter the annual championship event at the Queen's Club prior to Wimbledon, while the LTA event at Eastbourne in May 2009 failed to attract any of the top 20 ranked male players. There is also concern that some golfers will choose not to compete in the 2010 Ryder Cup in Wales and the 2014 event in Scotland due to tax issues. Taxing endorsement and sponsorship could ultimately damage the reputation of the UK and may determine whether international federations choose the UK to host an event in the future.

Pursuing athletes for tax liabilities

A second reason why UK income tax policy affects the competitiveness of UK NGBs when bidding is related to team sports and the refusal of HMRC to provide guarantees that they won't pursue individual athletes for tax liabilities. When an international team plays in the UK, there is no system whereby the tax on player prize money, bonuses or endorsements can be withheld. So whilst there is a tax liability, it is very difficult for HMRC to actually collect that tax. Many governments recognize this; when their NGBs are bidding for sport events, they provide exemptions from player tax and guarantee that they will not pursue the tax liability to give the players certainty over their tax position. The reasoning is clear:

> In terms of 80,000 fans coming to watch the [Champions League] final, the revenues that generates, they just take a sensible view that actually the amount of tax is immaterial compared to what it will do for the country hosting that event.[45]

This has not historically been the case in the UK. In 2008 the failure by the Football Association to secure the 2010 Champions League final at Wembley was precisely because the UK Government would not provide a guarantee to UEFA that they would not pursue the players for income tax on income earned in the UK, which could include a percentage of endorsement income:

> Most countries have taken the view that it's too difficult to collect anyway, there won't be much tax, therefore we will exempt you from the Champions League final. Whereas what the UK government have said is that these are the rules, we have to enforce them and therefore we can't give you a guarantee that we won't chase the players for tax.[46]

However the UK Government has subsequently given this guarantee to UEFA and Wembley has been chosen as the venue for the 2011 Champions League final. This decision, however, does not represent a change in taxation policy and instead represents a one-off decision that does not extend to other sport events. Nevertheless the fact that the Government has taken this decision sets a precedent for future events and perhaps indicates a willingness on the part of Treasury to consider tax exemptions on a case-by-case basis.

Underwriting tax liabilities

Underwriting tax liabilities is a prerequisite for hosting the Olympic Games. As part of the bid for the 2012 Olympics, the UK Government agreed in the 2006 Finance Act that the International Olympic Committee would not be liable for tax and that no competing athlete at the Games is liable to pay UK income tax on their games-related income. As competition during the bidding stage for many other sport events has increased, many other international federations are insisting that the host NGB underwrite tax liabilities:

> The international governing bodies are so powerful that they are insisting that if you have the event and there is any tax to pay, the local host city picks up the liability . . . . Our tax laws are not exempting these one-off events from all these taxes which means that we have got a huge burden on the governing bodies that bid for these events.[47]

These can include any taxation that the international federation is liable to incur. As well as increasing costs this can lead to issues over control. After a contract is signed whereby the NGB agrees to underwrite the tax liability of the international federation, the NGB will not have any control over the activities of the international federation and therefore it could potentially result in the creation of a large tax liability, for which the NGB is accountable. This demonstrates the need for a close working relationship between the NGB and the international federation, as well as an understanding on the part of the NGB as to how taxation issues affect the hosting of an event. As one of the tax consultants indicated:

> It's lack of control, because while you can control your own affairs you can't control an International Federation. You can work together, and I think the examples that we deal with where they are working together are great to see, but you can imagine some of the more arrogant International Federations would just say 'you have signed this, it's up to you. We don't really care if you go bust, it's your tax authorities' problem, they are chasing you.' So you can actually see there is some logic to these tax indemnity clauses but on the other hand there is an education process that is needed.[48]

Having to underwrite the costs of taxation from competitors' earnings from prize money is also an issue as it can lead to increasing the costs of hosting an event, which at the bidding stage can hinder the bid process. As the director of operations for an Olympic NGB stated: 'The International Federation in the end told us we could not deduct tax so we would have to pay the tax ourselves, so that inflates the price of running an event'.[49]

With securing funding for an event a key issue for NGBs during the bidding process, increasing the budget due to having to underwrite tax liabilities could ultimately have an adverse effect during the bidding phase and potentially determine whether an NGB decides to bid for an event and how competitive the bid is in relation to other countries. However, the analysis of the interview data indicated that some NGBs have found more tax efficient ways to work around this by paying prize money earned in the UK to the international federation who then pay the individual athletes to avoid the issue of taxation in the UK. It is possible however that HMRC may issue tax returns to the individual athletes and hope to collect income tax via self-assessment from the individuals in some cases.

VAT on sport events

In the UK, NGBs are registered for VAT. In the context of sport events, there are three key issues with VAT. First, as noted above, it is becoming more common that any VAT liability incurred by the international federation has to be underwritten by the host NGB. This is an increased cost that has to be considered during the bid process. The second issue is that there appears to be inconsistency about how VAT is applied to sport events, with it affecting governing bodies in different ways:

> The VAT seems to be dependent on which regional area you are in, in terms of how the VAT man treats entry fees .... That's been a big issue, and there is no consistency across the VAT areas.[50]

> VAT is not an issue for us at all. We've been successful in recovering VAT in relation to events ... we integrate it with our own VAT, it is just part of our activities and therefore it is just further elements of our inputs and outputs as far as VAT is concerned.[51]

The third issue is in the cases where HMRC charge VAT on ticket sales at the applicable standard UK rate of 15%. This is an issue that could potentially make the UK uncompetitive in relation to other EU countries when bidding for sport events, particularly if the VAT rate is higher in the UK. Over the past decade, VAT rates across the EU have been harmonized to some extent with the introduction of the VAT Directive in January 2007 which set out a mandatory minimum rate of VAT of 15% in EU states.[52] However, the EU Directive also allows for a reduced rate not less than 5%; admission to sporting events is one of the services to which the reduced rate can be applied.[53] In the EU *White Paper on Sport* in 2007, the Commission argued that it was important to maintain the possibility for reduced VAT rates for sport given its societal role.[54] However, with ticket sales for sport events in the UK often subject to VAT at the standard rate of 15%, this tax liability will increase the cost of hosting a sport event for a UK NGB. During the bidding stage, the need to raise funds to cover the VAT liability could therefore put UK NGBs at an additional disadvantage compared to other governing bodies within the EU.

Conclusions

Sport event bidding has become increasingly competitive and politicized over the last 20 years. This article has been structured around two key bidding-related issues. The first has looked at the ways in which the UK Government is supportive of NGBs during the bidding process. The analysis of the interview data has identified that there are four key government agencies that currently provide support to NGBs when bidding to host sport events. These include DCMS, which is particularly focused on mega events including the London 2012 Olympics. Local authorities are also shown to aid NGBs during the bid stage, while non-departmental public bodies including regional development agencies and UK Sport provide different types of support necessary for NGBs during the bid phase. Despite government support, the interview data also illustrated that NGBs and those stakeholders that are involved with the bidding process perceive that a lack of a joined-up strategic approach between government departments is currently undermining many NGBs during the bid process. The second issue that this article has considered is one such example. It has shown that government taxation policy and the tax environment in the UK has the potential to undermine the competitiveness of UK NGBs when bidding to host sport events. It was discussed how income tax policy can affect sport-event bidding due to the taxation of endorsement income of participating athletes, the pursuit of athletes for tax liabilities by HMRC, and the increasing need for NGBs to underwrite income tax liabilities. This latter point is also relevant in the context of VAT, while the rate of VAT charged on ticket sales can also impact on sport-event bidding.

In order to protect the reputation of the UK as one of the leading nations in the sport-event industry and to ensure that UK NGBs remain competitive during the bid process, the absence of any tax concessions could ultimately damage the long-term competitiveness and attractiveness of the UK as a venue and harm the ability of UK NGBs during the bidding process. It is clear that despite government support for sport-event bidding there is a fundamental conflict with taxation policy. To conclude, four key issues or questions are identified which require further research. First, should HM Treasury introduce legislation to relinquish the right to tax a percentage of worldwide endorsement income from overseas sportspeople? It could be argued that in doing so this ruling would reduce uncertainty and help to ensure that athletes are not discouraged from competing in sports events in the UK due to taxation. It would also mean that the UK falls into line with all other major nations. Second, when bidding for one-off sport events, should HM Treasury provide exemptions from player tax and HMRC guarantee that they will not pursue the tax liability? A precedent has been set with the guarantee that has been given to UEFA allowing the Football Association to succeed in the bid for the 2011 Champions League final. Third, although the Foreign Entertainers Unit within HMRC is responsible for issues surrounding the taxation of non-UK sportspeople, is there a need for HM Treasury to create a specialist sports-events unit? The purpose of this unit would be to consider tax issues in relation to sport events and should consist of representatives from HM Treasury, HMRC, DCMS, UK Sport and experts in corporation tax, income tax and VAT. It should also improve coordination across government in relation to how policy affects bidding for and hosting sport events. HM Treasury should also grant this unit the responsibility to look at sport events on a case-by-case basis and have the authority to offer tax exemptions to international federations to reduce the financial costs of staging events and ensure that UK NGBs are competitive during the bid process. Fourth, should a reduced VAT rate of 5% on spectator entry fees be introduced in line with the policy of reduced VAT rates in the EU VAT Directive and as recommended in the EU *White Paper on Sport*? This would ensure that UK NGBs are not at a competitive disadvantage when bidding in relation to other nations.

Given the small sample size and number of interviews, further research is required to determine whether these four key issues are valid and to what extent they could be implemented. For example, quantitative evidence is needed to demonstrate the impact of these recommendations on the revenues of HMRC and provide evidence to either support or oppose tax exemptions. Moreover a survey of all NGBs in the UK would enable more generalized conclusions as to the extent to which taxation impacts on NGBs and therefore provide support for the proposals. Further qualitative research looking at the advantages and disadvantages of each proposal and drawing on a wider range of interviews with taxation specialists and representatives from HMRC is also required to build on the four key issues that have been identified.

Notes

[1] Emery, 'Bidding to Host a Major Sports Event: The Local Organising Committee'; Westerbeek, Turner and Ingesson, 'Key Success Factors'.
[2] Roche, 'Putting the London 2012 Olympics into Perspective', 287.
[3] Masterman, *Strategic Sports Event Management: Olympic Edition.*
[4] DCMS, *Staging International Sport Events; DCMS, Game Plan; DCMS, Unpicking the Lock.*
[5] Kasimati, 'Economic Aspects'.
[6] Gratton, Dobson and Shibli, 'Economic Importance'.
[7] Ibid.
[8] Blake, *Economic Impact.*
[9] Crompton, 'Economic Impact Analysis'; Kirkup and Major, 'Reliability of Economic Impact Studies'.
[10] Baade and Matheson, 'Quest for the Cup'.
[11] Ibid.
[12] Emery, 'Bidding to Host: Strategic Investment'.
[13] Baade and Matheson, 'Quest for the Cup'; Baade, Baumann and Matheson, 'Selling the Game'.
[14] Gratton and Henry, *Sport in the City.*
[15] Gold and Gold, 'Olympic Cities'.
[16] Hall, 'Imaging, Tourism and Sports'.
[17] Gratton, Shibli and Coleman, 'Sport and Economic Regeneration'.
[18] MacRury, 'Re-thinking the Legacy 2012'.
[19] Masterman, *Strategic Sports Event Management: An International Approach.*
[20] Essex and Chalkley, 'Olympic Games'.
[21] Cochrane, Peck and Tickell, 'Manchester Plays Games'.
[22] Horne, 'Four "Knowns" of Sport'.
[23] Westerbeek, Turner and Ingesson, 'Key Success Factors'.
[24] Gratton, Shibli and Coleman, 'Sport and Economic Regeneration'.
[25] Swart and Urmilla, 'Seductive Discourse of Development'.
[26] Brown and Massey, *Sports Development Impact.*
[27] Masterman, *Strategic Sports Event Management: An International Approach.*
[28] Long and Sanderson, 'Social Benefits of Sport'.
[29] Sekaran, *Research Methods for Business.*
[30] Fetterman, *Ethnography.*
[31] HM Treasury, *Hosting the World Cup.*
[32] Ibid.
[33] Hall, 'Imaging, Tourism and Sports'.
[34] Director, non-Olympic development sport NGB.
[35] Competition Manager, Olympic NGB, 25 April 2008.
[36] Gratton, Shibli and Coleman, 'Sport and Economic Regeneration'.
[37] Northwest Development Agency, *A Strategy for Major Events.*
[38] Sports Events South East, *Major Sports Events Strategy.*
[39] Competition Manager, Olympic NGB, 25 April 2008.
[40] Chief Executive, Olympic NGB, 25 June 2008.
[41] Chief Executive, Olympic NGB, 25 June 2008.
[42] Chair, Olympic NGB, 13 May 2008.
[43] Chief Executive, Olympic NGB, 13 May 2008.
[44] Tax consultant, major accountancy firm, 8 April 2008.
[45] Tax consultant, major accountancy firm, 8 April 2008.
[46] Tax consultant, major accountancy firm, 8 April 2008.
[47] Tax consultant, major accountancy firm, 8 April 2008.
[48] Tax consultant, major accountancy firm, 8 April 2008.
[49] Director of operations, Olympic NGB, 15 April 2008.
[50] Competition Manager, Olympic Sport NGB, 25 April 2008.

[51] Treasurer, Olympic Sport NGB, 13 May 2008.
[52] European Union, Council Directive 2006/112/EC, 28 November 2006, on the common system of VAT.
[53] Commission of the European Communities, *White Paper on Sport*.
[54] Ibid.

References

Baade, R., R. Baumann, and V. Matheson. 'Selling the Game: Estimating the Economic Impact of Professional Sports through Taxable Sales'. *Southern Economic Journal* 74, no. 3 (2008): 794–810.

Baade, R., and V. Matheson. 'The Quest for the Cup: Assessing the Economic Impact of the World Cup'. *Regional Studies* 38, no. 4 (2004): 343–54.

Blake, A. *The Economic Impact of the London 2012 Olympics*. Christel DeHaan Tourism and Travel Research Institute: Nottingham University Business School, 2005.

Brown, A., and J. Massey. *The Sports Development Impact of the Manchester 2002 Commonwealth Games: Initial Baseline Research*. London: UK Sport, 2001.

Cochrane, A., J. Peck, and A. Tickell. 'Manchester Plays Games: Exploring the Local Politics of Globalisation'. *Urban Studies* 33, no. 8 (1996): 1319–36.

Commission of the European Communities. *White Paper on Sport*. Brussels: EC, 2007.

Crompton, J. 'Economic Impact Analysis of Sports Facilities and Events: Eleven Sources of Misapplication'. *Journal of Sport Management* 9 (1995): 14–35.

DCMS. *Game Plan: A Strategy for Delivering Government's Sport and Physical Activity Objectives*. London: DCMS, 2002.

DCMS. *Staging International Sport Events: Government Response to the Third Report from the Culture, Media and Sport Committee Session, 2000–2001*. London: DCMS, 2001.

DCMS. *Unpicking the Lock: The World Athletics Championships in the UK: Government Response to the First Report from the Culture, Media and Sport Select Committee Session 2001–2002*. London: DCMS, 2002.

Emery, P. 'Bidding to Host a Major Sports Event: Strategic Investment or Complete Lottery?'. In *Sport in the City: The Role of Sport in Economic and Social Regeneration*, edited by C. Gratton and I. Henry, 90–108. London: Routledge, 2001.

Emery, P. 'Bidding to Host a Major Sports Event: The Local Organising Committee Perspective'. *The International Journal of Public Sector Management* 15, nos. 4–5 (2002): 316–36.

Essex, S., and B. Chalkley. 'Olympic Games: Catalyst of Urban Change'. *Leisure Studies* 17, no. 3 (1998): 187–206.

Fetterman, D. *Ethnography: Step by Step*. London: Sage Publications, 1989.

Gold, J., and M. Gold. 'Olympic Cities: Regeneration, City Rebranding and Changing Urban Agendas'. *Geography Compass* 2, no. 1 (2008): 300–18.

Gratton, C., N. Dobson, and S. Shibli. 'The Economic Importance of Major Sport Events: A Case-Study of Six Events'. *Managing Leisure* 5, no. 1 (2000): 17–28.

Gratton, C., and I. Henry, eds. *Sport in the City: The Role of Sport in Economic and Social Regeneration*. London: Routledge, 2001.

Gratton, C., S. Shibli, and R. Coleman. 'Sport and Economic Regeneration in Cities'. *Urban Studies* 42, nos. 5–6 (2005): 985–99.

Hall, C. 'Imaging, Tourism and Sports Event Fever: The Sydney Olympics and The Need for a Social Charter for Mega-Events'. In *Sport in the City: The Role of Sport in Economic and Social Regeneration*, edited by C. Gratton and I. Henry, 166–86. London: Routledge, 2001.

HM Treasury. *Hosting the World Cup: A Feasibility Study*. London: HM Treasury, 2007.

Horne, J. 'The Four "Knowns" of Sport Mega-Events'. *Leisure Studies* 26, no. 1 (2007): 81–96.

Kasimati, E. 'Economic Aspects and the Summer Olympics: A Review of Related Research'. *International Journal of Tourism Research* 5 (2003): 433–44.

Kirkup, N., and B. Major. 'The Reliability of Economic Impact Studies of the Olympic Games: A Post-Games Study of Sydney 2000 and Considerations for London 2012'. *Journal of Sport Tourism* 11, nos. 3–4 (2006): 275–96.

Long, J., and I. Sanderson. 'The Social Benefits of Sport: Where's the Proof?'. In *Sport in the City: The Role of Sport in Economic and Social Regeneration*, edited by C. Gratton and I. Henry, 187–203. London: Routledge, 2001.

MacRury, I. 'Re-thinking the Legacy 2012: The Olympics as Commodity and Gift'. *21st Century Society* 3, no. 3 (2008): 297–312.

Masterman, G. *Strategic Sports Event Management: An International Approach*. London: Elsevier-Butterworth Heinemann, 2004.

Masterman, G. *Strategic Sports Event Management: Olympic Edition*. London: Elsevier-Butterworth Heinemann, 2009.

Northwest Development Agency. *A Strategy for Major Events in England's Northwest*. Warrington: NWDA, 2004.

Roche, M. 'Putting the London 2012 Olympics into Perspective: The Challenge of Understanding Mega-Events'. *21st Century Society* 3, no. 3 (2008): 285–90.

Sekaran, U. *Research Methods for Business*. New York: Wiley, 2000.

Sports Events South East. *Major Sports Events Strategy for the South-East Region*. Guildford: SEEDA, 2006.

Swart, K., and B. Urmilla. 'The Seductive Discourse of Development: The Cape Town 2004 Olympic Bid'. *Third World Quarterly* 25, no. 7 (2004): 1311–24.

Westerbeek, H., P. Turner, and L. Ingesson. 'Key Success Factors in Bidding for Hallmark Sporting Events'. *International Marketing Review* 19, nos. 2–3 (2002): 303–23.

What happens while the official looks the other way? Citizenship, transnational sports migrants and the circumvention of the state

Thomas F. Carter

Chelsea School, University of Brighton, Eastbourne, UK

The era of transnational sport migration (TSM) has been one of heady celebration, seemingly free movement across borders, and lucrative business. The predominant (and outmoded) models of sport migration currently ignore state controls of migration. This paper brings the state back into analyses of TSM and looks at strategies migrants have used to skirt governmental attempts to control their movements. Understanding the issues surrounding state constructions of national citizenship is essential – both for this paper but also for migrants themselves in order to manipulate these controlling mechanisms to work in their favour. After identifying classificatory themes for determining national and professional status, this paper draws on examples that highlight states' attempts to control the movements of sport professionals. Using a combination of ethnographic material gathered over the past decade along with interviews and investigative reports, this article argues that an updated theory for understanding transnational sport migration must incorporate and reflect the actual experiences, routes and roots of TSM *and* the multiple forces that contour these processes.

Introduction

In the spring of 2008, Alejandro Rojas[1] will travel from the Dominican Republic to the training facilities of the Chicago White Sox in Tucson Arizona.[2] He will, in all likelihood, travel on a passenger jet in relative comfort, pass through US Immigration with relative ease on his Dominican passport and US work visa, and continue his career as a professional baseball player. Rojas is not Dominican, however; he is Cuban. His ethnicity is not that remarkable. That Rojas will travel across the North American continent for his employment is not especially remarkable either. What is rather remarkable and is often absent from public discourse is the negotiated terms of his travel, terms set by a transnational corporation, Major League Baseball, in conjunction with a national government, the US Government, that regulates, legalizes, and constrains transnational sport labour migration. Even more remarkable and hidden is the means by which Rojas travelled to the Dominican Republic from Cuba. His and others' travels are what is of particular concern in this article.

A decade earlier, Alejandro Rojas was just a boy and I was in Havana. While I have never met Señor Rojas, I have known several other Cuban baseball players. On a brisk January day that Cubans consider cold, I was conversing with Román, a sports journalist and friend, in the street outside his office when he informed me that Juan Pablo was missing. Confused, I queried, 'Missing? What do you mean missing? He's got a game tonight. I just talked to him last week.'

Román shrugged his shoulders, 'He's gone. He's not at home, no one has seen him for three days.' His voice drops *sotto voce*, 'They [baseball officials] do not know where he is.'

'*Pinche*, he promised to give me an interview next week. Where do you think he is?'

Cocking his head to one side and looking at me out of the side of his glasses, Román smiles slightly and says, 'Who knows? All they know is that he is not where he is supposed to be.'

Two weeks later, Román and I meet again to catch up on news, gossip, and to discuss various local issues. Even as he sits down, he raises the subject of Juan Pablo again. 'Juan Pablo is in Costa Rica. So is Gutierrez.' Gutierrez is Juan Pablo's teammate on their *Serie Nacional* team.[3]

I splutter in disbelief, 'Both of them? How'd they get there? What are they doing there?'

Román orders the waiter to bring us two beers. 'No one here knows,' implying that that no Cuban official knows. 'They are investigating how they got there. *La Peña* says that Juan Pablo will sign with the [New York] Yankees for ten million'.[4]

I retort, 'The Yankees? Not without a tryout he won't. And I'm sure he'd have a tryout to show other clubs what he can do as well.' The waiter arrives with our drinks, takes our order, and wanders back to the kitchen leaving us in relative peace. I continue, 'You say no one knows. That's crap. Surely someone knows where he went and how.'

Román laughs briefly and smiles. 'Of course, Tomás. People know he went in a boat. What no one knows is who took him. Except those who organized it and some of them must still be here in Cuba.'

'Why do you say that?' I ask.

'It is simple, really. To do something like that, I imagine, requires coordination with people here and out there *(p'alla)*. So some of them, logically, must still be here.'

I finish his thought, 'And that is what the authorities are investigating . . . '.

Román finishes this conversational thread, 'Exactly.'

These two episodes, 10 years apart, serve to introduce the main themes of this paper. Both Rojas's sudden appearance in the Dominican Republic in 2007 and Juan Pablo's disappearance in 1997 illustrate the complexities of transnational sport migration and challenge our current understandings of these phenomena. Transnational sport migration (TSM), in all its forms, is dynamic and multifaceted, and capturing the intricacies of TSM requires more analytical sophistication than currently offered by the mainly ahistorical typologies that so far have been proposed.[5] At present, understandings about the transnational migration of sports professionals have been presented in atemporal dichotomies of sundered ties and new relations without any critical examination of the ties that are supposedly cut and the new ones used to replace those that allegedly disappear. These approaches oversimplify the migratory experience in both localities, origin and destination, consequently resulting in an overly simplified portrayal of the processes involved in TSM. The typologies currently on offer simply cannot account for the various factors that inform migratory processes, whether they are economic, political, familial, or one of several other potential factors informing decisions and strategies to move from one locale to another. They also tend to treat transnational sport migrants as individuals who operate in isolation when their decision-making processes clearly involve multiple individuals in the planning, implementation and effect of any such move.[6] Further, the choices of where, when and how to move from one place to another also are absent from these sorts of categorization. Another shortcoming, and the one that is the focus of this particular article, is the absence of the state in such migratory practices. The role of the state in TSM is essential despite pre-eminent texts' much greater emphasis on the global economic and political forces affecting sport in academic literature.[7] While certainly accurate in their accounts of the expanding roles that international non-governmental organizations (INGOs) like the International Olympic Committee (IOC) and FIFA play in shaping TSM, these leading works fail to account for the well established and ongoing effects that state governance of borders has on TSM. To begin to address these limitations, the complexities of Cuban TSM are used to illustrate these processes. Cuban TSM has a number of unique features specific to its recent history that further illuminate the importance of historical specificities that exist in all forms of TSM.

This paper brings the state back into analyses of TSM by looking at strategies migrant athletes have used to skirt bureaucratic attempts to control their movements. Excavating the strategies employed by transnational migrants draws attention to the means by which states channel the flow of TSM and to the particular contests over the control of the movement of individuals. By attending to these key aspects of how 'globalization' itself is ideologically articulated and received, it reveals the tenuously negotiated strategic positions held in the control of professionals' movements. Globalization is not merely the benign force its advocates claim it is; rather it entails conflicts over local ideologies and values that define personhood. Understanding the classificatory schema of citizenship that states construct is therefore essential – both for this paper and for migrants themselves in order to manipulate these controlling mechanisms in their favour. Adopting this perspective permits an investigative consideration of the various positions involved in this contested social process.

This essay is part of a larger project on TSM that attempts to humanize our understandings of these migrants by engaging in 'translocal research'.[8] Translocal research entails making a conscious methodological decision to exchange ethnographic depth for breadth of materials. This larger project makes use of a combination of ethnographic material gathered over the past decade, along with interviews and investigative reports. This was a conscious decision since it was unlikely that I would be able to obtain detailed observational data on the everyday lives of the particular migrants discussed in this paper.[9] Nor could I, realistically, make the same journeys under similar conditions since the migratory moves under scrutiny in this paper entail illegal activities. Consequently, every person identified in this article has been given a pseudonym, even if that person has appeared elsewhere in other publications (including my own) under other names, because the material presented here documents some of the reasoning for and strategies of engaging in illegal activities. Nevertheless, the examples presented here are results of primary fieldwork in which I followed migrants' routes (albeit not necessarily at the same moment in time or using identical methods of travel) and spoke with at least one person in each of the ethnographic anecdotes provided in this article at some point in their travels.

The strategic decision to engage in translocal research echoes Ian Henry's recent categorical rejection of the supposed diminished role of the nation-state in sports policy and supposed irreconcilable difference between the West and its Others.[10] Pursuing anthropologist George Marcus' suggestion to follow the subject and see where it leads shifts the analytic focus of transnational migration and global process from 'place of origin' and 'place of destination' to the strategic moves involved in sustaining a livelihood.[11] Such an approach is likely to take the researcher in unanticipated directions instead of the researcher imposing *sui generis* expectations of how 'global' practices form and adhere. My reliance on multi-vocal, translocal fieldwork sacrifices some of the usual ethnographic 'thick description' in favour of a broader expanse of transnational networks.[12] Tracing the movements of transnational sport migrants has led me to variously unanticipated places based on the routes taken by the individuals and not by any design I had on how this study should proceed. Instead, shorter visits to some, but certainly not all, of the other localities where the migrants were present (ideally while those individuals were in those locales) were made in an effort to obtain a better grasp of the routes and challenges migrants face in each state.

On sport and globalization

> At least 95 percent of all scholars and all scholarship from the period of 1850 to 1914, and probably even to 1945, originates in five countries: France, Great Britain, the Germanies, the Italies, and the United States. There is a smattering elsewhere, but basically not only does the scholarship come out of these five countries, but most of the scholarship by most scholars is about their own country.... This is partly pragmatic, partly social pressure, and partly ideological: these are the important countries, this is what matters, this is what we should study in order to learn how the world operates.[13]

Immanuel Wallerstein's comments on the historical patterns of scholarly production are undeniably important for those scholars concerned with the study of transnational sport. The vast majority of sport-related scholarship follows a similar pattern in which the predominant production of knowledge on sport is situated and produced within predominantly Anglophile, protestant, capitalist societies.

> [As] a product of modern European civilization, studying any problem of universal history, [a scholar] is bound to ask himself [sic] to what combination of circumstances the fact should be attributed that in Western civilization, and in Western civilization only, cultural phenomena have appeared which (as we like to think) lie in a line of development having universal significance and value.[14]

This tendency leads to a rather myopic position that the organization, values and practices found in sport in one culture compared with another are unequivocal evidence of some cosmopolitan universalism identified as 'global sport'. The prevalence of 'global sport' has been widely remarked upon and had a number of its facets addressed yet the methods, manner and meanings of the production and consumption of global sport are embedded in local power struggles and do not reign above them.[15] Globalization advocates speak about ways in which people are transcending localized, spatialized identities in order to become cosmopolitan citizens of a singularly imagined world.[16] Worryingly, the commentators and scholars examining all of these various aspects of what has come to be both popularly and academically called 'global sport' tend to adopt the particular rhetoric and logic of globalization. From this position, sport becomes a global social practice that transcends boundaries via 'diminishing contrasts and increasing varieties' yet simultaneously glosses over the specific disjunctures of hierarchy, power and agency in and across local contexts.[17] The muting of historically forged differences is particularly evident among scholars who have stressed the 'deterritorialized' nature of the contemporary world with respect to the organization of political economies and the reproduction of 'global sport'. Although 'global sport' arguments are frequently peppered with qualifications recognizing important differences among nations, cultures and transnational processes, these differences rarely rise to the level of analysis.

These suppressions of difference exaggerate the autonomy and determinacy of capital vis-à-vis states and leads to perspectives that locate anti-capitalist agency in cosmopolitan subjects who have the wherewithal, sophistication and power to negotiate national borders while calcifying those individuals who do not possess these capacities. It is precisely this lack of attention to the space-forming and space-contingent character of relations of production that has led some to regard late capitalist accumulation as being external to the political field of the state – as waves of 'global' capital that wash over states and, in the process, over important political questions.

> One thing is clear: globalization is not some great carnival of capital, technology, and goods where we are all free to walk away with what we want. What one gets and how much, where one finds a place in the global network of exchanges, indeed whether one finds a place in it at all, depends on several economic and political conditions.[18]

By stressing the deterritorialized character of contemporary capitalism, some have neglected not only the critical role played by states in constituting and disciplining labour power – Foucault's question of 'governmentality' – but also the multi-tiered spatial politics that enable and disable the transnational movement of capital.[19] 'The nation-state – along with its juridical-legislative systems, bureaucratic apparatuses, economic entities, modes of governmentality and war-making capacities – continues to define, discipline, control and regulate' all kinds of capital, including labour, whether in movement or in situ.[20] The tendency to exaggerate the deterritorialized nature of the contemporary world has important theoretical and political consequences. First, it has led to the assertion that globalization is a *fait accompli*. Irresistible and new, the projection of globalization is articulated as having superseded not only the politics of nation-states but their enduring asymmetrical relationships – asymmetries that are firmly rooted in the ongoing histories of imperialism. Second, the deterritorialization argument risks underestimating and obscuring political agency. The oppositional practices of those very agents who are experiencing, theorizing and struggling against 'globalizing' neoliberal economic policies, in particular, become hidden in supposedly hegemonic macro-scale phenomena.[21] Since states still monopolize the legitimate means of force within their borders, for the most part, it is problematic to conceptualize the 'deterritorialization of the state' as any kind of socio-political process entailing the deconstruction of state systems of rulership and power.[22] Far from dismantling state apparatuses and opening borders to free-flowing capital, it is apparent that many states, once presumed to be peripheral, are promoting the reproduction of transnational subjects and in the process reinventing their own role in the so-called 'new world order'.[23] What should be apparent is that the logic of globalization is not a foregone conclusion but is one politically informed ideological discourse engaged in a hotly contested ideological struggle. This contest over the constitution of global interests and identities in relation to the national is better viewed as an argument between multiple social agents instead of as a set of intractable, structural relationships between superstructural 'global' capital whose tentacles dangle and dip into base 'national' economies.[24] Finally, this same contest is one in which state authorities are prominent agents in the struggle and that condition cannot be ignored.

On citizenship and globalization

Globalization advocates speak about the ways people are transcending localized, spatialized identities and lives in order to become cosmopolitan 'citizens of the world'. This whole concept of a citizen of the world rests on the ideological construct of a singular global culture that supersedes the various spatial restrictions of movement entailed in crossing international boundaries. Quite simply, global citizenship is, as an aspect of globalization itself, an ideological project that is nowhere near fruition. Miller et al. survey the way in which global governance of sport appears to be creating such 'citizens of the world' while sport-related INGOs, such as FIFA, and other supranational bodies of governance define who shall be incorporated into this new form of citizenship through the establishment of transnational industrial labour regulations.[25]

In effect, these processes in TSM are part of the creation of a transnational capitalist class – a group of social actors comprising executives, professionals, bureaucrats and consumers who strive to sustain the dominance of capitalism as a social system.[26] These citizens of the world are primarily understood as individual rights holders and not members of a common or cohesive community.[27] Although incomplete, such projects nonetheless do impact states' attempts to regulate movement across borders and creates spaces in which individuals can manipulate those rules in their favour, thereby contravening the gate-keeping desires of the state.

These gate-keeping apparatuses are evident in various countries via the strategic interrogation of individuals requiring the proper kind of social capital. State bureaucracies, emblematic in the ubiquitous forms (filled out in triplicate) necessary to accomplish what should be basic interactions, facilitate the enforcement of a division of labour through the control of social spaces.[28] This gate-keeping work is not only an attempt to keep control of a state's populace, it serves to aid in the application of governmentality. The predominant form of this aspect of governmentality is the state's attempt to prevent unapproved individuals from entering the state's territory. States also attempt to prevent certain kinds of persons from leaving its domain as well.[29] In either direction, this work is partially accomplished through the definition of citizenship criteria and the identification of citizens.

Citizenship consists of disciplinary techniques comprising discourses and practices governing national belonging exercised by state authorities to channel access to social rights and regulate, among other things, the social division of labour. Those without the correct information on their identification often find themselves removed from certain spaces with utmost haste. Attending to the everyday struggles over labour, identity and national belonging highlights critical antagonisms within, and resistances to, the organization and specific practices of governmentality exercised in nation-states' attempts to produce and reproduce specific socio-spatial orders of capital accumulation.

Since the state itself is imagined as occupying a defined space over which it has nominal control of social experience, one of its goals and roles is to protect the sanctity of its borders from uncontrolled and unwanted presences. It does so through the invention and implementation of a variety of practices, one of the most prevalent being the forging of specific immigration policies and practices. The attempt to control entry and exit of this space is paramount to the performance of sovereignty, in which a state has to be seen by both its own peoples and outsiders, to be in control of its boundaries. In conjunction with a sport's national governing body (yet another bureaucratic arm of the state), quotas and definitions of citizenship, of who can and cannot represent the nation-state, are defined and enforced. Citizenship regulations determine who is and who is not a member of any given state. Acting as a 'continuing series of transactions between persons and agents of a given state in which each has enforceable rights and obligations, citizenship constitutes a critical and contested field of power relations and practices'.[30] Indeed, citizenship tests do not establish qualifications for such status but are instead a tool used to control the level and composition of immigration. These sorts of examinations have historically been introduced or modified in line with changing attitudes towards immigration in those states that utilize them.[31] Even with the introduction of 'European citizenship', access at 'this regional or supranational level is still defined at the member-*state* level'.[32] By controlling membership, a government can delineate who does belong, 'citizens', and who does not, 'foreigners'; and the contested processes of defining persons as one or the other determines access to various rights and goods, like political representation and employment. Yet citizenship is not portrayed as a categorical construct but as a 'natural' or 'biological' quality that effectively masks the actual relation between individual and state, and 'roots' people in territorial soil. Thus, people become 'naturally' linked to a specific space – a state's territory – and by creating 'lineages' of 'genetic material' passed down from generation to generation, the social fluid of 'blood' becomes a determining aspect of citizenship equated with a biological trait.[33] More recently, the concept of citizenship has shifted from inherent embodied right to negotiated commodity even as full membership remains crucial since it defines the scope of opportunity, security and sense of belonging within a state.

States actively recruit and deny citizenship of sports professionals through the use of quotas set by a sport's governing body in a given country. National governing bodies, on their own, with other bureaucratic aspects of the state and in consultation with an international governing body, are one bureaucratic limb of the state and often determine the quantity and quality of professionals allowed to enter and work in that country. These instruments of bureaucratic governmentality are a major restraint on a sport professional's ability to move around the world in search of employment.[34] Because the specificities of citizenship in each state are informed by historical particularities, any particular study of TSM must take the original state, the destination state and the historical political relationship between them into account. Thus, citizenship is a valuable piece of personal, social and political capital that can be deployed strategically within the global sport industry.

This is especially evident in the increasing attempts by athletes to switch nationalities in order to qualify for international competitions, what is euphemistically called 'code switching'. Indeed, this strategic switching of citizenship is becoming so prevalent the International Association of Athletics Federations (IAAF) and the IOC have both set up working groups to investigate the growing question of national representation and nation-switching.[35] One athlete who pursued this strategy of citizenship exchange is Graciela Yasmine Álvarez.[36] As is increasingly common among Cuba's star athletics athletes, Álvarez lived and trained in Europe in recent years. Since 2001 she had lived in the United Kingdom, training and competing in Europe on the IAAF sanctioned circuit. Álvarez applied for British citizenship in 2003 while living with her British husband so she could compete under the auspices of the Union Jack. While British athletics officials were privately thrilled with the potential addition of a world-class athlete, British immigration authorities denied her request for UK citizenship, in part because Cuban authorities refused to allow her to skip the required three-year waiting period for switching nationalities under IOC and IAAF regulations, which meant she would be ineligible to compete in the 2004 Athens Olympics. Having already missed the World Championships because she was effectively stateless, Álvarez decided that she could not accept her situation and pursued other possible nations to represent. Unwilling to return to Cuba, which would, in all likelihood, mean the end of her career and marriage, Álvarez reportedly entered into discussions with the Italian and the Czech governing bodies. When Sudanese officials suddenly approached her willing to grant her immediate citizenship, Álvarez readily accepted their offer.

Graciela Álvarez is one of the more recent world-class athletes in a variety of sports to decide to compete for a country with which she has no historical connection. While athletes can and do switch citizenship to facilitate their economic earning power, this is often done within state-defined rules of who is and who is not a member of the nation, particularly through the 'grandfather rule' as it is sometimes called, based on 'natural' or biological qualities of citizenship rather than based on the individual deployment of strategic capital. When pursuing this strategy, many athletes do not abandon their original 'natural' citizenship but become dual nationals, maintaining citizenship in two states, the country of their birth and the one which they represent in international athletic competition. Cuban athletes, however, do not have that particular option. The restrictions laid upon them by the Cuban state require that they choose rather than multiply their citizenship capital. This situation is by no means unique to Cubans; during the Cold War individuals often found it necessary to illegally migrate within an international political context that framed such moves. The peculiar historical circumstances that currently exist necessitating such strategies inform the particular patterns involved in Cuban TSM. Thus, they are required to renounce their citizenship and obtain new state membership. In short, they have to defect.

The whole concept of defection, a citizen's sundering of a relationship between state and citizen without that state authorities' consent, via a public renunciation of citizenship, is one that is firmly entrenched within Cold War ideological discourses. Ironically, it is not the framework in which the movement of Cuban athletes should be understood despite the vociferous trumpeting by right-wing Cuban exiles each time a baseball player leaves Cuba to try his luck as a professional abroad. Defection is itself an unusual context although political motivations are more prevalent than commonly assumed in TSM literature.[37] Álvarez's cross-border movements should be understood in the discourse of 'code-switching', found throughout the global governance of international sport, in which citizenship, effectively, is being used as a commodity that can be deployed for its use-value or even sold on to a government willing to sponsor the athlete. This is becoming more and more prevalent as citizenship parameters are being defined by non-state actors.[38] Citizenship is transforming from a condition of personhood to a resource, a form of capital, to be flexibly deployed.[39] While many of those who abandoned the Cuban state in the 1990s are baseball players, athletes in other sports have begun to flee the island within the past few of years thereby affecting the strategies used in the Cuban citizenship game.

The Cuban game of citizenship

The Cuban state's strategies for maintaining and utilizing its sporting excellence reveal the tensions found in the continual negotiation of citizenship. For most of the history of the Revolution, the control of Cuban athletes' movements was limited by Cold War contexts. Cuban athletes willingly accepted these controls as no active Cuban athlete defected in the first 30 years of Revolutionary rule. That situation changed with the onset of the *Periodo Especial en el Tiempo de Paz* (the Special Period in Times of Peace) in which the international relations the Cuban state had nurtured and cultivated over the previous three decades disintegrated along with the Berlin Wall and the Soviet Union. The collapse of European state socialism suddenly threw the ability of Cuban state bureaucrats to meet their obligations towards Cuban citizens into question, thereby causing a traumatic rupture in state-legitimating discourses. Through artful negotiation with its own population, authorities implemented the equivalent of war-time rationing without the experience of state-level violence. Officials positioned themselves, through various state institutions, to act as the primary distributor of imports within the domestic economy while maintaining a monopoly of exports in the global economy. In short, Cuban officials set themselves up as the gatekeepers of Cuban sport, as the structural control of sport moved from a centralized model run wholly under the Cuban Ministry of Sport to a more diffuse control through the creation of CubaDeportes, SA.[40]

During the 1990s, the restructuring of the economy included the following state-led strategic moves: the legalization of hard currency possession by individuals, changing entrepreneurship regulations, renegotiated international trade agreements, and the emergence of novel forms of foreign investment.[41] Many of these strategies emanated from within the government's hallowed halls but these strategies were also reactions to the situations on the ground in which citizens adopted alternative strategies and rejected the sacrifices for which authorities called. This led to the burgeoning of the already existing *bolsa negra*, the black market that thrived on petty theft from state warehouses and other forms of economic exchange that did not involve state institutions. Yet the dire straits in which both state leaders and everyday citizens found themselves led many to pursue alternative strategies to increase the likelihood of personal and familial survival. Numerous strategies were implemented at the behest of or, at the very least, with the tacit approval of state authorities. A few strategies, however, actively challenged the state's controlling mechanisms.

Cuban authorities created CubaDeportes, SA in 1993 to exploit the status and expertise of Cuban sports personnel. Its role over the past 15 years has been to cultivate and develop transnational economic relations with other sporting bodies for the economic benefit of the Cuban sports programmes. One of its primary strategies has been the export of Cuban technical knowledge through the contractual employment of Cuban coaches by foreign national governing bodies.[42] Yet while CubaDeportes officials work to create opportunities for sports professionals, not just anyone is provided the opportunity to become a Cuban transnational sport migrant. State officials keep a close eye on who they permit to leave the country for a number of reasons. The process was explained by several CubaDeportes employees in the following manner:

> Okay, let us say that you want to hire me to coach your team in whatever sport. You as an official of that club would either contact me who would tell you to contact CubaDeportes, or you would contact your sport's officials (of that national governing body) telling them that you want me or a coach with specific qualifications that I have, suggesting that I would be the best to get. Your officials would then contact CubaDeportes who would then check their list of available personnel. If I was the name at the top of that list, CubaDeportes would check on me, talk to my neighbors, to my coworkers, find out what kind of person I am. Is he an angry person? Does he show up for work on time? What's his family situation? Does he get along with others? Does he have *calidad*? And if all of that is positive then they would contact me and say, Señor Fulano, we have an opportunity for you, we want you to go over there.[43]

On the surface it would appear that Cubans would leap at the chance to work overseas. In a short span they could potentially earn five or six times what they normally make in a year, sometimes even more, depending on the country to which they would be sent. What one interviewee made clear though is that the offer of overseas employment is not really optional. 'If they ask you, you have an obligation to go . . . . If you do not, they can make your life *difficult*'. There are repercussions for not taking any opportunity presented since demonstrated reluctance to go can inhibit future opportunities to work overseas.[44] Not only is there an implicit obligation on the part of the individual to accept the offer the state has provided, it is nigh on impossible for a Cuban to find work independently from CubaDeportes. Indeed, it is all but impossible to organize one's own contract or offer. A couple of different individuals described situations in which they had been overseas and had maintained contact with foreign nationals while back in Cuba. They had obtained written invitations to return for further employment but because these offers did not follow proper channels, that is, through CubaDeportes representatives, state officials deemed the offers unacceptable and each individual in question was unable to leave Cuba to take up the offer of a post. This was true despite the glowing reviews their employers had written about their earlier work and the good relationship the migrant in question had developed with the foreign organization. An individual who attempts to play by other rules, so to speak, finds one's own willingness to be properly revolutionary, of one's willingness to engage in *lucha,* to struggle for the good of the Revolution, and be a staunch supporter of revolutionary ideals all called into question by those who do make the rules of the citizenship game. Demonstrating a public unwillingness to act in the manner expressed by state officials makes one's own social position in Cuban society open to reinterpretation vis-à-vis the Cuban state. In short, the relationship between citizen and state is called into question.

Consequently, many Cuban transnational sport migrants draw upon the *doble moral* of contemporary Cuban life in which it is necessary to demonstrate affections for a cause, in which one does not actually believe, all the while being forced to act in a contradictory manner in order to survive.[45] Those athletes who earn the honour of being able to represent Cuba in international competition have demonstrated not only outstanding athletic skill but also embody Cuban socialist ideals. The state's investiture in their bodies makes them essential to its legitimacy. By becoming part of this revolutionary vanguard, athletes demonstrate how the power of the socialist body can be made manifest. Their multiplying victories embody the idealized notion of the New Man and, by shaping their powerful bodies via rigorous discipline, their love for the Cuban people and their *patria.*[46] Patriotic fervour is supposed to provide greater motivation for the individual athlete, theoretically replacing monetary compensation. Ideally, the love of one's country replaces the fear of losing one's job. The problem is that most athletes' motivation for living overseas is the opportunity to earn some prize money (i.e., hard currency). Whether they are ever afforded this opportunity depends on their ability to 'produce' not just with their athletic bodies but also with their socialist bodies. These particular athletes must somehow find a way to incorporate and demonstrate that they embody socialist ideals to state authorities if they are going to earn an opportunity to compete at an international level. The irony is that those who eventually do leave or refuse to return must demonstrate socialist 'techniques of the body' in order to be allowed to compete overseas in international competition.[47] It is only by constructing, at the minimum, a 'revolutionary skin' – a façade that covers one's 'true' body – to demonstrate that one is a proper Cuban citizen that these same individuals can deny the primacy of the Revolutionary body through the act of nation-switching and citizenship exchange.

This *doble moral* leads some individuals to attempt to circumvent the state by engaging in unsanctioned TSM. Unsanctioned TSM refers to professionals who have crossed state borders or remained in a state's territory without the explicit consent of that government. Unsanctioned TSMs unquestionably affect Cuban sport. Two of the more common strategies Cubans employ are the refusal to return while working or competing overseas, or to be smuggled out of the country. While each is a distinct strategy, they share some similarities. They inherently contain a set of risks in that the refusal of state authority can have repercussions for those family members left behind. It can also inadvertently result in the termination of the very career one attempts to maintain. Plus, the uncertainty of finding further work and earning enough to survive makes taking such a decision a huge risk, with the rare exception of high-profile 'star' athletes. Most unsanctioned TSMs never make the international press, or even the national for that matter. Unfortunately, if such unsanctioned Cuban transnational sport migrants do obtain media coverage, they readily slide into a political context informed by Cold War politics.[48] The motivating factors for these unsanctioned movements are individual decisions based on family economics not political ideologies.[49]

The other form of unsanctioned Cuban transnational migration that needs to be addressed is migrant smuggling – the clandestine movement of groups of people from one state to another. Smuggling has a long history throughout the Caribbean and Cuba and continues to play a prominent role in the region.[50] People smuggling, in all its myriad forms, also continues to play a prominent role in transnational migration. Whereas slaves were smuggled past British naval ships into Cuba in the nineteenth century, twenty-first century smugglers attempt to evade US Coast Guard authorities to smuggle people out of Cuba. The popular perception of people smuggling is that globalization created the conditions for greater transnational trafficking of humans, conducted predominantly by violent and greedy professional criminals exploiting weak and (mostly) innocent migrants. That the specific actions by politicians and other state actors in both origin and destination states are largely responsible for creating these conditions remains largely unacknowledged. These smuggling operations are incredibly diverse in scope, scale and integration in local and regional social networks and structures.[51]

Migrant smuggling only began to be a viable and prominent migratory strategy in the 1990s when Cuba's economy changed rapidly and dramatically. The demise of the Soviet-led economic bloc resulted in the loss of 80–85% of Cuba's external trade and 50% of its purchasing power; and it has taken several years for the economy to climb out of that abyss.[52] Tourism replaced sugar as the island's primary source of hard currency.[53] Family remittances and foreign investment partially replaced the subsidies supplied by the Soviet Union. Family remittances increased from the comparatively paltry US$18 million in 1991 to estimates between US$500 and US$725 million in 1999.[54] Foreign investment strategies concentrate primarily on activities related to the use of natural resources, such as tourism, mining, petroleum and agriculture. A consequence of these changes has been a reordering of the class hierarchy in Cuban society with transnational ties suddenly becoming an eminently vital factor in determining one's position in Cuba. This new class is made up of those who played minimal roles in the state bureaucracy but now work with foreign investors in world markets as commercial intermediaries and service providers. Many of these managers are minor government officials who did not have much standing in the hierarchy of government but use their new found relations to augment and raise their own standard of living. This is evident in the changes in savings and new forms of employment. The number of small savings accounts dropped by 50%, yet the monetary value of the most affluent has nearly doubled.[55] In 1996, 12.8% of bank accounts represented 85% of private savings in the economy.[56] Professionals working in sport, however, did not have access to these new transnational links except through CubaDeportes. Sport professionals were losing socioeconomic position in this radical reshuffling of relationships and many individuals felt a need to either change careers or find another way to maintain their status.

As the following vignette illustrates, sport professionals have plans in place, strategies formulated, and a transnational network to implement those strategic moves. Those Cuban transnational sport migrants who take to the seas and risk life, limb, career and family in order to avoid the control of the Cuban state are not fleeing blindly, contrary to the popularly perpetuated myth of the *balsero*.[57] Rather, their moves are informed by the local political conditions in both Cuba and their destinations.

On a hot summer day in 1998, seven Cubans, five of whom claimed to be baseball players, suddenly arrived in a small town on the eastern shore of Nicaragua, aboard a 72-foot pleasure cruiser. The cruiser's tarpaulins were deliberately rigged to cover the vessel's name and the crew initially refused to give interviews when the luxury yacht arrived. Eventually, a convoluted story emerged, which, in each retelling of the circumstances of the Cubans' arrival in Nicaragua, gradually revealed that this arrival was more of a planned smuggling operation rather than a chance encounter at sea.

Allegedly, the group had launched a small boat from the western tip of Cuba with three gallons of water and two cans of tomato juice with the express hope of reaching the Yucatan peninsula, some 130 miles away. After only six hours at sea, they ran into a large pleasure cruiser supposedly on its way from Cozumel, Mexico to Costa Rica. The yacht took them to Nicaragua, where it so happened that four of these seven *balseros* had previously been offered visas by the Nicaraguan government months earlier.[58]

The Cubans claimed that they set out from Pinar del Rio province and encountered the pleasure cruiser by chance. Initially, the boat's owner corroborated the Cubans' story, claiming that they had accidentally happened upon the Cubans, even though he had told the boat's captain to make a several hundred mile detour from the usual route between Yucatan and Costa Rica so he could see the Cuban coast because 'a lot of people are investing in Cuba'. Months later, the owner claimed that he had received a call from an unidentified person asking him to help the players prior to his encountering them. He also claimed earlier that the athletes' escape was similar to a paramilitary operation involving around 20 people. Both statements clearly contradict his initial claims of accidental discovery.

Three months after arriving in Nicaragua, the Cubans suddenly vanished while waiting for their Nicaraguan visas. The current political climate in Nicaragua was in flux and their applications, previously guaranteed by President Alemán, were now being questioned.[59] The Cubans' disappearance was not really noted until they suddenly appeared in San José, Costa Rica. San José is in the middle of the country between two mountain ranges. How they got from the eastern coast of Nicaragua to the Costa Rican capital became another mystery. They fled to Costa Rica because they believed it was doubtful they would be able to obtain the necessary citizenship documents, whereas the differing local contexts in Costa Rica made it much more likely that they would be successful in obtaining a Costa Rican passport than a Nicaraguan one.[60]

In the end, two of those men eventually landed in the USA as legal migrants from Costa Rica and played professionally in the United States. Another secured a professional contract for one season in a Taiwanese professional league before returning to Costa Rica. The others, apparently, have never left Costa Rica and disappeared from sight.[61] The movements of this group from Cuba to Nicaragua, and then to Costa Rica, before pursuing their own separate routes hint at the importance local political contexts have in determining migratory strategies. It is clear from this example, along with others, that transnational migrants carefully consider shifting local conditions while planning their next move(s).[62]

Some concluding remarks

The importance of local conditions in both the origin state and the destination state of transnational sport migrants cannot be underestimated or ignored. Furthermore, the rules of citizenship are frequently manipulated and exploited to individual actors' own advantages. These manipulations are not done solely by marginalized individuals but by prominent individuals and by state authorities themselves to further their own specific interests. The repercussions of such actions affect sport and society as a whole in both localities thereby heightening the emphasis on historically specific connections rather than broad, sweeping generalized flows. This specificity is evident in the recurring concern over the territorial sanctity of state borders even as those borders become flexible, elastic and increasingly porous. This ever-present concern over the sanctity of state borders challenges the emphasis currently placed on the supposed deterritorialization of transnational sport processes.

The tendency to exaggerate the deterritorialized state risks obscuring political agency and those who are truly shaping the patterns of TSM. In particular, the focus on TSM lends itself to a picture of 'global sport' in which athletes readily move from location to location with relative ease because of 'globalizing' neoliberal economic policies of specific governments and international governing bodies. This projection of globalization is articulated as a *fait accompli* that supersedes not only the politics of nation-states but their enduring asymmetrical relationships – asymmetries that are firmly rooted in the ongoing histories of imperialism. Cuban state authorities act in direct contravention to these supposedly globalizing neoliberal strategies. At the same time, Cuban sports authorities attempt to control the movements of Cuban professionals thereby facilitating their own repositioning in transnational political economic relations within sport.

The constituency of the state is no longer simply a population of citizens defined by territorial borders who demand protection from forces outside of those borders. Increasingly, the global economy and its dominant actors and institutions themselves inform definitions of citizenship and citizenry. Various international actors, such as the IOC, FIFA and MLB, have all assumed some of the defining powers of citizenship within their respective domains. These reformulations are not accomplished despite states but in conjunction with state authorities. The emerging shape of TSM must, as a consequence, include considerations of the historical relationships between states since state-based actors continue to work at maintaining control of the entrance of individuals into their sovereign space and the movement through that geopolitical space. Through a variety of discursive bureaucratic processes, many states not only work at keeping certain individuals from entering the confines of the state's territory but actively attempt to prevent individuals leaving the country without the state's awareness. This is an especially prevalent strategy among those nation-states attempting to prevent the drain of educated and highly skilled citizens, as the loss of these individuals creates further restrictions on the ability of the state's leaders to sustain any economic stability. Thus citizenship is useful for not only keeping certain alien threats out but for state authorities to maintain control of the socioeconomic capital of its own citizens, whether resident or not.[63] Understanding how citizenship is conceived and deployed within the contemporary world system has important theoretical and political consequences that must be attenuated to any consideration of TSM.

The enduring role the nation-state plays in configuring global flows of capital, technology and labour, as well as in structuring the discourses about the nature and future of the 'global', cannot be discounted. However diminished the capacity of nation-states to govern their economies appears to be, the state nonetheless remains a central agent in structuring the specific manner in which transnational movements of capital, people and media are materialized in space, whether as multinational corporate initiatives or in alternative forms. 'Global sport', as an aspect of 'globalization' then, is less a description of the existing world system than a set of contested claims about how the world should be structured in relation to nation-states and their peoples. An assumption about TSM is that migration is predominantly based on individuals' economic decisions influenced by transnational corporate capital's penetration and shaping of domestic markets. Virtually ignored are other variables including the influence of families, state attempts to restrict the influx or flight of capital, including (especially) labour.[64]

The Cuban cases in this article make it apparent that the reach of global sport is not 'the world as it actually exists' but is more a reflection of how certain organizations and its members would like the world to be. Contrary to contemporary ideological discourses within the arena of international politics, whether the stultified remains of Cold War political ideologies or contemporary neoliberal globalization ideologies, Cuban TSM is based on a number of factors that includes individuals' economic decisions, corporate capital's penetration of domestic markets, and local political contexts.

As an initial step towards a greater understanding of the various forces that shape TSM, the ideological constructs and power struggles hidden within 'global sport' need to be extruded. The transnational structures of 'global sport' are historically specific power relations that are informed by and directly impact individuals' lives. How individuals support or challenge these structural relations loosely identified as 'global sport' is of utmost importance. Through their own actions, transnational sport migrants contour the very movements and flows of these processes. The evidence of these struggles may take numerous forms; one of which is the movements of transnational sport migrants. Approaching 'transnationalism from below' so that the apparent *fait accompli* of 'global sport' is taken as a problematic rather than as a sociological given would be an excellent start.[65]

Transnational migrants do not passively accept state-based definitions of citizenship: the surest indicator yet that there is much more work to be done on TSM. The current debates on sport-related labour migration are especially useful as long as it is emphasized that migration is not the rupture of social relations in one location and the forging of replacement ones in another but migrants' ability to transcend various borders and maintain social relations in two or more localities simultaneously – in some cases despite authorities' attempts to control these interactions.[66] What must be more thoroughly and critically documented are the means by which people continue to act while the 'official' looks the other way.

Notes

[1] All individuals identified in this article have been given pseudonyms to help protect their anonymity. Those Cubans who have given of their time, energy and knowledge freely have had their identities changed for two reasons: (1) it is standard ethnographic practice to do so unless the individual in question is someone well known and whose work and life are heavily reported in local if not international media; and (2) the potential repercussions for giving their assistance, which cannot be foreseen, when addressing social issues that involve questions of illegality and state power.

[2] Field research for this paper, funded by a British Academy Small Research Grant, SG-43107, examined the experiences of Cuban transnational sport migrants. Earlier fieldwork, informing that study and this paper, on various issues revolving around Cuban identity and sport was funded by the Latin American and Iberian Institute at the University of New Mexico. The Sports Council for Northern Ireland funded a long-range ethnographic study on the impact transnational sport migrants were having on local sports infrastructures after the 1998 Good Friday agreement. The support of all of these institutions is gratefully acknowledged.

[3] The *Serie Nacional* is the national baseball league.

[4] La Peña is a reference to the peña deportiva or sports group that meets everyday in Parque Central in Havana. Members of this group meet daily to argue about sport, especially baseball gossip, commiserate and socialize. See Carter, 'Baseball Arguments', for further discussion.

[5] Maguire, *Global Sport*, 97, 127, esp. 105–6; Magee and Sugden, 'The World at their Feet'. Unfortunately, space constraints preclude more detailed discussion of the strengths and weaknesses of these typologies.

[6] Carter, 'Family Networks'.

[7] Maguire, *Global Sport*; Maguire, *Power and Global Sport*; Miller et al., *Globalization and Sport*; Giulianotti and Robertson, *Globalization and Sport*.

[8] Hannerz, 'Being There'.

[9] This differs from other publications and research on TSM in which extended ethnographic fieldwork was carried out in numerous locales (see Carter, Donnan and Wardle, *Global Migrants*; Carter, 'Family Networks').

[10] Henry, *Transnational and Comparative Research*.

[11] Marcus, *Ethnography*, 79–104.

[12] Geertz, *Interpretation of Cultures*.

[13] Wallerstein, 'Open the Social Sciences', 3.

[14] Weber, *Protestant Ethic*, 13.

[15] A variety of topics from sport and the media to global governance, international migration, consumerism and commoditization all basically reproduce this theoretical encompassment of the local by the global. I argue that if the two can be separated into different social spaces, and I am highly sceptical that they can, the two are congruent with each other and national and regional spaces – all of which intersect, overlap, and inform each other.

[16] Beck, 'Cosmopolitan Society'; Held, *Democracy and the Global Order*; Robertson, 'Mapping the Global Condition'; Venn, 'Altered States'.

[17] Maguire, *Global Sport*, 213.

[18] Chatterjee, *Politics of the Governed*, 85–6.

[19] Foucault, 'Governmentality'.

[20] Ong, *Flexible Citizenship*, 15.

[21] This includes those states not willingly accepting the neoliberal dream of a global world made in their image. Cuba is one such state. See Carmona Báez, *State Resistance*.

[22] There are those exceptions, typically characterized as 'failed states', in which transnational organizations have sent military forces to act as 'peacekeepers'. Examples include NATO intervention in the Balkans, and African Union intervention in Darfur, Sudan.

[23] Guarnizo and Smith, 'Locations of Transnationalism', 8.

[24] Tsing, 'Inside the Economy of Appearances'.

[25] Miller et al., *Globalization and Sport;* see also Dabscheck, 'The Globe at Their Feet: FIFA's New Employment Rules – I'; Dabscheck, 'The Globe at the Their Feet: FIFA's New Employment Rules – II'. Parrish and McArdle, 'Beyond *Bosman*'.

[26] Sklair, *Transnational Capitalist Class*.

[27] Held, *Democracy and the Global Order*.

[28] Herzfeld, *Social Production of Indifference*.

[29] This particular aspect of state control is often overlooked and taken for granted by many people from Western liberal capitalist democracies, but is a fact of life in many places around the world, including Cuba. It is manifest in the passport checks undertaken at the airport BEFORE one is allowed to enter the gate area for boarding.

[30] Gregory, *Devil Behind the Mirror*, 39.

[31] Etzioni, 'Citizenship Tests'.

[32] Shachar and Hirschl, 'Citizenship as Inherited Property', 261. Italics in original.

[33] Malkki, 'National Geographic'.

[34] Clearly, states are not the only agents restraining professionals' movements. INGOs, the European Union and other international organizations also play significant roles in the shaping of migratory patterns through their own regulatory schema regarding national representation. The Bosman ruling also has had an impact on TSM, particularly in relation to European Union labour law. States, however, are the focus of this article and so the others will have to remain for later consideration.

[35] Poli has produced a similar discussion from a slightly different theoretical approach. Poli is addressing the question of nationality and ethnic nationalism whereas the concern here is the strategies and manipulations of citizenship. The two concepts are different yet interrelated and these distinctions need further explication sometime in the future. Where Poli and I diverge is the question of deterritorialization, which I argue is a distraction from actual processes of power and does not constitute an actual removal of spatial concerns, whereas Poli appears to support such claims. See Poli, 'Denationalization of Sport'.

[36] This is a pseudonym.

[37] Magee and Sugden, '"The World at their Feet": Professional Football and International Labour Migration.'

[38] This is apparent as FIFA sets the rules for transnational sports labour migration and was even more apparent when Bud Selig, the Commissioner of Major League Baseball, decreed that he would determine star player Alex Rodriguez's status over which team he would represent in the inaugural World Baseball Classic, the United States or the Dominican Republic, and that Rodriguez had no say in the matter.

[39] Ong, *Flexible Citizenship*.

[40] Instituto Nacional de Deportes, Educación Física y Recreación (National Institute of Sport, Physical Education and Recreation).

[41] Carmona Báez, *State Resistance*; Espinosa Martínez, 'Ethics'; Phillips, '"Cuentapropismo" in a Socialist State'; Ritter, 'Cuba's Economic Reorientation'.

[42] Carter, 'New Rules to the Old Game'.

[43] *Calidad* (quality) is a particular aspect of Cuban personhood evident in how one demonstrates expected morals, mores and values in everyday life. For a discussion on *calidad,* see Carter, *Quality of Home Runs*, 160–5.

[44] Carter, 'Family Networks'.

[45] Wirtz, 'Santeria in Cuban National Consciousness'.

[46] Guevara, *Socialismo y el Hombre en Cuba*.

[47] Mauss, 'Techniques of the Body.'

[48] See Bjarkman, *A History of Cuban Baseball*, 386–420; Fainaru and Sanchez, *Duke of Havana*; Jamail, *Full Count*, 73–101; Price, *Pitching Around Fidel.*

[49] This has been emphasized repeatedly in interviews I have conducted and in press conferences in which Cuban athletes publicly declare their motivations for 'fleeing' as 'to be able to provide for my family' and not in any overt repudiation of the Castro regime. It could be argued that these statements mask migrants' true feelings because of fear for family members still in Cuba. However, considering the anonymity of my consultants I find this particular argument unlikely.

[50] Rogozinski, *A Brief History of the Caribbean*; Williams, *From Columbus to Castro*.

[51] Kyle and Dale, 'Smuggling the State Back In'.

[52] Carmona Báez, *State Resistance,* 86.

[53] Monreal, 'Development as an Unfinished Affair'.

[54] Ritter and Rowe, 'Cuba', 104.

[55] Burchardt, 'Contours of the Future', 61.

[56] Hamilton 'Whither Cuban Socialism?', 27.

[57] A *balsero* (rafter) is a Cuban who clandestinely builds a homemade raft and then either alone, or (usually) with a few others, launches it into the Florida Straits, a particularly dangerous and swift moving stretch of water.

[58] There is insufficient space to provide full detailed accounts for the reasons why these four had already obtained visa offers from another state. Suffice it to say, for the purposes of this article, that those four had made a previously unsuccessful attempt to leave Cuba that had received some publicity thereby attracting the attention of then Nicaraguan president Arnoldo Alemán.

[59] Ex-President Alemán is currently serving a 20-year prison sentence in Nicaragua for money laundering in which he used roughly 60 Panamanian bank accounts to launder about US$58 million allegedly stolen from Nicaraguan government coffers.

[60] Unfortunately, there is insufficient space to detail the methods used to travel from Nicaragua to Costa Rica in this article. The reasons for their belief are complicated and the space of this article prevents an accurate chronicle of all of the machinations that were involved in their illegal move from Nicaragua to Costa Rica and why they engaged in a second risk-laden journey. Those details will be forthcoming in a larger publication.

[61] Anyone's sight, it appears, since I have been unable to trace them since they arrived in San José.

[62] Brettell, 'Adjustment of Status'; Chavez, *Shadowed Lives*; Ong, *Flexible Citizenship*.

[63] Margheritis, 'State-led Transnationalism'.

[64] Corrales, 'Gatekeeper State'; Carter, 'New Rules to the Old Game'.

[65] Smith and Guarnizo, *Transnationalism from Below*.

[66] I am thinking here of the work of Nina Glick Schiller and Michael Peter Smith, among others, who make this point abundantly clear. See Glick Schiller, 'Transnational Social Fields'; Glick Schiller and Fouron, *Georges Woke Up Laughing*; Smith, 'Power in Place/Places of Power', Smith and Guarnizo, *Transnationalism from Below*.

References

Beck, U. 'The Cosmopolitan Society and Its Enemies'. *Theory, Culture and Society* 19, nos. 1–2 (2002): 17–44.

Bjarkman, P.C. *A History of Cuban Baseball, 1864–2006*. Jefferson: McFarland & Co, 2007.

Brettell, C.B. 'Adjustment of Status, Remittances and Returns: Some Observations on 21st Century Migration Processes'. *City & Society* 19, no. 1 (2007): 47–59.

Burchardt, H-J. 'Contours of the Future: the New Social Dynamics in Cuba'. *Latin American Perspectives* 29, no. 3 (2002): 57–74.

Carmona Báez, A. *State Resistance to Globalization in Cuba*. London: Pluto Press, 2004.

Carter, T.F. 'Baseball Arguments: Aficionismo and Masculinity at the Core of Cubanidad'. *The International Journal of the History of Sport* 18, no. 3 (2001): 117–38.

Carter, T.F. 'Family Networks, State Interventions and the Experiences of Cuban Transnational Sport Migration'. *International Review of the Sociology of Sport* 42, no. 2 (2007): 371–89.

Carter, T.F. 'New Rules to the Old Game: Cuban Sport and State Legitimacy in the Post-Soviet Era'. *Identities: Global Studies in Culture and Power* 15, no. 2 (2008): 1–22.

Carter, T.F. *The Quality of Home Runs: The Passion, Politics, and Language of Cuban Baseball*. Durham, NC: Duke University Press, 2008.

Carter, T.F., H. Donnan, and H. Wardle. *Global Migrants: The Impact of Migrants Working in Sport in Northern Ireland*. Belfast: Sports Council for Northern Ireland, 2003.

Chatterjee, P. *The Politics of the Governed: Reflections on Popular Politics in Most of the World*. New York: Columbia University Press, 2004.

Chavez, L.R. *Shadowed Lives: Undocumented Immigrants in American Society*. New York: Wadsworth, 1997.

Corrales, J. 'The Gatekeeper State: Limited Economic Reforms and Regime Survival in Cuba, 1989–2002'. *Latin American Research Review* 39, no. 2 (2004): 35–65.

Dabscheck, B. 'The Globe at Their Feet: FIFA's New Employment Rules – I'. *Sport in Society* 7, no. 1 (2004): 69–94.

Dabscheck, B. 'The Globe at the Their Feet: FIFA's New Employment Rules – II'. *Sport in Society* 9, no. 1 (2006): 1–18.

Espinosa Martínez, E. 'Ethics, Economics, and Social Policies: Values and Development Strategy, 1989–2004'. In *Cuba in the 21st Century: Realities and Perspectives*, edited by J. Bell Lara and R.A. Dello Buono, 57–100. La Habana: Editorial José Martí, 2005.

Etzioni, A. 'Citizenship Tests: A Comparative, Communitarian Perspective'. *The Political Quarterly* 78, no. 3 (2007): 353–63.

Fainaru, S., and R. Sanchez. *The Duke of Havana: Baseball, Cuba, and the Search for the American Dream*. New York: Villard, 2001.

Foucault, M. 'Governmentality'. In *The Foucault Effect: Studies in Governmentality*, edited by G. Burchell, C. Gordon, and P. Miller, 87–104. Chicago, IL: University of Chicago Press, 1991.

Geertz, C. *The Interpretation of Cultures*. New York: Basic Books, 1973.

Giulianotti, R. and Robertson, R., eds. *Globalization and Sport*. Oxford: Wiley-Blackwell, 2007.

Glick Schiller, N. 'Transnational Social Fields and Imperialism: Bringing a Theory of Power to Transnational Studies'. *Anthropological Theory* 5, no. 4 (2005): 439–61.

Glick Schiller, N., and G.E. Fouron. *Georges Woke Up Laughing: Long-Distance Nationalism and the Search for Home*. Durham: Duke University Press, 2001.

Gregory, S. *The Devil Behind the Mirror: Globalization and Politics in the Dominican Republic*. Berkeley, CA: University of California Press, 2007.

Guarnizo, L.E., and M.P. Smith. 'The Locations of Transnationalism'. In *Transnationalism from Below*, edited by M.P. Smith and L.E. Guarnizo. 3–34. New Brunswick, NJ: Transaction Books, 1998.

Guevara, E. *Socialismo y el Hombre en Cuba*. Atlanta: Pathfinder Press, 1992 [1965].

Hamilton, D. 'Whither Cuban Socialism? The Changing Political Economy of the Cuban Revolution'. *Latin American Perspectives* 29, no. 3 (2002): 18–39.

Hannerz, U. 'Being There . . . and There . . . and There! Reflections on Multi-Site Ethnography'. *Ethnography* 4, no. 2 (2003): 201–16.

Held, D. *Democracy and the Global Order*. Cambridge: Polity Press, 1995.

Henry, I. *Transnational and Comparative Research in Sport: Globalisation, Governance and Sport Policy*. London: Routledge, 2007.

Herzfeld, M. *The Social Production of Indifference: Exploring the Symbolic Roots of Western Democracy*. Chicago, IL: University of Chicago Press, 1993.

Jamail, M.H. *Full Count*. Carbondale, IL: Southern Illinois University Press, 2000.

Kyle, D., and J. Dale. 'Smuggling the State Back In: Agents of Human Smuggling Reconsidered'. In *Global Human Smuggling: Comparative Perspectives*, edited by D. Kyle and R. Koslowski, 29–57. Baltimore, MD: Johns Hopkins University Press, 2001.

Magee, J., and J. Sugden. '"The World at their Feet": Professional Football and International Labor Migration'. *Journal of Sport and Social Issues* 26, no. 4 (2002): 421–37.

Maguire, J. *Global Sport: Identities, Societies, Civilizations*. Oxford: Polity, 1999.

Maguire, J. *Power and Global Sport: Zones of Prestige, Emulation and Resistance*. London: Routledge, 2005.

Malkki, L. 'National Geographic: The Rooting of Peoples and the Territorialization of National Identity among Scholars and Refugees'. In *Culture, Power, Place: Explorations in Critical Anthropology*, edited by A. Gupta and J. Ferguson, 52–74. Durham, NC: Duke University Press, 1997.

Marcus, G.E. *Ethnography Through Thick and Thin*. Princeton, NJ: Princeton University Press, 1998.

Margheritis, A. 'State-led Transnationalism and Migration: Reaching Out to the Argentine Community in Spain'. *Global Networks* 7, no. 1 (2007): 87–106.

Mauss, M. 'Techniques of the Body'. *Economic Sociology* 2 (1973): 70–8.

Miller, T., G. Lawrence, J. McKay, and D. Rowe. *Globalization and Sport*. London: Sage, 2001.

Monreal, P. 'Development as an Unfinished Affair: Cuba After the Great Adjustment of the 1990s'. *Latin American Perspectives* 29, no. 3 (2002): 75–90.

Ong, A. *Flexible Citizenship: The Cultural Logics of Transnationality*. Durham, NC: Duke University Press, 1999.

Parrish, R., and D. McArdle. 'Beyond Bosman: The European Union's Influence upon Professional Athletes' Freedom of Movement'. *Sport in Society* 7, no. 3 (2004): 403–19.

Phillips, E. '"Cuentapropismo" in a Socialist State'. In *Cuba in Transition? Pathways to Renewal, Long-Term Development and Global Reintegration*, edited by M. Font and S. Larson, 107–24. New York: Bildner Center for Western Hemisphere Studies, CUNY, 2006.

Poli, R. 'The Denationalization of Sport: De-ethnicization of the Nation and Identity Deterritorialization'. *Sport in Society* 10, no. 4 (2007): 646–61.

Price, S.L. *Pitching Around Fidel: A Journey into the Heart of Cuban Sports*. New York: Ecco, 2000.

Ritter, A.R.M. 'Cuba's Economic Reorientation'. In *Cuba in Transition? Pathways to Renewal, Long-Term Development and Global Reintegration*, edited by M. Font and S. Larson. New York: Bildner Center for Western Hemisphere Studies, CUNY, 2006.

Ritter, A.R.M., and N. Rowe. 'Cuba: From "Dollarization" to "Euroization" or "Peso Reconsolidation"?'. *Latin American Politics and Society* 44, no. 2 (2002): 99–123.

Robertson, R. 'Mapping the Global Condition: Globalization as the Central Concept'. In *Global Culture: Nationalism, Globalization and Modernity*, edited by M. Featherstone, 15–30. London: Sage, 1990.

Rogozinski, J. *A Brief History of the Caribbean: From the Arawak and the Carib to the Present*. New York: Meridian, 1992.

Shachar, A., and R. Hirschl. 'Citizenship as Inherited Property'. *Political Theory* 35, no. 3 (2007): 253–87.

Sklair, L. *The Transnational Capitalist Class*. Oxford: Wiley-Blackwell, 2000.

Smith, M.P. 'Power in Place/Places of Power: Contextualizing Transnational Research'. *City & Society* 17, no. 1 (2005): 5–34.

Smith, M.P. and Guarnizo, L.E., eds. *Transnationalism from Below*. New Brunswick, NJ: Transaction Publishers, 1998.

Tsing, A. 'Inside the Economy of Appearances'. *Public Culture* 12, no. 1 (2000): 115–44.

Venn, C. 'Altered States: Post-Enlightenment Cosmopolitanism and Transmodern Socialities'. *Theory, Culture and Society* 19, nos. 1–2 (2002): 65–80.

Wallerstein, I. 'Open the Social Sciences'. *ITEMS, Social Science Research Council* 50, no. 1 (1996): 1–7.

Weber, M. *The Protestant Ethic and the Spirit of Capitalism*. New York: Routledge, 1992 [1904].

Williams, E. *From Columbus to Castro: The History of the Caribbean*. New York: Vintage Books, 1970.

Wirtz, K. 'Santeria in Cuban National Consciousness: A Religious Case of the *Doble Moral*'. *Journal of Latin American Anthropology* 9, no. 2 (2004): 409–38.

Sport, development and aid: can sport make a difference?

Grant Jarvie

Vice-Principal, University of Stirling, Stirling, UK

It is the ability to combine sport with other social forces such as education that has facilitated an increased profile for sport with international aid and humanitarian organizations. This article recognizes the role that sport has to play in the field of international development, the promise and possibilities brought about by presidential elections in the United States of America and the distinct poverty traps that some countries continue to face. The lack of growth in those countries that make up the bottom billion of the world's poorest people requires particular strategies for particular circumstances and it is open to question as to whether sport can bring about change or be a resource of hope. Improving life chances requires a coordinated effort and as such any contribution that sport can make must also build upon a wider coalition of sustained support in order to narrow the gap between rich and poor. In a substantive way this article, drawing upon international evidence, notes the potential of education through sport to help with influencing life chances, if not levels of poverty, in the world today.

The international flow of athletes from parts of Africa has been referred to as a global trade in muscle in which Kenyan and Ethiopian athletes have switched allegiance from the country of their birth to oil-rich states such as Qatar and Bahrain.[1] This scramble for African talent, write Simms and Rendell, may be equated with the exploitation of Africa's mineral wealth during different periods of colonial rule.[2] The assertion being that those living in poverty provide the muscle while the rich countries of the world capture the benefits. The scramble for Africa started as early as the 1960s with athletes being lured to American colleges, but now the oil-rich countries of the world simply buy athletic talent that is then lost to Africa. Gyulai, athletics correspondent for the IAAF (International Association of Athletics Federations) News, commented that the freedom of movement of athletes may give rise to conflicting interest between different member federations of the IAAF, but believes that there should be no exception to the increased mobility of individuals within the rules of free-market trade and global sporting capitalism.[3] The IAAF notes that the rules with regard to the movement of athletes should not be to the detriment of the member federations. Kenya recently moved to try to stem the flow of athletes out of Kenya by tightening up on the circumstances and conditions under which athletes may be granted visas to leave the country.[4]

There are initially two ways of reflecting about sport and capitalism. The first is to think of capitalism in terms of what it represents as a set of contemporary relationships between people and countries. The truth about sport as a universal creed is that it is also an engine of injustice between nations and peoples. The second is to think of the relationship between sport and capitalism in historical terms. Sport potentially provides a resource of hope for many people and places but it also runs the danger of aligning itself with historical calls proclaiming the principles of equality, justice and the eradication of poverty. Past interventions through sport have not sufficed to make a reality of any of these aforementioned possibilities.

In early 2009 international communities were struggling to understand the significance of the New Depression – its causes, its duration, its consequences and its possible solutions. The global crisis that began in the summer of 2007 with the onset of a credit crunch and the unravelling of the world financial systems also marked a potential fundamental shift in the balance of international power. While the financial crisis began in the United States, the changing balances of power provided a further challenge to a neo-liberal ideology that has influenced broader western thinking since at least the 1970s. The value of the dollar and its future as the world's reserve currency perhaps depends on China. Some have suggested that such shifts constitute the most profound, financial, economic, political and ideological crisis facing the West since the 1930s.[5]

Many of the poorest countries in the world continue to defy repeated attempts by international communities to provide sustainable help. Sport has historically been used as a key facet of humanitarian aid and a proven avenue of social mobility for many athletes from developing countries. The historical writings on sport and capitalism are rich with proven examples of how sport has intervened in the past.[6] The focus of this article limits itself to a reflection on an emerging body of research arising out of a more evidence-based approach to sport and international development in the context of a potential shift to a new world order.[7] The article also draws upon observations made by Collier, Fraser and the Fabian Society all acknowledging that the real development challenge is one of closing the gap between a rich world and a poor world in which the world's poorest people – the bottom billion – face a tragedy that is growing inexorably worse.[8] Helping the bottom billion remains one of the key challenges facing the world in the twenty-first century. This article questions whether sport has a part to play in this process.

A new sports agenda and international development

As noted, a very recent and significant contribution to research into sport in society has been made by those who have started to address and critically question the role of sport in development.[9] Much of this research talked to a world that existed before the emergence of credit crunch, economic recession, the election of a new American president and the emergence of a New World Order symbolically represented by the G20.

The role that sport has to play in the field of international development has been advanced through the work of Levermore and Beacom.[10] The aim of this work was to initiate debate, in primarily academic international development circles, upon the 'use of sport based initiatives to establish and assist development'.[11] The collection of essays remains the most comprehensive coverage of a potential new sports agenda in the field of international development and provides a body of evidence that testifies to the idea that power in world sport has become increasingly dispersed. The dispersal of power in world sport means that the control, management and organization of sport does not simply occur at local or global levels. The global era of sport has presented fundamental challenges for sporting governance but it has also created the opportunity for sport to be a social force for internationalism, reconciliation and international development.[12]

The research associating sport with international development tends to rely on some or all of the following arguments, that: (i) sport represents a number of theoretical positions within the field of development; (ii) sport can be part of the process for development in a diverse range of different circumstances and contexts; (iii) the evidence to support the claim that sport can produce social change is at best limited and that we need to be clear about the limitations of sport as well as the possibilities; (iv) sport has only recently figured within the goals of modernization/neo-liberal development thinking; (v) sport reproduces and helps to sustain the gap in resources between different parts of the world; (vi) sport has some capacity to act both as a conduit for traditional development but also as an agent of change in its own right; and (vii) new forms of internationality and cooperation between countries provide a more realistic opportunity for progress rather than those that simply emanate from Westphalia or state-organized capitalism.

Historically sport and education have been key avenues of social mobility and an escape from poverty for some.[13] Thinking systematically about emancipatory alternatives and the part played by sport is only one way, or element in the process, by which the limits of the possible can expand and the promise and possibilities of the power of education through sport can become more of a reality for more people. Educational sport projects have long since been viewed as agents of social change with the rationale being that they can: (i) increase knowledge and skills and in a broader sense contribute to the knowledge economy; (ii) help to provide opportunities for lifelong learning and sustain not just education but an involvement in sport and physical activity; (iii) make a voluntary contribution to informal education through sport that can make a positive contribution to helping young people; (iv) help foster and develop critical debate about key public issues; (v) support programmes in different parts of the world which involve sport as part of an approach to tackling HIV education; and (vi) help to foster social capital through fostering relationships, networking and making connections. These networks through education and sport have the potential to act as a form of human resource.

A valuable and much needed corrective to the social role of sport has been provided through the work of, most recently, Kidd but also Sugden in that they both tend to indicate that sport can be used to promote and contribute to change within borders while acknowledging that sport might be less effective across borders. While acknowledging this point, examples such as Gebrselassie in Ethiopia, Weah in Liberia, Keino in Kenya and Mutola in Mozambique all provide evidence to suggest that while some athletes and sporting celebrities may leave their country of origin they nonetheless remain committed to the social and economic development of their country of origin.[14] Increasingly athletes such as George Weah, Haile Gebrselassie and others have realized that African countries are increasingly electing their leaders, and as athletes on the world stage they command a degree of visibility, loyalty and in some cases increased credibility because they have got rich honestly by their own efforts and have not forgotten the local context. Sport in these cases has helped to fashion resources of hope in many different ways.

Inequality is a complex issue and varies both within and *between* countries and communities. An important although not causal determinant would be the inequality of opportunity or lack of access to good education, healthcare and clean water; poor economic and social services, lack of access to markets and information and the lack of democratic right to participate in the key decision-making processes. Often the root cause of poverty, marginalization and injustice is the unequal power distribution that impacts upon many regions and areas of the South. There are historical causes linked to colonial impositions and extraction of resources (human and natural), and the reality of globalization and international affairs only seems to perpetuate certain benefits of power. Within the South there are cultural, social, political and historical reasons today for poor governance and power in certain groups and places. Most noticeable are the major fault lines between the North and South. This is to say that there exists a very definite tension, sometimes ideologically based and sometimes intuitively based between the demands of those from the wealthy countries and those from the poorer countries.

Writers such as Coalter continually remind us of the substantive basis for such claims.[15] If there is any doubt about the potential of trade to reduce poverty far more effectively than aid then it will not be because of the efforts to alleviate poverty within certain parts of Africa. If the main aim of Millennium Development Goals – to half the proportion of people of the world living in poverty by 2015 – is likely to be met then it will not be because of Africa but because China, Brazil and India have been making progress on the back of increased trade with Western markets. Yet the major unanswered question remains whether the structures through which we manage trade, as a world community, give poor countries a real chance to help themselves. While China, India and Brazil continue to develop, the very poorest countries of the world may lack the economic power to negotiate favourable trading terms. OECD research suggests that the emigration of highly skilled workers, including athletes, may in fact prevent the poorest countries in the world from reaching the critical mass of human resources necessary to foster long-term development.[16] What is undeniable is that part of the root of the problem lies in countries in the West failing to manage their own needs and poorer countries paying the price in terms of the emigration of national talent. It is often the poorest countries with the fewest opportunities and smallest salaries who suffer most. India, Brazil and China are reckoned to be losing about 5% of their highly skilled workers while in countries such as Mozambique, Ghana and Tanzania the figure is closer to 50%.[17]

The promise and possibilities arising out of any new world order of power should not detract from the fact that increasing competition within some of the poorest areas of the world often depletes social capital and leaves its potential fragmented. The informal sector (often in the form of voluntary or professional associations) often transnational, sometimes dissolves self-help networks and solidarities essential to the survival of the very poor and it is often women and children who are the most vulnerable. An NGO worker in Haiti describes the ultimate logic of neo-liberal individualism in a context of absolute immiseration:[18]

> Now everything is for sale. The women used to receive you with hospitality, give you coffee, share all that she has in her home. I could go get a plate of food at a neighbour's house; a child could get a coconut at her godmother's, two mangoes at another aunt's. But these acts of solidarity are disappearing with the growth of poverty. Now when you arrive somewhere, either the women offers to sell you a cup of coffee or she has no coffee at all. The tradition of mutual giving that allowed us to help each other and survive – this is all being lost

Sport, poverty and the bottom billion

Nelson Mandela described child poverty as modern slavery; thousands have demonstrated against it; New Labour on coming to power in Britain in 1999 vowed to eliminate child poverty within a generation; eradicating it has been viewed as been one of the most successful strategies to halt terrorism and it has been the object of fundraising campaigns by some of the world's top musicians and sportsmen and women. James Wolfensohn, head of the World Bank, noted in July 2004 that, in terms of expenditure, the priorities were roughly $900 billion on defence, $350 billion on agriculture, and $60 billion on aid of which about half gets there in cash.[19] Oxfam recently noted that it would cost £3.2 billion to send all the world's children to school. Poverty may be one of the few truly global phenomena in that, in relative and absolute terms, it exists worldwide and while governments and policies change, the needs of the world's poor invariably remain the same.

The notion of poverty is not new but it is often suppressed, not just in the literature and research about sport and society. However, it is highlighted here as a fundamental reason and motivation for why some athletes run. Many NGOs have been at the forefront of initiatives involving sport as a facet of humanitarian aid in attacking the social and economic consequences of poverty. The Tiger Club Project in Kampala Uganda is one of many such initiatives using sport. The objectives of the Tiger Club include: (i) helping street children and young people in need; (ii) providing children with food, clothing and other physical needs; (iii) help with education and development; (iv) enabling children to realize their potential so that they can gain employment; (v) providing assistance to the natural families or foster carers of children and young adults; and (vi) providing medical and welfare assistance.[20] The 2003 Annual Report reported that, in 2002, 263 children had been offered a permanent alternative to the street; a further 116 street children and young people were in the START programme which meant full-time schooling; and 161 young people resettled in their village of origin and were provided with the means for income generation. Seventy-six per cent of those resettled children have remained in their villages.[21]

Every year about 200 million people move in search of employment – about 3% of the world's population.[22] Legal migrants who leave their homes in poor countries to provide labour or entertainment in other parts of the world are generally regarded as privileged. Many African runners have provided an exhilarating spectacle for sports audiences but what is often forgotten is that the money raised from these performances often provides pathways of hope for other people. Sociologists such as Maguire have helped pave the way for an extensive body of research into the causes of sports labour migration across different parts of the world and yet very little has been written about the part played by some athletes in earning money to support whole families and even villages in their country of origin.[23] When the career of a leading world athlete from a developing country is brought to a premature end, the consequences often extend far beyond the track. Maria Mutola, the Mozambican, former Olympic and five-time world indoor 800m champion and world-record holder, routinely sends track winnings back to her country of origin. Chamanchulo, the suburb of Maputo in which Mutola grew up, is ravaged by HIV, passed on in childbirth or breast milk to 40% of the children.[24] In 2003 when Mutola became the first athlete to collect $1 million for outright victory on the Golden League Athletic Grand Prix Circuit, part of the cash went to the foundation she endowed to help provide scholarships, kit, education and coaching for young athletes.[25] Farms and small businesses have often been sustained by her winnings on the circuit, which have provided for the purchasing of tractors, fertilizers and the facilities to drill small wells.

The 3000m steeplechase at the 2005 World Athletic Championships held in Helsinki was won by Saif Saaeed Shaheen in a time of eight minutes 13.31 seconds. The official world championship records will show that the gold medal went to Qatar, a country in which Saif Saaeed Shaheen is viewed as an athletic icon. The athlete's successful defence of this world championship 3000m steeplechase gold medal was his 21st successive victory since 2002.[26] His elder brother Chris Kosgei won the gold for Kenya in 1999 but unlike Shaheen did not defect to Qatar. Saif Saaeed Shaheen, born Stephen Cherono, won his first world steeplechase title 17 days after defecting to the oil-rich state which had granted him a passport.[27] In that same race Shaheen's brother ran for Kenya, refused to call him anything other than Stephen and did not congratulate him after the race. Kenyan athletic officials, writes Gillon, were so upset at losing this steeplechase world title for the first time since 1987 that they stopped Shaheen running for Qatar at the 2004 Athens Olympics through enforcing athlete eligibility rules following his migration.[28] Kenya won gold, silver and bronze medals in the men's 3000m steeplechase at the 2004 Athens Olympic Games.

Athletes such as Shaheen are single minded and mono-causal when it comes to explaining both personal and Kenyan athletic success. It is important here not to be confused by simple western stereotypes about non-western cultures. The context is such that as a boy Shaheen's family 'had 60 cows and 30 goats until a drought...left the family with 7 cattle and 3 goats...and it cost him his education', since the animals would have been sold to pay for his school fees.[29] As Stephen Cherono he was raised in Kamelilo, a village in Keyo in which there was no water-tap and every day after school, which cost two dollars for three days, he walked three kilometres to collect 10 litres of water. The move to Qatar was allegedly based upon an offer of a least $1000 dollars a month for life.[30] About 50 people now depend upon that athlete's success for their livelihoods. He puts eight children through school with two at college in America and, when asked to explain Kenyan running success said that the answer is simple, 'an athlete in Kenya runs to escape poverty' and 'I fight to survive'.[31]

In the same way that the all-too-easily accepted truths about globalization have ignored the uneven and differentiated forms of capitalism emerging in the twenty-first century, so too it is crucial not to ignore the injustices and uneven patterns of sports labour migration.

It is essential that any contemporary understanding of sport must actively listen and engage with other sporting communities, places and voices. Perhaps it is impossible for humanity or sport to arrive at an understanding of the values that unite it, but if the leading capitalist nations ceased to impose their own ideas on the rest of the sporting world and started to take cognizance of 'other' sporting cultures, then the aspiration of sport may become more just and less charitable. It is not charity which Africa or African runners want but the tools by which Africans can determine their own well-being and life chances in a more equable sporting world.[32] If large parts of Africa are kept poor as a result of unfair trade arrangements, which facilitate cheap European and American imports that keep parts of Africa poor and dependent, then why should the resources afforded by running not be viewed as a viable route out of poverty for those that can make it?

The issue is put more explicitly in the work of Collier, who asserts that single-factor theories about development fail to recognize that a one-size-fits-all theory of development fails in part to acknowledge the distinct poverty traps that some developing countries face.[33] For the past 50 years or more, what we have defined as developing countries tends to encompass about five billion of the six billion people in the world. Those whose development has failed face potentially intractable problems and account for the bottom billion people and about 50 failing states. This bottom billion live on less than a dollar a day and, while the rest of the world moves steadily forward, this forgotten billion is left further behind and the gap between rich and poor fails to diminish in economic terms. Conventional international aid has been unable to impact in areas of the world in which corruption, political instability and resource management lie at the root of many problems.[34]

The lack of growth in the countries of the bottom billion needs particular strategies for particular circumstances. The object of international development should not be aid but growth. The politics of the bottom billion is not a contest between the rich developed world and a number of economically poorer worlds, but it is difficult for parts of Africa, Haiti, Bolivia, Laos, Cambodia, Yemen, Burma, North Korea to compete with the likes of China, India and Brazil. The 58 countries which make up Collier's bottom billion people have fewer people than China or India combined.[35] One of the few forums where the heads of the major governments meet is the G20.

Capitalism, a new world order and the audacity of hope

An important priority in any contemporary discussion of capitalism is to firstly acknowledge that it still exists but perhaps more importantly to acknowledge that it exists in new forms. Capital today is much more fluid, it flows much more readily, looking for the optimum conditions with which to reproduce itself and in turn accumulate greater capital. Sports businesses continue to look around the world, not just around the locale, the region or the nation, for greater profit. Capitalism is marked by the rise to pre-eminence of the transnational corporations that, in terms of their size and power, are able to take advantage of whatever opportunities exist to lower the costs of production, typically by shifting aspects of sports production from wealthier to relatively poorer countries, or through consolidation, merger or take over. Contemporary capitalism also takes place within an alleged regime of international governance that seeks to accommodate the interests of nation-states and the needs of transnational capital.

At the same time there is the almost unquestionable challenge that sport in many ways is part of the hallmark of the triumph of capitalism coupled with the growing ascendancy of economics over politics, of the corporate demands for sport over public policy and of private sporting interest over public sporting interests. Neo-liberal thinking about sport in many ways implies the end of politics because of the centrality of the market as the resource allocator and the submission of public life and the commons to commodification. Even transnational corporations (TNC) who take on increased social responsibilities and use sport as a positive tool for help acknowledge that the overall operating rationale for the organization remains one of profit. TNCs often fail to recognize that alternative common frameworks for sport to operate within do exist.

But what happens when the market collapses – albeit temporarily? It is tempting to suggest that globalization represents but a further acceleration towards the capitalization of the sporting world but to accept such an analogy would be to acknowledge *uncritically* the rhetorical promotion of globalization as capitalism and the submission of public life and the commons to commodification. That is to say that at one level the services that remain in the public sector according to neo-liberalism have to be compelled to run themselves as private enterprises and the role of different sporting worlds is simply to compete for customers. At another level neo-liberalism also advocates a clear path towards economic convergence between the richest and poorest parts of the world if the governments of poor countries strictly adhere to liberal policies. While neo-liberalism is an intellectually complex body of knowledge involving diverse strands of argument its politics are pristinely simple in that politics ceases to have any meaning beyond terms prescribed by the market.

To accept such logic would be to deny or reduce to a matter of insignificance the many opportunities for social change and social reform that are presented by and through contemporary sport. To deny that such opportunities for social change do exist would be just as utopian as thinking that older variants of capitalism remain the way of the twenty-first century – this is not the case. It would also crucially fail to acknowledge that contemporary capitalism is itself at a crossroads. New parameters of geo-global politics and socio-economic cooperation exist. That is to say that policies are forged and implemented and that political ideas wax and wane within an increasingly global space that at one level is geopolitical and at another level is socio-economic. Opportunities for social change in and through sport exist at both these levels.

Capitalism is in itself a good example of a contested concept or idea. It is contested along two dimensions – explanatory and normative. Capitalist sport, often synonymous with global sport, is also a contested idea but all too often the alternatives to it remain silent; as a result there are key silences about sports' role within alternative debates about internationalism, anti-globalization, anti-capitalism, social movements and the power of the social within the world past and present. Football managers such as Wenger at Arsenal and Ferguson at Manchester United have recently questioned whether the credit crunch facing the world economy may in fact be an opportunity for football to regain a more noble vision for the game, one that is not solely dependent upon wealth creation at the same levels.[36] Neo-liberalism, some have suggested, is dead but the values often associated with neo-liberalism may still have residual influences.[37] Freedom has often been reduced to the right to buy and sell and reduces opportunities for solidarity to privatized individualism. The meeting of the G20 world leaders was also meant to be symbolic of the coming of a new social order and a more humane form of capitalism, in response to a crisis brought about in part by the collapse of US-led global finance and the American state.[38] President Barack Obama acknowledged that the old Washington consensus of unfettered globalization and deregulation was now outmoded and a more balanced approach to regulating markets rather than letting them run free was required.[39] Set against this background the potential of sport cannot be seen to reside within the values promoted by sport or particular forms of capitalism. The possibilities that exist within sport are those that can help with radically different views of the world, perhaps based upon opportunities to foster trust, obligations, redistribution and respect for sport in a more socially orientated humane world. This has to be part of any debate about sport and international development. Sport's transformative capacity must not be overstated but possibilities do exist within sport to provide some resources of hope in a new world order.

The audacity of hope is Barack Obama's call for a new kind of politics – a politics that builds upon shared understandings to make a difference and pull people together. *The Audacity of Hope* is about the idea that we might begin to renew the process of changing politics and civic life and it is grounded in a notion of a common good.[40] It is interesting to note that on the eve of the election for the new President of the United States of America (USA) both Barack Obama and John McCain were interviewed on the half-time show of Monday Night Football. Asked the same questions, they differed significantly on only one: if you could change one thing about American sports what would it be? McCain offered something worthy about sorting out the steroid problem while Obama wanted a college football play-off. Obama is not only the first black President of the USA but the first President to identify himself primarily as a basketball fan. Reagan played football at college, Bushes senior and junior are both baseball men, Clinton did play basketball at Oxford, but Obama's basketball credentials are good. It has been widely reported that he shook off election-day nerves playing basketball. In *Dreams of my Father*, Obama writes 'that I was trying to raise myself to being a black man in America and, beyond the given of my appearance, no one around me seemed to know what that meant'.[41] What Obama's election means for the United States of America is that, at very least, the decades of American conservatism that have tended to define global politics maybe about to witness a seismic liberal change – or will it?

The possibilities that exist through sport are those that can help with radically different views of the world and this has to be part of any understanding which underpins the complexity of the sport-in-development relationship. It also suggests that perhaps capitalism itself is at a critical crossroads and that the global financial crisis, a decidedly post-neo-liberal response and the election of an American president perhaps points to the fact that we may stand poised at the brink of a period of transformation. If so then the shape of any successor society will be the object of intense contestation.

There are still no easy answers while conditions of acute exploitation, market irrationality and economic crisis are manifest everywhere albeit often in new forms. The new world order represented at the London summit was evident in the countries invited to the global summit. Unlike the former G8 countries, the wider representation of the G20 group, in which the presence of Ethiopia represented Africa and Thailand represented

South East Asia alongside the more sizable emerging economies like India, China and Brazil, ensured that wider issues were discussed.

Narrowing the gap or resource of hope?

Improving life chances requires a coordinated effort and as such any contribution that sport can make must also build upon a wider coalition of sustained support for social and progressive policies. The life-chances approach to narrowing the gap between rich and poor has a key role to play in producing social change.[42] It requires harnessing a strong political narrative and action plan that fits with many people's intuitive understanding that life should not be determined by socio-economic position and that people do have choices, whilst drawing attention to the fact that some people and places face greater risks and more limited opportunities. Equalizing life chances and focusing on areas such as poverty should sit together as part of a vision for a better society, better sport and any progressive approach to sport and international development.

Sport, it has been suggested, should be thought of more as a potential resource of hope, in that sport has some limited capacity to assist with development, can have an impact on life chances, and can be part of a holistic approach to what a recent report by a international think-tank referred to as 'narrowing the gap'.[43] Intervention can come in many forms, legislation, policy, writing, investigating, uncovering silences, pressure groups, social forums, campaigns and activism, re-allocation of resources, not accepting injustice in sport, and intervention through projects designed stimulate aid. Historically sport, often linked with education, has been a key avenue of social mobility and an escape from poverty for some. Thinking systematically about emancipatory alternatives and the part played by sport is only one way or element in the process by which the limits of the possible can expand and the promise and possibilities of sport can become more of a reality for more people. Sociologists and those interested in the role that sport has to play in social policy and international development still have to think about the transformative capacity of sport to contribute to equalizing life chances.

The promise of education through sport to narrow the gap should not be overestimated. The right of all people to have access to education and/or sport and the small contribution that education through sport can make to this goal is not insignificant. With the international campaigns against world debt in a state of flux, new ideas and progressive ideas are needed to cure the problems in part caused by international finance institutions attempting to solve the debt problem of the global South and other places. Football is popular in places such as Brazil, where it is estimated that some 25 million children work and a further 25 million who are not working are in school. The need to raise money for the family unit through the informal economy means that children often do not have access to education and the failure to study only serves to maintain poverty.[44] Some of the projects presented through the work of Levermore and Beacom highlight both the promise and possibilities but also the limits of education through sport to make a difference.[45] Sport cannot do this on its own but swapping international debt for education, including education through sport, maybe one of the possible strategies open to a progressive, humanitarian international approach to education through sport which could challenge the very values at the heart of capitalism's impact upon sport. It may assist in creating the conditions that allow education through sport to thrive. In short, swapping debt for education, including education through sport, may assist millions of children and others to gain substantive education, transferable skills and enable some ultimately to become more active participants in a national economy, secure better life chances and escape the cycle of poverty.

Narrowing the gap through education in sport is about the significant intervention and potential that the dynamic combination of higher education and sport has, if not determining the life chances and activity levels certainly influencing them. Improving life chances requires a coordinated effort and as such any contribution that sport can make must also build upon a wider coalition of sustained support for social and progressive policies. The life chances approach to narrowing the gap between rich and poor has a key role to play in producing social change. It requires harnessing a strong political narrative and action plan that fits with many people's intuitive understanding that life should not be determined by socio-economic position and that people do have choices, whilst drawing attention to the fact that some people and places face greater risks and more limited opportunities.

Conclusion

Sport needs to be more just and less charitable but it also continues to provide a pathway for hope for some in different parts of the world. Improving life chances requires a coordinated effort and as such any contribution that sport can make must also build upon a wider coalition of sustained support for social and progressive policies. The life chances approach to narrowing the gap between rich and poor has a key role to play in producing social change. It requires harnessing a strong political narrative and action plan that fits with many people's intuitive understanding that life should not be determined by socio-economic position and that people do have choices, whilst drawing attention to the fact that some people and places face greater risks and more limited opportunities. Certainly we may possibly be seeing the development of capitalism with a more human face, the early stirrings of a new wave of change aimed at articulating alternative views of the world, and sport can make a limited but popular and very public contribution to an open future. The audacity of hope thesis acknowledges that unfettered globalization and deregulation are now outmoded and a more balanced approach to regulating markets is needed rather than letting them run free.

The Ethiopian athlete and politician, once Olympic champion and former world-record holder, Haile Gebrselassie has left us in no doubt about both the social and political responsibility of the athlete and the limits and possibilities of sport in relation to poverty in his country. In an interview Haile Gebrselassie drew attention to the context and circumstances that were his early life.[46] Talking of his life aged 15, 'This was all at a time when my father was cross with me because I was doing athletics and my country was going through famine in which millions died and all I had was running – I just ran and ran all the time and I got better and better'. Talking of the necessity to run –'I only started running because I had to – we were six miles from school and there was so much to be done on the farm that I ran to school and back again to have enough time to do farming as well as school work'. Finally, his talking about the political responsibility of the athlete left one in no doubt about the priorities:

> eradicating poverty is all that matters in my country. When I am training I think about this a lot; when I am running it is going over in my mind – as a country we cannot move forward until we eradicate poverty and whereas sport can help – the real problems will not be overcome just by helping Ethiopians to run fast.[47]

In reality sport can only make a small contribution, but small contributions can sometimes make a difference. How sport can help in the fight against poverty should not be shelved as a historical question until much more has been done to fight both relative and absolute experiences of poverty worldwide and to note what sport can or cannot do to help.

Notes

[1] Pitsiladis et al., *East African Running*.
[2] Simms and Rendell 'Global Trade in Muscle'.
[3] I. Gyulai, 'Transfers of Nationality', *IAAF News* 64, 2003, 2–4.
[4] Pitsiladis et al., *East African Running*.
[5] Jacques, 'No One Rules the World'.
[6] See, for example, Kidd and Donnelly, 'Human Rights in Sport'; Bass, *Not the Triumph*; and Bellos, 'President Wins'.
[7] Jacques, 'No One Rules the World'.
[8] See Collier, *Bottom Billion*; Fraser, 'Feminism Co-Opted'; Levermore and Beacom, *Sport and International Development*; and Fabian Society, *Narrowing the Gap*.
[9] Coalter, *A Wider Social Role*.
[10] Levermore and Beacom, *Sport and International Development*.
[11] Ibid., 5.
[12] Jarvie, *Sport, Culture and Society*.
[13] Jacques, 'No One Rules the World'.
[14] See Kidd, 'A New Social Movement'; Sugden, 'Teaching and Playing Sport'.
[15] Coalter, *A Wider Social Role*.
[16] OECD, *Education at a Glance 2008*.
[17] Bolton. *Aid and Other Dirty Business*.
[18] Davis, *Planet of Slums*, 15.
[19] Bolton, *Aid and Other Dirty Business*.
[20] The Tiger Club, *Annual Report*.
[21] Ibid.
[22] Seabrook, 'Don't Punish the Poor'.
[23] See Maguire, *Power and Global*; Maguire, 'Sport Labour Migration Research'.
[24] D. Gillon, 'Candle Who Brings a Ray of Hope', *The Herald*, 3 May 2004, 24.
[25] Ibid.
[26] D. Gillon, D, 'View From Man Who Races to Escape Poverty', *The Herald*, 15 January 2005, 10.
[27] Ibid.
[28] Ibid.
[29] D. Gillon, D. 'No Barriers to Shaheen's Success', *The Herald*, 10 August 2005, 34.
[30] Ibid.
[31] Ibid.
[32] J. McAlpine, 'Africa Has Spoken, But Did Any of Us Bother to Listen?', *The Herald*, 7 July 2005, 20.
[33] Collier, *Bottom Billion*.
[34] Ibid.
[35] Ibid.
[36] See Rees, 'Global Soul'; Campbell, 'New Statesman Interview'; Tormey, *Anti-Capitalism*.
[37] Fraser, 'Feminism Co-Opted'.
[38] Obama, *The Audacity of Hope*.
[39] Ibid.
[40] Ibid.
[41] Obama, *Dreams of my Father*, 54.
[42] Fabian Society, *Narrowing the Gap*.
[43] Ibid.
[44] Bolton, *Aid and Other Dirty Business*.
[45] Levermore and Beacom, *Sport and International Development*.
[46] H. Gebrselassie, 'Triumph and Despair', *The Times*, 10 March 2003, 12.
[47] Ibid., (this and the preceding two quotes).

References

Bass, A. *Not the Triumph But the Struggle: The 1968 Olympics and the Making of the Black Athlete*. Minneapolis, MN: University of Minnesota Press, 2002.
Bellos, A. 'The President Wins the Midfield Battle'. *New Statesman*, 3 November 2003, 32–4.
Bolton, G. *Aid and Other Dirty Business*. Reading: Edbury Press, 2008.

Campbell, A. 'New Statesman Interview with Alex Ferguson'. *New Statesman*, 23 March 2009, 20–3.

Coalter, F. *A Wider Social Role for Sport?* London: Routledge, 2008.

Collier, P. *The Bottom Billion*. Oxford: Oxford University Press, 2007.

Davis, M. *Planet of Slums*. London: Verso, 2006.

Fabian Society. *Narrowing the Gap: The Fabian Commission on Life Chances and Child Poverty*. London: Fabian Society, 2006.

Fraser, N. 'Feminism Co-Opted'. *New Left Review* 56 (2009): 97–118.

Jacques, M. 'No One Rules the World'. *New Statesman*, 30 March 2009, 22–5.

Jarvie, G. *Sport, Culture and Society*. London: Routledge, 2006.

Kidd, B. 'A New Social Movement: Sport for Development and Peace'. *Sport in Society* 11, no. 4 (2008): 370–80.

Kidd, B., and P. Donnelly. 'Human Rights in Sport'. *International Review for the Sociology of Sport* 35, no. 2 (2000): 131–48.

Levermore, R. and A. Beacom, eds. *Sport and International Development*. Basingstoke: Palgrave Macmillan, 2009.

Maguire, J. *Power and Global Sport: Zones of Prestige, Emulation and Resistance*. London: Routledge, 2005.

Maguire, J.A. 'Sport Labour Migration Research Revisited'. *Journal of Sport and Social Issues* 28, no. 4 (2004): 477–82.

Obama, B. *Dreams of my Father*. New York: Three Rivers Press, 2004.

Obama, B. *The Audacity of Hope*. New York: Three Rivers Press, 2006.

OECD. *Education at a Glance 2008*. OECD Indicators, 2008.

Pitsiladis, Y., J. Bale, C. Sharp, and T. Noakes, eds. *East African Running*. London: Routledge, 2007.

Rees, B. 'The Global Soul'. *New Statesman*, 15 December 2008, 24–6.

Seabrook, J. 'Don't Punish the Poor for Being Poor'. *New Statesman*, 23 September 2003, 6–7.

Simms, A., and M. Rendell. 'The Global Trade in Muscle'. *New Statesman*, 9 August 2004, 24–5.

Sugden, J. 'Teaching and Playing Sport for Conflict Resolution and Co-Existence in Israel'. *International Review for the Sociology of Sport* 41, no. 2 (2006): 221–40.

The Tiger Club. *Annual Report*. Kampala: Uganda, 2003.

Tormey, S. *Anti-Capitalism*. Oxford: One-World, 2004.

Transferring national allegiance: cultural affinity or flag of convenience?

Michael Holmes[a] and David Storey[b]

[a]Department of Politics, Liverpool Hope University, Liverpool, UK; [b]Department of Geography, Institute of Science and the Environment, University of Worcester, Worcester, UK

In international sport in recent years there has been a growing tendency for sportspeople to represent a country other than the one in which they were born. Most international sporting bodies allow people to represent either the country of their birth or one to which they have an attachment through ethnicity, residency or marriage. This article explores the senses of national identity and belonging felt by sportspeople competing for a country other than the one in which they were born and grew up. It does so through a focus on the case of the Republic of Ireland soccer team since the 1980s. It examines perceptions of national identity amongst the so-called 'Anglo' contingent, players who were born in Britain but were eligible to play for Ireland under FIFA rules relating to parentage. The article is based on self-evaluations recorded in newspaper and magazine interviews and in players' 'auto' biographies. It further examines the reactions by various individuals outside Ireland to this phenomenon and the views of Irish fans towards player eligibility and selection.

The article places this work in an analytical context of sport and nationalism, with particular emphasis on the complex relationships between sport and nationalism in Ireland. The article argues that there is evidence of significant attitudinal differences between players; that players' attitudes are by no means uniform but range from the 'careerist' to the 'nationalist' position. Responses to this phenomenon have been sharply divided between those who view it as a dilution of the authentically Irish nature of the team to those who see it as a pragmatic response to an otherwise limited player pool.

Introduction

The crowd joined in, every one of them, from Dublin and Cork, from London and from Stockholm. And suddenly I knew this was the only country I still owned, those eleven figures in green shirts, that menagerie of accents pleading with God ... I raised my hands and applauded, having finally found the only Ireland whose name I can sing, given to me by eleven men dressed in green.[1]

Sport has become a prism through which political identities, and especially national identities, are frequently viewed and it might be argued that sport is, in some ways, uniquely well suited to an examination of national identity. In Benedict Anderson's insightful phrase, the nation can be seen as an 'imagined community' which allows people to perceive a common bond, a shared identity with others who might be from completely different class backgrounds or geographical locations or religious groups.[2] While there can be material components (such as language) at the root of a sense of national identity, fundamentally it rests on a subjective sense of affinity. For Anderson, part of the appeal of nationalism is its ability to create this sense of community amongst people who would almost certainly never meet each other. Therefore, most nations find it useful to have symbolic markers or moments where the 'imagined community' becomes a little more concrete. In this sense, it becomes important to have opportunities in which something fundamentally subjective can gain the appearance of an objective reality. And sport is particularly adept at creating such opportunities.

Sport could be said to make the nation exist or to make the imagined community become something closer to a manifest reality.[3] Senegal's triumph over France in the opening match of the 2002 soccer World Cup finals was an important affirmation of identity for many Senegalese but it was also a means through which the country became 'known' by many non-Senegalese around the world.[4] Palestine's membership of both the International Olympic Committee (IOC) and *Fédération Internationale de Football Association* (FIFA – the sport's governing body worldwide) provides the nation with a form of international recognition, while Bosnia was admitted to membership of FIFA prior to obtaining a seat at the United Nations. Furthermore, sport provides an excellent arena for political socialization, one where 'the presence of national flags, banners, anthems and other patriotic symbols, coupled with the inherently competitive nature of sport, can transform total strangers into a unified collectivity struggling against a common adversary'.[5] Little wonder then that Bairner contends that 'sport has been one of the most valuable weapons at the disposal of nationalists'.[6]

Many countries have invested in sport in order to promote political goals. Politicians may seize on sporting triumphs and utilize them as symbols of political success while sporting failures may be seen to reflect badly on the wider nation. A further indicator of this link between sport and national identity is the way in which such things as playing styles are taken by journalists, sports pundits and others to illustrate or reflect supposed traits of 'national character'. For example, at every World Cup, the same old clichés are trotted out about 'Brazilian flair', 'German efficiency', 'typical English spirit' and 'the luck of the Irish' – even when the observable reality of team performance clearly belies the stereotype.[7] Even sports stars themselves occasionally give voice to these constructions. Commenting on the Republic of Ireland soccer team of the 1990s, former international Niall Quinn suggested that 'the sheer urgency of our play somehow contained a degree of our Irishness. We are the country of gaelic football, of hurling; we are not Holland'.[8]

Representing the nation

While much has been written on the way in which sports, and especially team sports, can be used as a surrogate representation of 'the nation' and on the linkages between sets of supporters and their outlook on national identity, one relatively neglected aspect is the perspectives of participants. While there is now a significant academic literature exploring the importance of sport in reproducing the nation, much less attention has been given to the views of international sportspeople themselves, those who could be said to embody the nation (albeit quite often only for the duration of their participation in a specific sporting event).[9] The teams themselves are often treated as relatively undifferentiated collectives, rather than as groups of individuals in their own right. The fact that each member of the team can have their own unique variation on identity has very rarely featured in academic analyses of sport. While the intersections between sport and national identity as publicly expressed by sportspeople do not often amount to much more than assertions of pride in representing the country, occasionally more explicit connections are made. The significance of a soccer match between Croatia and the 'rump' Yugoslavia in the late 1990s, following the bloody Balkans conflict, was not lost on Croatian international Davor Suker who felt that 'this is not to be regarded as just another football match . . . there are too many women in Zagreb crying over lost husbands and sons for that'.[10]

The concepts of nation, nationality and nationalism are complex and controversial and (as well as being central to many territorial disputes) continue to be the subjects of considerable academic debate.[11] Traditionally a division between ethnic and civic nationalisms has been proposed whereby a distinction is made between national affiliation in terms of birth within the boundaries of the state (civic-territorial) or through descent (ethnic-genealogical). The former is the more inclusive in terms of who can be accepted into the 'nation', but the latter can be interpreted in a more exclusive fashion – one has to be part of the appropriate ethnic community to belong to the nation. And for some nations, that exclusivity is particularly important, and is marked by a strong sense of the 'other' – a rival group or culture or nation against which one's own national identity is assumed to stand out.[12]

A growing phenomenon in international sport is the amalgamation of both civic and ethnic senses of national identity, together with other criteria such as residency. Sportspeople representing a country other than the one they were born or raised in has become a more common phenomenon. This has been particularly noticeable in soccer where shifting regulations have allowed players to represent the country of a parent or grandparent's birth. Soccer's world governing body, FIFA, decided in the early 1960s to openly accept that players could choose the nationality not just of their place of birth, but also that of their parents or grandparents. For many countries this was simply an acknowledgement of what was already happening – for example, throughout the 1930s, 1940s and 1950s Italian soccer had tapped into the large Italian-descent pool in Argentina. In some ways, the new FIFA regulations were seen as a way of bringing some degree of order to international soccer. In particular, the new rules made it clear that once footballers had played for one country, they could no longer change allegiance and play for another at a later stage. There have been a number of subsequent changes regarding eligibility, allowing players who have played non-competitive under-age games for one country to subsequently switch allegiance but, in essence, current regulations effectively permit players to play for a country whose citizenship they are eligible for whether through birth, descent or residency.[13]

Notwithstanding these regulations, the rules governing eligibility for participation in international sports are not always straightforward. FIFA have made a number of attempts to clarify the regulatory environment in relation to eligibility but their rules have lagged behind national citizenship criteria, and that creates two problems. First of all, national criteria for eligibility for citizenship vary widely from country to country, and there is no prospect for any internationally agreed set of rules. Second, national eligibility criteria have always been open to manipulation, with many countries being prepared to twist their own rules in order to attract sports stars.

It is increasingly the case that some countries rely heavily on these more flexible regulations. A number of African countries now select players from their national diasporas. In the past France was happy to choose the likes of the Ghana-born but French-raised Marcel Desailly. Indeed the multi-ethnic background of France's successful team of the late 1990s and early 2000s drew the ire of the French far right, though some comments by members of the team reflected a more progressive and complex understanding, as exemplified by Zinedine Zidane (born in Marseille to Algerian parents): 'Everyday I think about where I come from and I am still proud to be who I am: first a Kabyle from La Castellane, then an Algerian from Marseille, and then a Frenchman'.[14]

More recently players such as the French-born Frédéric Kanouté have elected to play for the country of their parent's birth (in his case – Mali). French-born players represented Benin, Côte d'Ivoire, Ghana, Guinea, Mali, Morocco, Senegal and Tunisia in the 2008 African Cup of Nations.[15] The claim to African migrants is exemplified by Nigeria's selection of Peter Odemwingie, who was born in Uzbekistan to a Nigerian father and Russian mother. Elsewhere teams like Turkey and Croatia have displayed an increasing willingness to tap into their extensive emigrant pool, while the Argentinian-born Mauro Camoranesi won a World Cup winners' medal with Italy (where his grandfather was born) in 2006. Jamaica's team in the 1998 World Cup finals and that of Trinidad and Tobago in the finals of 2006 both selected second-generation players born in Britain for their squads. As the English-born Jamaican international Robbie Earle put it, 'many exiled Jamaicans are realising their dreams through the team, and that means a lot to us'.[16]

Elsewhere, periods of residency have been the mechanism through which some sportspeople have become 'naturalized'. Two English examples are the Irish-born Ed Joyce who has played test cricket for England and the Tongan Lesley Vainikolo who was included in England's rugby union team in 2008. Elsewhere, the Brazilian-born Francileudo dos Santos has become a star of the Tunisian soccer team. The fluidity of qualification rules has also given rise to some scandals – most notably the so-called 'grannygate' affair in rugby union in 2000 when Wales selected New Zealand-born players who it transpired were not qualified to play for them. In 2004 Qatar attempted to select a number of Brazilian soccer players by granting them citizenship although they did not live in the country and had no family connection to it. From the Qatari perspective this was seen as a device to enhance their prospects of success, while for the players there was the chance of making a lot of money and gaining international recognition. One of the Brazilians involved, Ailton, was quoted as saying: 'if Brazil ignores me for 2006, then I have to find another way to get there'.[17] From a FIFA perspective this development was seen to be against the spirit of their regulations and it prompted the introduction of emergency measures to prevent players assuming a new nationality where there was no clear connection to the country concerned. FIFA acknowledged that 'from a strictly legal point of view... [a player] may assume another nationality', but went on to assert that players should not be allowed to play for a country 'for no obvious reason'. They stipulated that players must either be born in a country, have a biological parent or grandparent born in that country, or have lived continuously in that country for the previous two years.[18] The situation in respect of Qatar was deemed to be in breach of a statute of FIFA which states that an objective shall be 'to prevent all methods or practices which might jeopardise the integrity of matches or competitions or give rise to abuse of Association Football'.[19]

Interesting anomalies do occur however and the newly independent Kosovo is currently endeavouring to tempt Kosovan-born players who presently represent Albania to 'return' to play for them.[20] In other instances close relatives may find themselves representing different countries. In the 2007 rugby world cup the So'oialo brothers played for different teams, Rodney for New Zealand and Steve for Samoa. Tim Cahill, the Australian soccer international who played for Samoa at under-20 level (and who was also eligible to play for England, Scotland and Ireland) has a brother who plays for Samoa (where their mother was born). Franck Songo'o is a French under-19 international, born in Cameroon but raised mainly in France, and is the son of former Cameroon goalkeeper Jacques Songo'o. In the 2010 World Cup the Berlin-born Kevin-Prince Boateng played for Ghana against a German team which included his half brother Jérôme.

This increasingly complex scenario with regard to national representation, coupled with the international migration of soccer players and the associated increasingly multinational nature of the players in major European leagues, links into broader debates over globalization, nationalism and sport.[21] It has been characterized by some as contributing to the denationalization of sport with elements of both de-ethnicization and deterritorialization in the selection of international sportspeople who have no ethnic and/or direct territorial connection to the entity they represent.[22] This will of course depend on the specific circumstances but it is certainly the case that we are seeing a broadening and transnationalization of the pool available for countries from which to select.

Methods and sources

This paper uses the example of non-Irish-born Republic of Ireland international soccer players to explore issues of player's senses of national identity. It further explores the reactions of fans, the media and other observers to this phenomenon. It is concerned with how the players themselves respond to these multiple, conflicting notions of national identity. Do they see themselves as Irish or English or British? Are they motivated by a sense of national identity or by career or economic considerations? In order to explore these issues three types of source material were utilized. Firstly it was necessary to obtain biographical information on Irish international football players. While many internet sources are available there is also a range of useful published sources used to establish the place of birth and career details of players. In this research, biographical information on Irish international soccer players is derived mainly from three sources: McGarrigle's *The Complete Who's Who of Irish International Football 1945–96*, Ward's *Republic of Ireland: Gifted in Green* and Hayes' *The Republic of Ireland: International Football Facts*.[23] The perspectives of the players is based on stated perceptions of their identity as reflected in self-evaluations recorded in newspaper and magazine interviews and in players' 'auto' biographies. There are obvious limitations in using these as definitive sources. Books by players are generally ghostwritten and are likely to be presented in a way which will appeal to fans rather than unsettle them. Sports autobiographies in general tend to be written with a view to commercial success and, as such, are likely to reflect what fans want to hear rather than straying too far into potentially controversial territory. Nevertheless, they do provide some indication of a player's feelings. Media interviews with players can be useful source material though they tend to focus on aspects of the game, such as the player's or the team's performance, rather than their feelings of playing for Ireland. Even when players enthuse about the team, the nature of team sport is such that this reflects a team loyalty as much as an automatic identification with Ireland.

The fan responses utilized here were gleaned from a perusal of a variety of online discussion forums on soccer websites or sports sections of more general sites. There are obvious limitations to this approach. These relate to issues of reliability, selectivity, the nature of the sources and their target audience. These forums are utilized by some fans and not by others and those who participate are not necessarily representative of the broad swathes of opinion amongst Irish football fans. Nevertheless such sources do provide pointers towards issues and allow some insights into competing strands of thought with regard to player selection and eligibility.[24] They provide a flavour of the reaction to the inclusion of non-Irish-born players in the Irish team. Before proceeding with the analysis it is useful to place the discussion within the broader context of sport and national identity in Ireland.

Sport and nationalism in Ireland

The links between sport and nationalism have been played out in a particularly complex fashion in Ireland and have been discussed extensively elsewhere.[25] Irish nationalism (like any other nationalism) is a complex and multifaceted phenomenon exhibiting a wide range of perspectives and quite often contradictory narratives.[26] Central to any consideration of Irish nationalism is the fact that, until the early years of the twentieth century, the island as a whole was under British rule. Thus, Irish nationalism initially emerged as a challenge to British colonial rule. From the time of independence in 1922, the island has been divided into two distinct political entities, the Republic of Ireland, which is a fully independent state, and Northern Ireland, which is a region of the United Kingdom with devolved institutions and powers. Subsequently the 'unfinished business' of partition, has been a central issue for many nationalists.

The irredentist claim on the north is, of course, complicated by the fact that there is a large unionist community in Northern Ireland that opposes the nationalist goal of Irish unification. The tensions inherent in sport in the north of Ireland are exemplified by such things as the tendency in recent decades for many Northern Irish Catholics to support the Republic's soccer team rather than that of Northern Ireland and a loyalist death threat (which appears to have been a hoax) faced by the Catholic former Northern Ireland international Neil Lennon leading to his retirement from international soccer.[27] Indeed the relationships between national identity and sporting allegiance are particularly complex within the north, even amongst both nationalists and unionists as well as between them.[28] Irish nationalism has also had to try to negotiate between competing views of the 'other', of Britain. As Garvin argues, there is an aspect of Irish nationalism which accepts the existence of a natural affinity between the neighbouring islands, but another one which is more strongly antipathetic to Britain and British influences.[29]

A further complicating factor – and one that is crucial for this research – is that Ireland has a long history of out-migration resulting in sustained population loss through the latter half of the nineteenth century and much of the twentieth.[30] This has created a large Irish diaspora, including a very significant Irish community living in Britain.[31] It is only with the economic boom that commenced in the mid-1990s that Ireland's traditional role as a migrant-exporting country has been reversed. Ireland's president in the early 1990s, Mary Robinson, stressed the importance of seeing the Irish diaspora as part of the broader national collectivity. At roughly the same time, the 'reclaiming' of the offspring of previous generations of migrants was a policy actively pursued by the Republic of Ireland's soccer team. From the mid-1980s onwards, sons and grandsons of Irish emigrants were increasingly selected for the national team. In Poli's terms those selected could be seen to have an ethnic link to Ireland though a rather weak territorial one in that they had not lived in the country. The big challenge is that these players can also be seen to represent a link to the 'other' of Irish nationalism, to a British identity, since the identity of some Irish nationalists is at least partly conditioned by opposition to links with Britain and British identity.

Although a British colonial presence in Ireland can be traced back many hundreds of years, a key date is 1800, when an Act of Union was imposed which abolished an autonomous Irish parliament and imposed direct rule from London. Therefore, Irish nationalism developed particularly strongly throughout the nineteenth century. This was not just a political campaign; as with nationalist movements elsewhere in Europe during this time, there was a very strong cultural dimension as well. Attempts were made to revive and strengthen the Irish language, to develop a 'national' literature, to establish a 'national' theatre, and so on. Within this cultural realm, sport played a key role as an arena in which demands for a separate Irish identity could be played out.

Towards the end of the nineteenth century, a number of codes were drawn up for what were distinctive and (supposedly) historical Irish games, and a nationalist sports association, the Gaelic Athletic Association (GAA) was founded in 1884. Not only did this organization attempt to set up and run its own games, it also specifically sought to challenge what were termed 'foreign' games – in other words, games and sports that had been codified in Britain. A ban on GAA members playing 'foreign' sports or even attending them as a spectator was maintained until 1971.[32] Alongside this was a ban on Gaelic sports grounds being used for 'foreign' games, a rule temporarily suspended in 2007 to allow rugby and soccer to be played at the national stadium, Croke Park, in Dublin during the refurbishment of Lansdowne Road. The GAA still regards itself as much more than just a sporting organization, and explicitly acknowledges its contribution to an Irish national identity. The association asserts that it 'has as its basic aim the strengthening of the National Identity in a 32 County Ireland through the preservation and promotion of Gaelic Games and pastimes [and it will] actively support the Irish language, traditional Irish dancing, music, song, and other aspects of Irish culture [and] foster an awareness and love of the national ideals in the people of Ireland'.[33] Not surprisingly, GAA games are almost totally exclusive to nationalists, especially in Northern Ireland where until recently formal rules dissuaded participation by members of the Northern Irish security forces.[34] However, while the GAA has been very successful in establishing and maintaining its own games, it has been less effective in dissuading people from participating in other games.

In Ireland most international sports are organized on an all-island basis, with a single Irish team with representation drawn both from the Republic and Northern Ireland. However, that in itself masks huge variety, complexity and debate. The all-Ireland nature of the GAA represents a nationalist claim, while for sports such as rugby, hockey and cricket it represents an accommodation between two states. But even in such circumstances, the effort of accommodating Northern Irish unionists alongside nationalists from the north and from other parts of the island creates unusual stresses and strains. This complexity is evidenced by the display of separate non-political insignia to allow this accommodation. Thus, the Irish rugby union authorities commissioned a separate anthem, 'Ireland's Call'. This is used solely at matches played by the Irish rugby team, although to complicate matters further, the anthem of the Republic of Ireland, 'Amhrán na bhFiann', is still played in addition to 'Ireland's Call' at matches played in Dublin.[35] Controversy surrounded a friendly encounter between Ireland and Italy played at Ravenhill in Belfast in 2007, with calls in some unionist quarters for 'God save the Queen' to be played. In the event 'Ireland's Call' was the only anthem permitted for the team.[36] Similarly, the Irish cricket team competes under the flag of the Irish Cricket Union, thereby again avoiding offence to unionists who might have difficulty identifying with the green, white and orange tricolour of the Republic of Ireland. Perhaps some of the most complicated scenarios have emerged in relation to hockey. This is one of the few team games where a single United Kingdom team exists, albeit only for the Olympic Games. At other times, separate English, Scottish and Welsh hockey teams compete, while players from Northern Ireland can play for an all-island Irish team. This has resulted in situations where the top players from Northern Ireland have represented Ireland in World Cup competitions and the UK in the Olympics.

By way of contrast, Irish soccer is the only major game that is split between northern and southern bodies. Initially, there was an all-Ireland team and an all-Ireland association, the Irish Football Association (IFA) based in Belfast. But in 1925, shortly after Irish independence, the southern part broke away and established the Football Association of Ireland (FAI) based in Dublin. Both associations laid claim to representing soccer on a single all-island basis, and up to the 1940s they both selected players from the whole island. Thus, there are examples of players turning out for the IFA-controlled 'Ireland' in Belfast, then catching the train down to Dublin to play for the FAI-controlled 'Ireland' a few days later.[37]

In a relatively disorganized international structure, such peculiarities did not arouse too much attention. But as international soccer grew in status and importance, the game's international body, FIFA, began to impose more strict rules governing the eligibility of players for national teams. By the 1950s, the lure of participating in the FIFA-controlled World Cup meant that the IFA and FAI had to regularize their selection policies. Disputes rumbled on about which association had the right to use the name 'Ireland' – FIFA's archives in Zurich are full of letters from the IFA and FAI sniping at each other on these grounds. But it was clear that they could no longer choose the same players, and from that time more consistently differentiated Northern Ireland and Republic of Ireland teams began to emerge. More recently issues of player selection have re-emerged as some northern-born players from a nationalist background have elected to play for the Republic. The 'defection' of Derry-born Darron Gibson to the Republic in 2007 generated considerable tension between the two associations and led to FIFA intervention to adjudicate and clarify the eligibility criteria.[38]

Although both the IFA and FAI team selections have always drawn players from clubs outside Ireland due to the poorly developed state of both domestic leagues, it was only successive changes and modifications to FIFA rules that led to the recruitment of players from amongst the huge Irish-descent population in Britain.[39] The Republic of Ireland's association began to exploit what became known as the 'granny rule'. (Although the IFA have also utilized these more flexible eligibility criteria, they have used them more sparingly.) Starting in the early 1960s with Manchester-born Shay Brennan, they began to select players who had been born and bred in Britain but were of Irish origin. This approach reached its pinnacle during the 1990s, when the Republic of Ireland national team was being managed by an Englishman, Jack Charlton. This, together with the subsequent six-year reign of Mick McCarthy to 2002, was a period of heretofore unprecedented success for the Republic in soccer, featuring qualification for the finals of four major international tournaments, the European Championships in 1988 and the World Cup in 1990, 1994 and 2002. Charlton, who at his very first game in charge of the Republic had been greeted by a banner at Lansdowne Road declaring 'Go Home Union Jack', subsequently became better known as 'St Jack'.[40]

During his time in charge, Charlton used a total of 56 players, 33 of whom had been born outside Ireland. He gave 33 first 'caps' to players, 21 of whom had been born abroad. Between 1988 and 1995, the end of Charlton's reign, the Republic played 79 full internationals. On only six occasions were the majority of the team Irish-born, and on four occasions the team featured as many as 10 non-Irish-born players on the field. Non-Irish-born players formed the majority of the squads for the 1988 European finals and the 1990 and 1994 World Cup finals, while they constituted just under half of the 2002 finals squad. This heavy reliance on ancestry as an instrument in team selection led some people to refer (somewhat disparagingly) to the FAI as 'Find Another Irishman'. The result was what might be seen as something of a transnational team in the sense of the origins of the players, many of whom had never lived or played football in Ireland but who could be deemed ethnically Irish in being the sons and grandsons of Irish emigrants.

As suggested earlier, sport is an arena where the nation becomes embodied, and a great deal of significance is attached to the identities of the players. Therefore, it is well worth asking what the objects of these debates – players themselves – think and feel about their identity choices. Do they think of themselves as mercenaries, or do they have a strong sense of Irishness and patriotism, or do other considerations apply? This paper is concerned with the ways in which players have rationalized their decision to elect for Ireland and with the subsequent reactions by supporters, journalists and others to their selection.

The politics of national identity in the Irish soccer team

In this section, we explore the statements that have been made by a number of 'Anglo' players – players born and bred in Britain who have had the option of choosing to play for the Republic of Ireland. Within this it is apparent that some players express views which seem to suggest a functional or 'careerist' motivation, players who admit they chose to play for the Republic for professional reasons and whose sense of Irish identity appears somewhat weak. Second, there is a 'patriotic' strand, players whose comments suggest an affinity with Ireland that predates their decision to play for the national team. However, we need to be wary of overly simplistic generalizations and the views expressed by some players suggest an evolving sense of identity through which an initially professional motivation becomes tempered by a growing sense of Irishness.

It can certainly be argued that some players appear to have chosen to play for Ireland for professional reasons and their justification reveals little apparent allegiance to any Irish identity. The classic case, for long thought to be apocryphal but now apparently substantiated, is that of Terry Mancini, a Londoner with an Irish father, who opted to play for Ireland in the early 1970s. Standing for the national anthems before his first game for his 'new' country, Mancini wasn't impressed.

> All the pre-match ceremony seemed to go on forever. Then the music started playing and it went on and on, and I turned to Don Givens and said 'for fuck's sake, their national anthem don't half go on!' And he said 'that's ours, Terry!' I didn't have a clue![41]

To some extent Tony Cascarino appears to be another example of this position. He was born in London with Italian origins and relied on an Irish grandparent to earn qualification for the Republic of Ireland. Cascarino admits the mercenary dimension in relation to opting for Ireland and suggests he chose them 'I suppose because they chose me'.[42] In fact, it transpired that he was not a direct bloodline descendant of his Irish 'grandfather' and, although international rules were later altered to allow this, at the time Cascarino acquired his Irish passport, he does not appear to have been eligible. But this only came to light at the end of his career, during which he represented Ireland at two World Cup finals and earned a then-Irish-record number of international caps. Cascarino's own 'auto' biography is revealing in this regard. He acknowledges some genuine sense of an Irish identity saying he 'grew up with a strong sense of "Irishness" and got to know Michael [his Irish grandfather] quite well when he came to live with us'.[43] But he also admits openly 'my mum wasn't an O'Malley as I'd always believed. I didn't qualify for Ireland. I was a fraud. A fake Irishman'.[44]

A similar functional attitude can be discerned in the case of Clinton Morrison. He was born in England, but again FIFA regulations meant that he was also eligible for both the Republic of Ireland (via his grandmother) and Jamaica (where his father was from). At the time that he was pondering his international options, his agent was quoted as saying that 'as yet no approach has been made by any association ... but for the last few days, Clinton has been feeling very Irish'.[45] Morrison's own opinion reinforces this sense of a mercenary, career-based view of international soccer in which 'I could pull on an Ireland shirt and feel passionately about it because it's international football and everyone wants to play international football'.[46] Morrison subsequently elected to play for Ireland and proved a popular figure amongst supporters. In a later interview Morrison reflects on the experience, he suggests:

> it was obviously hard. I was born in England. When someone approaches from another country and asks you to go and play and all the time your heart's been set on playing for England, it's difficult. But I think this is the best decision I've made. The Irish fans have accepted me, shown me love and it feels good.[47]

Some other cases provide further evidence. One player who emerged in the late 2000s was Alex Bruce, son of Manchester United legend Steve Bruce, who was qualified to play for either association in Ireland (by virtue of an Irish grandmother) but opted for the Republic. Again, around the time he was making his decision, his attitudes show a highly career-driven outlook. He stated that he was 'very flattered that Northern Ireland and the Republic are both showing an interest in me. But I think I'm going to pick the Republic purely because I think they are a better team. That's no disrespect to Northern Ireland'.[48]

Finally, as a further illustration of the careerist side, we can add the case of Zat Knight. In 2004 Knight was touted as another who might be eligible for the Republic (through yet another Irish grandmother), even though he was born and raised in England. Again, his motivations appeared to be career-based. As it became clear that he was not really in the running for an England call-up, he began to push the possibility of playing for the Republic to a greater degree. Knight's comments were not particularly well received by many Irish fans.[49] As it transpired, Knight was never called into the Irish set-up, nor was he included in the England squad for the 2006 World Cup finals, though he has gained two caps for England in friendly internationals. It is possible that hostility or antipathy towards players such as Knight might of course be racially motivated. Allegations emerged in 2006 that black players representing Ireland had received racist mail and Knight himself claims to have received racist letters from Irish fans.[50] The extent to which the selection of British-born black players such as Morrison, Terry Phelan or Phil Babb may have contributed to a more racially tolerant conception of Irishness (or conversely solidified the racist attitudes of some) remains a matter for conjecture.

However, for each Englishman enticed to the Irish colours by the prospect of advancing their career through playing international soccer, there are others whose desire to play for the Republic of Ireland and commitment to the Irish cause appear to be far stronger. Take, for example, John Aldridge, born in Liverpool and again with a grandparent as his nearest Irish family connection. Aldridge states that 'I might have been born in England but I felt as Irish as any of the five million or so who lived in the Republic'.[51] By way of reinforcing his Irishness, Aldridge further asserts that 'among my proudest possessions is a small book which is of little monetary value ... it is my Republic of Ireland passport and it means everything to me'.[52]

Another interesting case is that of Preston-born Kevin Kilbane. Again, he was born and raised in England, but claims to have always felt a sense of affinity with Ireland. 'All my life, I'd been supporting Ireland. I still remember how special Ray Houghton's goal against England in Stuttgart was to me .... All my friends were the same, in school there were the lads who supported Ireland and the ones who supported England. It all seemed completely normal'.[53] Kilbane is particularly interesting because he had the opportunity to play for England as well, and had been called up for a training camp with the English youth team. By his own account,

> I went down and trained with England for three days but never had any intention of getting picked...my heart just wasn't in it. It's just that I always wanted to play for Ireland and no other country. My dad is from Mayo and my mum is from Waterford. So despite the way I speak I've always felt Irish.[54]

Kilbane's comments about his accent are interesting, because one of the issues for the 'Anglos' in the Irish team is how well they fit in, how well they are accepted, and their accent may render them 'different'. There is a very interesting case provided by Séamus McDonagh, who played in goal for Ireland in the 1980s. For McDonagh, born and raised in Yorkshire, his Irish name marked him out as different throughout his school days, but when he visited Ireland on family holidays, his Yorkshire accent marked him out from the kids he would meet there. There was therefore a double sense of exclusion reflecting the larger sense of 'betwixt and between' two countries and cultures felt by many Irish people (and others) in Britain.[55]

Finally, it should be noted that not all those 'Anglos' with very strong Irish cultural connections actually did choose to play for Ireland. The best example of 'one that got away' is Martin Keown, born in Oxford to Irish parents but who ended up having a distinguished international career with England in the 1990s. Keown asserts that 'when I play for England there is nobody more English than me', but also acknowledges his very strong Irish family links, admitting,

> I think I felt Irish when I was young...people have told me I'm probably more Irish than half the Irish team...I grew up in what was very much an Irish community. I had to listen to the Chieftains every Sunday morning with my cooked breakfast.

He notes how his decision to declare for England caused a frisson of family tension where he

> had a lot of relations, cousins and uncles who said to my father: 'You know, we can't believe you let him play for England'. But my dad says: 'this is the country you were born in and you make all your own decisions'.

Keown shows an awareness of the complex issues of national identity among diaspora communities where 'a generation had come over and the children, like myself, adopted the English culture'.[56] An interesting current example is Scottish-born Ryan O'Leary who, despite being closely related to two former Irish internationals (he is the son of Pierce O'Leary and nephew of David O'Leary), has recently turned down an offer of a place in an Irish under-21 squad in favour of Scotland.

So we can see that there are some players who appear to have joined the Republic of Ireland because they have a strong sense of attachment and allegiance to Ireland while others have expressed sentiments which seem to suggest more functional, career-based motivations. However, while it might be tempting to accept this binary distinction, the reality may be more complex. While the examples above seem to reflect a view of national identity and allegiance that is static, one in which individuals either think of themselves as Irish, or else acknowledge that their Irishness is a somewhat temporary, acquired identity that allows them to achieve certain professional goals, other examples suggest a relationship to Ireland and Irishness that evolves rather than being fixed.

The first example is Mick McCarthy, captain of Ireland at the 1990 World Cup and subsequently the manager who took over at the end of Jack Charlton's reign. He was born in Barnsley, the son of an Irish father. At the start of his international career, McCarthy suggests that his affinities were not indisputably Irish in that, although, 'I was aware of my

Irishness ... it wasn't my country. I wasn't born there, I lived in England all my life. But to get the opportunity to represent my dad in Ireland was brilliant'.[57] Here we can see a kind of second-hand identification through his father, but at the same time a clear sense of being English first. But as his Irish career developed, so did his attitudes change. When manager of the team at the 2002 World Cup finals, he wrote: 'We stand for *Amhrán na bhFiann*. I sing the anthem in Irish, having learned it phonetically, proud of the song, proud to sing it in our native tongue in a Yorkshire brogue'.[58]

A similar shift can be identified in Andy Townsend (born in England but with an Irish grandmother), who took over from McCarthy as captain of the Republic's team and led them to the 1994 World Cup finals in the USA. Townsend freely admits that initially, 'the thought of playing football for Ireland just didn't seem ... right'. When he was first called up for the Irish team, he felt unease as 'in my twenty-five years, I had never set foot in Ireland before and was feeling just a touch uncomfortable when our flight touched down in Dublin. Technically Irish, I was never more conscious of my Englishness and my South London accent'. But over time, something emerged so that 'the wearing of a green shirt didn't suddenly make me Irish; my affinity towards the team, the nation and its people would be a slowly evolving thing ... the more I travelled to Dublin, the more I felt at home with my new identity'.[59]

Finally, there is the example of Andy O'Brien, who perhaps provides one explanation of how and why attitudes and senses of identity can change. O'Brien is another 'Anglo' (born in Yorkshire with Irish grandparents) who, like Kevin Kilbane, had been involved in training sessions with English youth teams, and indeed played for both the Republic of Ireland and England at under-21 level before committing fully to the Republic. He declares that he

> decided to play for Ireland because I experienced both camps and I thoroughly enjoyed the Ireland camp, more than the England one. In the English camp it was colder. There was just a feeling to it that didn't feel right to me.

He contrasts that with how he felt in the Irish set-up where 'it was amazing how I felt warm in the Irish camp .... On the whole the Irish lads were more pleasant towards me'. And perhaps aware that having played for England in the past might not endear him to his new colleagues (or to the readership of an Irish newspaper) he points out 'I didn't sing the English national anthem, if that's anything'![60]

There are a number of players whose international allegiances have (at the time of writing) yet to be determined. The English-born Kevin Nolan and Dave Kitson have both been sounded out by Ireland but appear to be awaiting England call-ups. Kitson (who has an Irish grandfather) asserted in one interview that he had no wish to opt for Ireland as he felt himself to be English and players should play for their country of birth.[61] However, later he appears to have had something of a rethink and suggests 'if you want to play international football and you're eligible for two countries you have to have a serious think'.[62] This appears to a case of a player weighing up his options in a highly instrumentalist manner.

Through the examples above we can see cases of shifting identities, of players adapting, changing and developing their sense of association. While some responses may suggest a static idea of identity, many reflect a sense of multiple or hybrid identities. We can also see clearly that national identity is just one factor influencing players' attitudes. They are also susceptible to professional calculations about career choices, and by very individual and subjective factors such as how they get on with other players, and how much they enjoy their experiences.

Reactions

The selection of non-Irish-born players for the team has, over the years, prompted a variety of responses ranging from the deeply hostile, through the purely pragmatic to the openly accommodating. Some have been quick to disparage the Irish approach with (inevitably perhaps) jokes suggesting that to qualify for an Irish cap, all you needed was to have drunk a pint of Guinness or to own an Irish wolfhound. During the 1994 World Cup finals one journalist referred to the former Irish international Liam Brady as 'an unusual beast – an Irish international with an Irish accent', while during the 2002 World Cup finals a newspaper heading posed the question: 'the Irish – were they unlucky, plucky – or just a bunch of Englishmen?' and a letter writer to the same newspaper set another poser: 'these players can claim to be Irish until the cows come home, but does anyone believe them?'.[63]

Much of this reaction appears to rest on an assumption of mercenary motivations underpinning players' decisions to opt for Ireland. Indeed, the 'mercenary' tag was explicitly used by the then Northern Ireland manager Billy Bingham prior to a World Cup qualifying game between the Republic and Northern Ireland in 1993 – a game with special significance given Ireland's complex history and played against the backdrop of a particularly violent period in the Northern Irish conflict. Elements of this attitude still permeate some reactions to Irish team selection. An article in the *Guardian* newspaper by Steve Claridge in April 2007 about a promising young player – Sean St Ledger, born and bred in England but eligible to play for Ireland through one of his grandparents – threw in an aside that 'the Irish must have more grandmothers than any other nation'.[64]

More recently tensions have also emerged surrounding the decision of some players born in Northern Ireland to opt for the Republic as noted earlier. Reactions may also depend on the particular player. One player whose decision to opt for Ireland provoked particular controversy was the Glasgow-born Aiden McGeady.[65] He elected to play for the country of his grandparent's birth leading to denunciation from some sections of Scottish supporters and the media. For one Scottish supporter this was all a bit too much, 'If the wee turncoat wants to play for Ireland so much, he should be made to live there . . . Traitorous scum!'. While another asserted 'I would fucking ban him from ever entering our beautiful country ever again'. The fact that McGeady had chosen Ireland was a particular bone of contention for some who are not particularly well disposed towards Irish nationalism or territorial claims over Northern Ireland. This is exemplified in the following comment: 'if he wanted to play for Northern Ireland or Wales, I wouldn't have a problem, but he wants to play for a foreign country that didn't help us during World War 2 and supported organisations that tried to kill British people. I would take his passport from him quicker than Abu Hamza'.[66] This intense, politically related resentment was compounded by McGeady's 'defection' at a time (2004) when the fortunes of the Scottish team were at a low ebb.[67]

At one level, the reaction to these kinds of jibes in the Republic has been to take a certain delight in them. Prior to one crucial World Cup qualifying match against The Netherlands in 2001, one advertising campaign featured mock images of Irish passports for the grandparents of some of the top international soccer stars of the day, such as Zinedine Zidane, Roberto Carlos and Ronaldo. However, some reactions in Ireland echo the hostility or scepticism of external observers. A scan through online discussions reveals some Irish supporters themselves have negative reactions to the selection policy, with arguments that 'we should . . . put a stop to these mercenaries jumpin' on the bandwagon' alongside highly essentialized notions of Irishness whereby 'if you're not Irish, you shouldn't be playing for Ireland'. The idea of players' expressions of cultural affinity is seen to be important for some supporters, so that, for one, 'I'd prefer to see some fella on the pitch who sings the national anthem and means it rather than some fella who'll spend a few hours learning it as a front'. Alongside this are distinctions between different perceived degrees of Irishness so that 'If somebody has a direct link, i.e. his parents are Irish, then fair enough, but anything else is a complete joke' while another supporter does not think 'players such as Morrison or Knight [referred to above] should be allowed play for Ireland, it's different with lads whose parents are Irish or who have stayed in touch with their Irishness!' In this way some cultural awareness of their Irish origins is seen as legitimating their decision so that 'if a player is born outside of Ireland, but is of Irish parentage, and displays a *genuine* [italics added] desire to play for us, then bring them on'.

Other fans appear to adopt a more relaxed attitude, so that for one 'If they qualify for an Irish passport then they're Irish', while there are those who express a functionalist justification, in that if the player pool or the quality of Irish-born players was deep enough then 'it would be great if we had 11 born and bred Irishmen playing for the side', but in the absence of that then selecting others is justifiable. For other supporters, a purely pragmatic attitude is expressed so that 'if someone can add something to the squad, I don't give a fuck how he qualifies'.

Intriguingly there is also a school of thought that the liberal selection policy was acceptable as a means of allowing Ireland to gain initial success but that 'now we've moved on we don't need the granny rule'. This viewpoint has also been expressed by one of Ireland's leading sports journalists who suggests 'the Granny Rule served us well in the growth stages . . . but surely we should start imposing limits on ourselves now in terms of where we trawl and how deeply we fish'.[68]

These varied responses by Irish supporters reveal the impact that soccer has on shaping ideas of identity. They also suggest a wide range of attitudes from an insular view of Irishness, largely predicated on place of birth, through to a more open and accepting response that sees Irishness as something broader than being born or brought up on the island. For others the identity of the player is secondary to the pragmatic concern of the contribution they might make to the team.

Conclusions

This paper has endeavoured to cast some light on a neglected issue, that of sportspeople's senses of national identity, concentrating on the self-identification of the 'Anglo' contingent in the soccer teams of the Republic of Ireland. The paper has shown that there is a considerable degree of flexibility and fluidity in relation to senses of identity. Rather than being locked into one identity or another, people can be quite happy to swap and switch their national affiliations and therefore, to at least some degree, their own national identities. The paper has also illustrated the overlapping multiplicity of identities that can apply in such situations. Again, people can be quite comfortable with more than one sense of identity, finding an accommodation between place of birth and place of ancestry, between Britishness and Irishness, reflecting a cultural hybridity that transcends more narrowly defined accounts of national identity. The issues of identity and the 'choosing' of identity for some non-Irish-born players reflect the complexity of ethno-national and cultural identity faced by other members of minority groups in Britain and elsewhere.[69] More broadly, these insights cast further light on the multilayered, dynamic, shifting and contingent nature of social identities.

This complexity and fluidity is not just worthy of interest born of a certain curiosity value. If we accept the idea that people can think of national sports teams as embodying the nation, and the players as exemplars of national identity, then we must also accept that the individual nuances and deviations to be found amongst those players must also carry some weight for senses of identity. The fact that the Irish soccer team has been composed of players drawn from both within and outside the country, and with differing levels of connection to the country, means that it allows a much more multifaceted image of the 'embodied nation' to emerge, set within the context of broader transformations in Irish economy, society and culture.[70] Given that the Irish case is but one example of the increasing cultural hybridity of national sporting teams, it may be the case that this will continue to play an important role in nurturing more open and inclusive interpretations of nationality. Paradoxically, alongside these sporting developments, legislation in Ireland (and elsewhere) seems to be increasingly concerned with more rigidly defining and circumscribing nationality and citizenship.

We started this paper with a quotation taken from Dermot Bolger's play about Irish soccer supporters, *In High Germany*. His vision of the impact of the success of the Irish soccer team in the late 1980s is a very useful starting point for considering the current circumstances. Bolger's play highlighted how that success brought all kinds of different Irish identities together and the way that it allowed Ireland's diaspora communities to engage with an Irish identity in a way they knew and understood, reflected in second-generation support for the team.[71] This is significant from the point of view of understanding Irish identity and Irish nationalism for a number of reasons. First of all, it has created a much stronger and more balanced bond between the Irish 'homeland' and the Irish diaspora community. In the past, such bonds were maintained on the basis of the homeland exporting its culture to the diaspora, and the diaspora community being expected to cling to that culture. But the evidence from the soccer players is that the diaspora community is now in a far better position to feed the cultural experiences of their new homelands in to their Irish homeland, thereby promoting much greater integration and exchange on both sides. The Bolger play captures the way in which the Irish diaspora community had often felt left out if it did not subscribe to a limited, traditional view of Irishness. He talks about the generations of emigrants being represented by the players: 'and suddenly it seemed they had found their voice at last, that the Houghtons and McCarthys were playing for all those generations written out of history'.[72] Furthermore, it can be argued that members of a diaspora have options from which to choose. As Patrick West (himself English-born of Irish parentage) puts it: 'some of us over here in England like to feel we are Irish; some like to feel we are English; others choose, on grounds of expediency, to become technically Irish'.[73]

Furthermore, from an Irish point of view, issues of the multiplicity and variety of identities are going to become much more complicated in the near future. The rapid growth of the Irish economy over the 15 years prior to the recent crash saw large-scale migration into Ireland, reversing a trend of many years of emigration. This has led to heightened debate in Ireland over immigration, citizenship and belonging.[74] Within a sporting context, as one Irish sports columnist has pointed out, 'we are coming fast towards a time when there will be kids born and raised in Marino [a suburb of Dublin] who will be declaring to play soccer for Latvia or Lithuania or Nigeria. Good luck to them'.[75] The new multicultural Ireland is one where people with surnames likes Zurawski and Ladevicius and Mpanwa will start to appear in the green jerseys of the national team – and in the multicoloured jerseys of local GAA and soccer and rugby teams. And it is one that may also find itself having to become accustomed to seeing O'Briens, Murphys and Kellys opting to represent Poland, Lithuania or Nigeria.

Notes

[1] Bolger, 'In High Germany', 97.
[2] Anderson, *Imagined Communities.*
[3] Duke and Crolley, *Football, Nationality and the State.*
[4] In general, 'soccer' is used throughout this paper in order to distinguish the game from the specifically Irish sport of Gaelic football. However, please be aware that many of the quotations we use will still refer to 'football'.
[5] Sack and Suster, 'Soccer and Croatian Nationalism', 35.
[6] Bairner, *Sport, Nationalism, and Globalization*, 177.
[7] Crolley, Hand and Jeutter, 'Playing the Identity Card, 107–28.
[8] N. Quinn, 'Ireland are not Holland, and Kerr Must Realise This', *Guardian*, 7 October 2005.
[9] For a rare example see Tuck and Maguire, 'Making Sense'.
[10] Quoted in *The Irish Times*, 9 October 1999.
[11] See for example Gellner, *Nations and Nationalism;* Hobsbawm, *Nations and Nationalism since 1780;* Smith, *Nationalism;* Ozkirimli, *Contemporary Debates on Nationalism;* Guibernau, *Identity of Nations.*
[12] For various insights on constructions of 'nation' and 'other' see Gruffud, 'Remaking Wales'; Penrose and Jackson *Constructions of Race*; Winichakul, 'Siam Mapped'.
[13] The regulations governing 'eligibility to play for representative teams' are set out in section VII, articles 15–18 of the *FIFA Statutes* (FIFA, *FIFA Statutes*).
[14] Quoted in A. Hussey, 'ZZ Top', *Observer Sport Monthly,* April 2004. See also Dauncey and Hare, *France and the 1998 World Cup;* and Mignon, 'French Football'.
[15] See B. Oliver, 'New World Order', *Observer*, 20 January 2008.
[16] Earle and Davies, *One Love*, 108.
[17] 'FIFA Rules on Eligibility', http://news.bbc.co.uk/sport1/hi/football/africa/3523266.stm
[18] See FIFA Circular Letter no. 901, Zurich, 19 March 2004, available at http://www.fifa.com/mm/document/affederation/administration/ps_901_en_90.pdf
[19] FIFA, *FIFA Statutes,* Statute 2e.
[20] B. Andoni, 'Kosovo "Declares War" on Albania…In Sport', *The Bridge* 6, 2007. Available at http://www.bridge-mag.com/pdf/vol6/bridge06.pdf
[21] Bairner, *Sport, Nationalism, and Globalization*; Lanfranchi and Taylor, *Moving with the Ball*; McGovern, 'Globalization or Internationalisation'.
[22] Poli, 'Denationalization of Sport'.
[23] McGarrigle, *Complete Who's Who;* Ward, *Republic of Ireland;* Hayes, *Republic of Ireland.*
[24] For a discussion of the potential advantages and disadvantages of these sources see, amongst others, Millward, 'True Cosmopolitanism'.
[25] Cronin, *Sport and Nationalism in Ireland.*
[26] See for example Boyce, *Nationalism in Ireland;* MacLaughlin, *Re-Imagining the Nation-State.*
[27] Sugden and Bairner, *Sport, Sectarianism and Society*; Fulton, 'Northern Catholic Fans'; Lennon, *Man and Bhoy.*
[28] See Bairner, 'Political Unionism and Sporting Nationalism'.
[29] Garvin, *Evolution of Irish Nationalist Politics*, 149.
[30] Amongst many accounts see MacLaughlin, *Ireland.*
[31] One estimate suggests that in 1991 there were over 830,000 Irish-born people living in Britain, with of course many more second or third-generation Irish as well. Courtney, 'A Quantification of Irish Migration'.
[32] See Rouse, 'Politics of Culture and Sport'.
[33] The Gaelic Athletic Association, www.gaa.ie/.
[34] Doak, '(De)constructing Irishness; Cronin, 'Global, Parochial'.
[35] For more on the complexity of rugby and national identity in Ireland see Tuck, 'Making Sense of Emerald Commotion'.
[36] Amongst many newspaper accounts see G. Mair, 'Why it's Time to Take a Stand on Anthems', *Belfast Telegraph*, 23 August 2007.
[37] Hannigan, *Garrison Game*; Ryan, *Boys in Green.*
[38] See a series of articles by E. Malone: 'Gibson is Not One for Turning', *Irish Times*, 7 September 2007; 'Delaney Upbeat on FIFA Proposal', *Irish Times*, 7 November 2007; 'Some FIFA Members More Equal Than Others', *Irish Times*, 13 November 2007.
[39] McGovern, 'Irish Brawn Drain'.

[40] All aircraft of the national airline, Aer Lingus, are named after saints, and when the airline supplied one of its planes to fly the team home from their World Cup campaign in Italy in 1990, it was temporarily renamed 'St Jack'.

[41] Terry Mancini quoted on QPRnet.com, www.qprnet.com/interviews/mancini.shtml.

[42] Cascarino with Kimmage, *Full Time*, 16.

[43] Ibid.

[44] Ibid., 80.

[45] Neil Fewings, Clinton Morrison's agent, quoted in M. Walker, 'McCarthy Eyes Palace Striker', *Irish Times*, 13 January 2001.

[46] Clinton Morrison quoted in N. Moxley, 'Morrison Yet to Decide on Future', *Irish Times*, 27 January 2001.

[47] Quoted in B. Doogan, 'Morrison Puts Down New Roots to Strike Happy Balance', *Times Online*, 13 October 2002. Available at http://www.timesonline.co.uk/tol/sport/article1170663.ece.

[48] Quoted on www.ireland-mad.co.uk, 31 January 2006.

[49] See I. McCullough, 'Back of the Net', *Irish Post*. Available at http://www.irishabroad.com/news/irishpost/sport/Backofnet.asp.

[50] C. Lally, 'Kerr Handed Over "Vile" Racist Hate Mail to Gardai', *Irish Times*, 20 January 2006; L. O'Connor, 'Race Thugs Smash Zat's Irish Dream', *Sunday Mirror*, 10 February 2008.

[51] Aldridge with Jawad, *My Story*, 203. Of course, the population of the Republic of Ireland is lower than the 5 million mentioned by Aldridge – between 3.5 and 4 million would be a more accurate figure at that time.

[52] Ibid, 145.

[53] Kevin Kilbane quoted in E. Malone, 'Young Guns Go For It', *Irish Times*, 13 November 1999. Kilbane is referring to the winning goal scored in the Republic of Ireland's first-ever match at the finals of a major international soccer tournament, the 1988 European Championship finals in Germany. Not only was this Ireland's first such game, it was also against the 'old enemy', England.

[54] Kevin Kilbane quoted in B. Pierce, 'Kilbane Showing His True Colours', *Irish Examiner*, 17 November 1999.

[55] See Rowan, *Team that Jack Built*; West, *Beating Them*.

[56] Martin Keown, all quotes from M. Walker, 'In Defence of the Realm', *Irish Times*, 13 May 2000.

[57] Quoted in the *Irish Independent*, 24 March 2001.

[58] McCarthy with Dervan, *Ireland's World Cup 2002*, 227.

[59] All quotes from Townsend with Kimmage, *Andy's Game*, 74–8

[60] Andy O'Brien, all quotes in the *Irish Times*, 13 January 2001.

[61] See T. Humphries, 'Granny Rule is Mother of Dependency', *Irish Times*, 23 January 2006.

[62] Quoted in Ludzik, 'Kitson: I Could Answer Ireland's Call', *Irish Examiner*, 27 January 2006.

[63] White, 'Wily Waddle's Dextrous Dribble Dazzles Amid the Drivel', *Independent*, 20 June 1994; headline in the *Observer*, 23 June 2002; reader's letter in the *Observer*, 23 June 2002.

[64] S. Claridge, 'Scouting Report', *Guardian*, 3 April 2007.

[65] See D. Alexander, 'Bhoy Who Would be King', *Times Online*, 4 April 2004. Available at http://www.timesonline.co.uk/tol/sport/football/article1055553.ece.

[66] Quotes in this section taken from a range of on-line soccer forums (www.extratime.org; http://footieheads.com; http://www.pieandbovril.co.uk; http://www.spaotp.com; http://www.peoplesrepublicofcork.com). See also T. Humphries, 'Identity is a Sense of Place Not Birthplace', *Irish Times*, 10 January 2005.

[67] It is also highly probable that the more vitriolic responses emanated from supporters of Celtic's arch-rivals Rangers.

[68] T. Humphries, 'Granny Rule is Mother of Dependency', *Irish Times*, 23 January 2006.

[69] See, for example, Burdsey, 'If I Ever Play Football'.

[70] Kirby, Gibbons and Cronin, *Reinventing Ireland*.

[71] See Free, '"Angels" with Drunken Faces?'.

[72] Bolger, 'In High Germany', 97.

[73] West, *Beating Them*, 207.

[74] See special edition, *Irish Geography* 41, no 2 (2008).

[75] T. Humphries, 'Identity is a Sense of Place Not Birthplace', *The Irish Times*, 10 January 2005.

References

Aldridge, J., and H. Jawad. *My Story*. London: Hodder & Stoughton, 1999.

Anderson, B. *Imagined Communities. Reflections on the Origin and Spread of Nationalism*. Revised edition. London: Verso, 1991.

Bairner, A. 'Political Unionism and Sporting Nationalism: An Examination of the Relationship Between Sport and National Identity Within the Ulster Unionist Tradition'. *Identities: Global Studies in Culture and Power* 10 (2003): 517–35.

Bairner, A. *Sport, Nationalism, and Globalization: European and North American Perspectives*. Albany: State University of New York Press, 2001.

Bolger, D. 'In High Germany'. In *A Dublin Quartet*. Harmondsworth: Penguin, 1992.

Boyce, D.G. *Nationalism in Ireland*. 3rd edition. London: Routledge, 1995.

Burdsey, D. '"If I Ever Play Football, Dad, Can I Play for England or India?": British Asians, Sport and Diasporic National Identities'. *Sociology* 40, no. 1 (2006): 11–28.

Cascarino, T., with P. Kimmage. *Full Time: The Secret Life of Tony Cascarino*. London: Simon and Schuster, 2000.

Courtney, D. 'A Quantification of Irish Migration with Particular Emphasis on the 1980s and 1990s'. In *The Irish Diaspora*, edited by Andy Bielenberg, 287–316. Harlow: Longman, 2000.

Crolley, L., D. Hand, and R. Jeutter. 'Playing the Identity Card: Stereotypes in European Football'. *Soccer & Society* 1, no. 2 (2000): 107–28.

Cronin, M. 'Global, parochial, Still Anti-Imperialist and Irish'. *Peace Review* 11, no. 4 (1999): 517–22.

Cronin, M. *Sport and Nationalism in Ireland: Gaelic Games, Soccer and Irish Identity since 1884*. Dublin: Four Courts Press, 1999.

Dauncey, H. and Hare, G., eds. *France and the 1998 World Cup: The National Impact of a World Sporting Event*. London: Frank Cass, 1999.

Doak, R. '(De)constructing Irishness in the 1990s – the Gaelic Athletic Association and Cultural Nationalist Discourse Reconsidered'. *Irish Journal of Sociology* 8, no. 1 (1998): 25–48.

Duke, V., and L. Crolley. *Football Nationality and the State*. London: Addison Wesley Longman, 1996.

Earle, R., and D. Davies. *One Love: The Reggae Boyz: An Incredible Soccer Journey*. London: Andre Deutsch, 1999.

FIFA. *FIFA Statutes: Regulations Governing the Application of the Statutes*. Zurich: FIFA, 2008. Available at http://www.fifa.com/mm/document/affederation/administration/01/09/75/14/fifa_statutes_072008_en.pdf.

Free, M. '"Angels" with Drunken Faces? Travelling Republic of Ireland Supporters and the Construction of Irish Migrant Identity in England'. In *Fanatics! Power, Identity and Fandom in Football*, edited by A. Brown, 219–32. London and New York: Routledge, 1998.

Fulton, G. 'Northern Catholic Fans of the Republic of Ireland Soccer Team'. In *Sport and the Irish. Histories, Identities, Issues*, edited by A. Bairner, 140–56. Dublin: University College Dublin Press, 2005.

Garvin, T. *The Evolution of Irish Nationalist Politics*. Dublin: Gill and Macmillan, 1981.

Gellner, E. *Nations and Nationalism*. Oxford: Blackwell, 1983.

Gruffud, P. 'Remaking Wales: Nation-Building and the Geographical Imagination, 1925–50'. *Political Geography* 14, no. 3 (1995): 219–39.

Guibernau, M. *The Identity of Nations*. Cambridge: Polity Press, 2007.

Hannigan, D. *The Garrison Game: The State of Irish Football*. Edinburgh: Mainstream Publishing, 1998.

Hayes, D. *The Republic of Ireland: International Football Facts*. Cork: Collins Press, 2008.

Hobsbawm, E.J. *Nations and Nationalism since 1780: Programme, Myth, Reality*. Cambridge: Cambridge University Press, 1990.

Kirby, P., L. Gibbons, and M. Cronin, eds. *Reinventing Ireland: Culture, Society and the Global Economy*. London: Pluto Press, 2002.

Lanfranchi, P., and M. Taylor. *Moving with the Ball: The Migration of Professional Footballers*. Oxford: Berg, 2001.

Lennon, N. *Man and Bhoy*. London: HarperSport, 2006.

McCarthy, M., and C. Dervan. *Ireland's World Cup 2002*. London: Simon and Schuster, 2002.

McGarrigle, S. *The Complete Who's Who of Irish International Football 1945–96*. Edinburgh: Mainstream Publishing, 1996.

McGovern, P. 'Globalization or Internationalisation: Foreign Footballers in the English League, 1946–95'. *Sociology* 36, no. 1 (2002): 23–42.

McGovern, P. 'The Irish Brawn Drain: English League Clubs and Irish Footballers, 1946–1995'. *British Journal of Sociology* 51, no. 3 (2000): 401–18.

MacLaughlin, J. *Ireland: The Emigrant Nursery and the World Economy.* Cork: Cork University Press, 1994.

MacLaughlin, J. *Re-Imagining the Nation-state: The Contested Terrains of Nation-building.* London: Pluto Press, 2001.

Mignon, P. 'French Football After the 1998 World Cup: The State and the Modernity of Football'. In *Football Culture: Local Contests, Global Visions*, edited by G.P.T. Finn and R. Giulianotti, 230–55. London: Frank Cass, 2000.

Millward, P. 'True Cosmopolitanism or Notional Acceptance of Non-National Players in English Football: Or, Why "Bloody Foreigners" Get Blamed When "Things Go Wrong"'. *Sport in Society* 10, no. 4 (2007): 601–22.

Ozkirimli, U. *Contemporary Debates on Nationalism: A Critical Engagement.* Basingstoke: Palgrave Macmillan, 2005.

Penrose, J., and P. Jackson. *Constructions of Race, Place and Nation.* London: UCL Press, 1993.

Poli, R. 'The Denationalization of Sport: De-ethnicization of the Nation and Identity Deterritorialization'. *Sport in Society* 10, no. 4 (2007): 646–61.

Rouse, P. 'The Politics of Culture and Sport in Ireland: A History of the G.A.A. Ban on Foreign Games, 1884–1971'. *International Journal of the History of Sport* 10, no. 3 (1993): 333–60.

Rowan, P. *The Team that Jack Built.* Edinburgh: Mainstream, 1994.

Ryan, S. *The Boys in Green. The FAI International Story.* Edinburgh: Mainstream Publishing, 1997.

Sack, A.L., and Z. Suster. 'Soccer and Croatian Nationalism: A Prelude to War'. *Journal of Sport and Social Issues* 24, no. 3 (2000): 305–20.

Smith, A.D. *Nationalism: Theory, Ideology, History.* Cambridge: Polity Press, 2001.

Sugden, J., and A. Bairner. *Sport, Sectarianism and Society in a Divided Ireland.* London: Leicester University Press, 1993.

Townsend, A., with P. Kimmage. *Andy's Game: The Inside Story of the World Cup.* London: Stanley Paul, 1994.

Tuck, J. 'Making Sense of Emerald Commotion: Rugby Union, National Identity and Ireland'. *Identities: Global Studies in Culture and Power* 10, no. 4 (2003): 495–515.

Tuck, J., and J. Maguire. 'Making Sense of Global Patriot Games: Rugby Players' Perceptions of National Identity Politics'. *Football Studies* 2, no. 1 (1999): 26–54.

Ward, A. *Republic of Ireland: Gifted in Green.* London: Hamlyn, 1999.

West, P. *Beating Them at their Own Game: How the Irish Conquered English Soccer.* Dublin: Liberties, 2006.

Winichakul, T. 'Siam Mapped: The Making of Thai Nationhood'. *The Ecologist* 26, no. 5 (1996): 215–21.

Never forget you're Welsh: the role of sport as a political device in post-devolution Wales

Russell Holden

Director, In the Zone Sport and Politics Consultancy

This paper considers the role of sport in post-devolution Wales in terms of how an important policy concern that permeates a range of government portfolios has operated in an environment where the notion of 'Othering' has given way to the advance of neo-liberal ideas in the way in which sport is perceived by policymakers. This is achieved through a discussion of four elements of Welsh sport: the opening of Cardiff's Millennium Stadium, the significance of the Welsh contribution to the 2005 Ashes victory, the continued playing of Welsh baseball and the attention given to the successful Welsh participants at the Olympic and Paralympic Games in 2008, with particular reference to the victory celebrations which followed the homecoming of the Welsh athletes. However, throughout the discussion it is regularly acknowledged that much of Welsh sport is framed within the context of Britishness.

Introduction

The display and projection of identity (local, regional and national) is a characteristic central to all sporting contests. However, with sport so tightly interwoven with political questions concerning finance, health, identity and national well-being, sport emerges as a critical policy tool at the disposal of politicians. As Polley remarks, sport does not function in either a socioeconomic or political-cultural vacuum.[1]

This discussion considers the impact of how sport is utilized in policy terms in Wales and whether it has altered in the context of the dynamics of Welsh politics as prescribed in the devolution process and constitutional settlement laid down in the Government of Wales Act 1998. This is not, however, an assessment of the effectiveness of the roles of the ministers who have had responsibility for managing and developing sport in Wales.

Sport and the Welsh

For small states and stateless nations such as Wales, sport has long provided an 'avenue for self-esteem and external recognition'.[2] It is both a creative and reflexive force. The rich cultural and political traditions of Wales, from the Eisteddfod, religious non-conformism, male-voice choirs, and its distinct language, provide expressions of national pride that also speak of geographic, political and ethnic pluralities.[3] However, sport has been a central tenet in inventing, maintaining and projecting the idea of a single Welsh identity in and outside its blurred borders. It has helped gloss over the different meanings that the people of Wales attach to their nationality, enabling them to assert their Welshness in the face of internal division and the all-encompassing shadow of England.[4] With players and spectators united in song, colour and contest, sport provides an ideal vehicle to express a singular (constructed) identity of a nation unified, distinct and special.[5] In Hoberman's oft-repeated truism, the 'imagined community' feels more real when manifest through a national team, be it of 11, 13 or 15 personnel.[6]

No more so was this expressed than in the famous 1905 victory of Wales over New Zealand in rugby union.[7] Halting a string of defeats for the home nations, Wales beat the world's best rugby nation (albeit in controversial circumstances) heralding combative displays of a (racialized) cultural nationalism in the press. For instance, the editorial of the *South Wales Daily News* triumphed:

> These men – these heroes of many victories that represented Wales embodied the best manhood of the race.... We all know the racial qualities that made Wales supreme on Saturday.... 'Gallant little Wales' has produced sons of strong determination, invincible stamina, resolute, mentally keen, physically sound.[8]

The surprising victory highlighted not only the pluck and determination of the Celt, the fact that a small nation could take on the big boy(o)s, but also projected a modern identity for Wales. The victory is etched on Welsh sporting memory and is always recalled at every home Wales–New Zealand encounter. The victory of a small nation reaping unexpected success (Welsh sport had never scaled such heights previously) against all odds was a message that Wales was, and remains, happy to project. Further, it cemented within Welsh culture an idea that sporting success could also play critical social functions of generating and sustaining community well-being and promoting social integration. For instance, it is important not to overlook the fact that the team was heavily reliant on the contribution of immigrants. Wales was showing itself willing to embrace outsiders, and rugby was an agent of acculturation, incorporating outsiders into an: 'idealized notion of a socially integrated Welsh nation'.[9] This tradition has continued in the post-1998 era, with the successful Grand Slam side of 2008 coached by a New Zealander, assisted by an Englishman and Welshman, whilst an English elite performance director took overall control of the development of Welsh rugby in 2008.

The links between sport and nationalism have been fertile grounds for the academic study of sport politics. Sport plays a pivotal role in the evolution and consolidation of civil society, provides symbolic resources that sustain a community's sense of itself – a national identity – and a form of identification against others, providing the social glue that brings individuals and communities together and a resource upon which to draw upon for political claim.[10] As Hoberman reminds us, a nation's sporting stature, which often exceeds its political stature, creates a fantasy place in which competition can produce miracles on the level field of play.[11] This may even help in eroding a country's historical inferiority complex.[12] It can, of course, spawn: 'fantasies of national grandeur, xenophobia and triumphalist celebrations that appear to be cathartic releases of popular emotion'.[13] These are dramatic reactions and for the Welsh nation they have only been relevant in respect of rugby union, and even then, only the expression of triumphalism has been evident with respect to victory over England.[14]

As Jarvie maintains, the promotion of national identity and the symbolism of sport are very closely connected; whilst Jackson valuably takes the analysis further, arguing that sport has long served as a critical source of collective identification and remains one of the most powerful and visible symbols of national identity and nationalism as proven in Wales.[15] Since the advent of the 1998 Government of Wales Act, the process of redefining Welsh identity has speeded up. This has occurred within the dual context of the continuing accommodation of the notion of 'Otherness' and the burdgeoning neo-liberal government agenda of New Labour. However, the reality of sport in Wales is yet more complex because of the desire in some sports to happily accept Wales's Britishness (aside from those sports that have their own existing Welsh administrative structures).

As Morgan and Pritchard comment, notions of conflict, foreignness and 'Otherness' have defined Wales and the Welsh both historically and culturally.[16] Wales's relationship with England has been pivotal in this process, as one of the defining characteristics of the Welsh is the sharing of a common ethnic boundary. Furthermore, the 1536 Act of Union defined Wales's lack of political independence and the incorporation of Wales into the English state resulted in the attempt to eradicate the Welsh language, the most obvious symbol of a culturally distinct country. As Rose notes, this helped not only to define Wales and the Welsh but also England and the English through the process of 'Othering'.[17]

Yet the significance of 'Otherness', beyond the merely symbolic, has been dampened by the process of devolution and the realization of Wales' lack of economic strength coupled with its persistently underperforming economy. As far back as 2005, the Welsh Assembly Government (WAG) acknowledged that Wales lagged behind the rest of the United Kingdom in terms of economic activity rates and income levels and, furthermore, possessed some of the most economically deprived areas in the whole of Europe.[18] However, the collective and community solidarity evident in Wales contributed to the Welsh Labour Party attempting to mark out a distinctive policy path in line with the traditions that Wales had long cherished. This resulted in the Welsh Labour Party advocating 'Clear Red Water', to emphasize its independence of thought from the rest of the Party in the United Kingdom.[19] This was attempted with its references to radicalism and collectivism. Yet, the reality of the WAG policy approach has not been particularly different to its English counterpart. For instance, when it came to celebrating Olympic achievement Rhodri Morgan was selling Wales in the US, seeking to secure investment for Wales's post-industrial economy, duly adhering to neo-liberal tenets. Although Wales has had a greater immediate challenge since 1998 in seeking to resist or temper the forces of neo-liberalism as a central plank of economic thinking and government strategy because of the limited powers granted, Wales has sought to project itself through a range of popular cultural spheres with sport as one of the key aspects of this strategy.[20] In so doing neo-liberal thinking has featured prominently in WAG thinking as Wales has striven to gain some form of renewed economic strength.

The limitations of the devolution settlement coupled with the lack of a burning desire for Wales to extricate itself from the continuing existence of the UK sporting umbrella and the Olympic movement (where an emphasis on Welsh achievement is played out in the political and media spheres) there is no major objection to being wrapped within the Union flag. Wales and Welsh individuals are content, in the most part, to reconcile themselves with Wales's Britishness, Welsh cricket has benefited from integration with, rather than separateness from England, hence the support for the England cricket team throughout the successful 2005 Ashes campaign, whilst selection for the British and Irish Lions has long been deemed as the pinnacle of achievement for many Welsh rugby union players.

Sport has been a central tenet in inventing, maintaining and projecting the idea of a single Welsh identity in and outside its blurred borders. It has helped gloss over the different meanings that the people of Wales attach to their nationality, enabling them to assert their Welshness in the face of internal division and the all-encompassing shadow of England.[21] Although rugby has immense financial impact on the Welsh economy if only in terms of the revenues generated on International days, Welsh politicians with a measure of increased decision-making power need to think about the commercial gains to be made from other sports and how these can be linked into developments such as tourism, retailing, heritage and entertainment.[22] In generating economic strength using sport as a catalyst the WAG is linked into what Stead refers to as a 'Performance Culture', in which energy is channelled via enterprise and excellence through sport as well as the arts. This generates positive publicity and external recognition.[23]

This paper therefore considers sport in post-devolution Wales in terms of a movement from an 'othering' to a neo-liberalized policy environment. This is achieved through a discussion of four elements of Welsh sport: the opening of Cardiff's Millennium Stadium, the significance of the Welsh contribution to the 2005 Ashes victory, the continued playing of Welsh baseball and the attention given to the successful Welsh participants at the Olympic and Paralympic Games in 2008, with particular reference to the victory celebrations which followed the homecoming of the Welsh athletes. Although Royles argues that Wales is less dependent on sport to express its identity since 1999, as it now possesses a set of new political institutions, this analysis will argue that this fails to acknowledge the significance of sport to everyday existence.[24] It also ignores the fact that political institutions need to interact with a range of interest and consumer groups in the construction, delivery and review of policy. Rather, this analysis subscribes to Redeker's claim that sport should be viewed as a significant historical development permeating societies at all levels.[25] In Wales this extends beyond the confines of rugby, which, for many, continues to be the pre-eminent sporting interest as International match days always illustrate, to a modern sporting infrastructure of a new political and economic arrangement.

Impetus for the discourse

The essence of this study proceeds from the theoretical standpoint that nations are historically specific geographic constructions. What follows is also based on the principle that national identity is shaped very considerably in Wales by sporting achievement and prowess. Nations are consciously created and temporally specific social products that emerge from power struggles between various social classes and ethnic groups as complex, composite, negotiated entities that project the imagery of homogeneity and unity, all the while constantly being challenged, reformulated and reworked. They are, in essence, particularly modern structures that came to prominence in conjunction with the emergence of industrial capitalism and the mass media in western Europe and the United States. These developments allowed diverse and often spatially disparate populations to conceive of themselves as belonging to some larger entity through the sharing of an historical past, present interests and a mutually beneficial future. Thenceforth, the making and remaking of Welsh identity was, and continues to be, made up of a number of complementary and competitive discourses that influence and shape the imagined entity that is Welshness.

Whilst creating this social fact, the construction and reproduction of the nation is an ongoing process in which connections are forged and broken, as the flow of social and political debate informs the power struggle over what it means to be Welsh. The notion is not a natural outcome of some biological or inherent capacity of the people who presently call themselves Welsh. Rather, contemporary Welshness is taken to be a culmination and combination of various historical, political, economic and social factors that unite to form a construct identifying the majority of people living in a small region of Britain as being Welsh. Sport is central to this evolution as it is a critical component of both the mass media and popular culture: hence the importance attached to how success is portrayed in cultural terms with respect to identity and the political process. This is a reality that the subsequent examples will prove.

Devolution

As Bogdanor remarks, devolution is an explicitly constitutional act, which involves: 'the transfer to a subordinate electoral body, on a geographical basis, of functions at present exercised by ministers and Parliament'.[26]

Although the pro-devolution swing between 1979 and 1997 was greater in Wales than Scotland, the pro-devolutionists only secured a wafer-thin majority. As Wyn-Jones suggests, the devolutionists 'got lucky'.[27] Their advantage was secured through an alignment of factors – a popular government at Westminster, an opposition in Wales that was wiped out at the 1997 general election, a determined Secretary of State and the benefit of the Welsh vote following on from the Scottish referendum. Wales was thus the recipient of New Labour's desire to placate Scottish nationalism which, as Day suggests, carried Wales along with it, albeit within a context of Britishness.[28] However, the Welsh pro-devolutionists lacked the advantages of a more complex civil society (no separate legal framework, limited educational autonomy and a weak media framework) in the struggle to advance their case as compared to Scotland.[29]

Bradbury comments that the hallmark of devolution is legislative decentralization, be it of primary legislative powers or of secondary powers.[30] In the case of Wales, the latter has applied, with the contents of the 1998 Act based on a series of proposals developed by the Welsh Labour Party between 1992 and 1997 under the direction of Ron Davies, Labour's then Shadow Secretary of State for Wales. Although the settlement was more limited than that provided for Scotland because of Wales's historical limitations as a distinctive political arena, the arrangements put in place for the founding of the Assembly and the devolving of powers to it were innovative. As Day Dunkerley and Thompson comment:

> the devolution of decision-making powers to the National Assembly for Wales signifies political recognition of the distinctiveness of Wales as a place that merits independent representation, which has its own voice and its own problems and concerns. In other words, it is accepted as forming a distinct, though not totally separate society.[31]

However, the process towards devolution in Wales was different to the Scottish experience. Whereas in Scotland pressure for change was essentially attributable to bottom-up political forces, in Wales the process was driven more overtly by the New Labour project.[32] Ron Davies, Secretary of State for Wales, was fortunate in being able to cash in on the Scottish momentum as he lacked the support of a distinctive Welsh civil society, as that which existed had been constructed and nurtured within the context of Britishness.

Powers were delegated to the National Assembly as a corporate body rather than to ministers as mere representatives of the Crown. The Assembly would delegate its powers to secretaries (later ministers) but it retained the legal responsibility for decisions carried out in its name. More significant, however, was the rhetoric of 'new politics' which accompanied the process – this pointed towards greater cross-party working and the possibility of coalition administrations, a development which has come to pass. (As the legislation progressed at Westminster, the bill was amended to include provision for a Cabinet composed of Assembly secretaries in order to provide executive leadership). The Assembly was also granted the right to formulate Wales-only bills and bid for Westminster parliamentary time to have them enacted, thus empowering the Assembly in specified areas. This confirmed (with other developments) that Welsh devolution was to be a process rather than an event.

The theoretical significance of the powers (as opposed to the reality) devolved to the National Assembly tends to be underrated. The secondary powers granted included responsibility for the NHS, education and lifelong learning, economic development, environmental policy and a wide range of social justice, arts and cultural matters including sport and recreation. The settlement provided for the transfer of powers previously under the remit of the Welsh Office and the Secretary of State for Wales to the National Assembly. In governmental terms, sport is lodged under the auspices of the Ministry for Heritage. Yet, in possessing a First Secretary, Rhodri Morgan (for the bulk of the period since 1999), who is genuinely interested in sport, the overburdened ministerial brief of the Heritage Minister, Alun Fred Jones and his predecessors, has been aided, as the First Secretary seeks to promote the profile of Wales whilst attracting visitors and benefits for sporting and Welsh cultural organizations. Whenever possible, the First Secretary has helped to place sport (as opposed to rugby alone) in a more central role in national life, in which the high performance of athletes is not the primary concern.

However, the role of Heritage Minister does resemble that of his English counterpart running the Department of Culture, Media and Sport. Although appearing outwardly glamorous, the brief is too wide and needs rethinking as the minister has too many competing demands on his time and budget. As the National Assembly consolidates, some considered reflection on the nature of this role would be useful as both the minister and the WAG could then play an even more valuable role than it currently undertakes. Thus, as will be demonstrated, the devolution settlement creates new opportunities for national promotion. The new political institutions have helped to spur sporting ambition, fund elite athletes via the Sports Council for Wales, as well as promote increasing participation in the effort to boost national and international recognition in addition to improved health.

Although the potential role of sport as a positive contributor to national well-being is not altered by the process of devolution, the central concern to both politicians and academics seeking to understand the importance of sport to society in national terms is to see sport in the context of an evolving identity moulded by globalization, which is forever shaping and reshaping identities in the twenty-first century.[33] This presents a considerable challenge to a set of decision-makers who, by their Welshness, should be more in tune with the needs of the national population. Sport thus remains key to Wales and the Welsh nation; however, sport is now being projected with a sense of coherence (aided by the cooperation between the WAG Cabinet members) facilitated by the new political institutions in place, and the broad consensus that exists between the political parties and permanent officials that are responsible for the governance of the nation. Yet finance remains a problem and WAG's capacity to respond to both financial pressures and to resist Westminster inspired neo-liberal measures is hampered by its denial of tax raising powers.

Having inherited responsibility for this policy area from the Welsh Office, the WAG, through its succession of Ministers, has preferred to offer pronouncements of encouragement to Welsh sportspersons and sporting initiatives through collaborative programmes whilst ensuring that much of the critical work with respect to sport policy and administration is undertaken by the Sports Council for Wales, which the WAG funds. This is illustrated in the WAG's 2005 document; 'the Assembly Government is totally committed to bringing sport and physical acts from a peripheral part of our administration to centre stage'.[34] As early as 2002, the Culture Minister Jenny Randerson (Liberal Democrat), declared that her aim was to maximize the role of sport in Wales, whilst acknowledging that sport already helps address key issues such as health and the economy.[35]

At the heart of the WAG's philosophy regarding sport has been the dual aim of developing mass participation whilst working towards systematic success in international competition; though as the then Culture Secretary, Alun Pugh admitted, this was no easy task.[36] The 2005 Strategy for Sport entitled 'Climbing Higher' underlined a wish to move sport and physical activity from a peripheral part of government to a more central role. This document sought to build on the previous strategy 'Creative Future'.[37] The reality is that sport has not stood separate from other aspects of government, as the WAG has sought to facilitate links between sports and a range of ministerial portfolios. This is substantiated by the evidence of cross-cutting departmental activity involving economic regeneration, health and social justice portfolios in particular.

Devolution is a project that New Labour was happy to take on as it linked with the concept of modernization, very much at the heart of the New Labour project dating back to Kinnock's overhaul of economic and European policy.[38] It represented a clear strand of modernization which, as Day notes, was intended to deliver more effective and responsive government; bringing decision-making wherever possible closer to the people, thus applying the concept of subsidiarity.[39] This legitimized New Labour's readiness to concede to demands for a greater recognition of national and regional interests within an evolving United Kingdom. The approach also theoretically empowered the people. But, as Mooney and Williams remark, this strand of domestic modernization has to be couched in terms of globalization and europeanization (Wales has been highly successful in attracting funds from the European Regional Development Fund).[40] Devolution was thus central to New Labour's willingness to accommodate demands for increased recognition of national and regional interests within the United Kingdom as a means of seeking to retain the unity of the nation. What this also did was to erode the notion of 'Otherness' whilst providing Westminster with the capacity to extend the tentacles of neo-liberalism as a response to the failings of previous Labour governments in their efforts to boost economic prosperity. This was of course far more achieveable for New Labour with its main opposition party weak at Westminster and absent from governing coalitions in both Wales and Scotland. However, in granting limited powers to the National Assembly, WAG's potential power was curtailed and the desire for greater political control was quashed was deferred in the short term.

In charting change by using a set of major sporting events as illustrations, coupled with the establishment of a critical historical context, the conclusion reached is that the awareness of the place and recognition of the importance of sport has grown, with the role of the WAG as that of a facilitator of political and commercial decisions. However, to develop the discussion further it is now necessary to examine the historical context and the sporting development events identified earlier as key to the analysis. Although rugby will be mentioned in subsequent sections, as it is vital to any discussion on the role of sport in post-industrial Wales as a tool of soft cultural policy, a more complete picture is required and this is gained by extending the discussion to incorporate sports from a wider range of activity undertaken across the nation.

Opening of the Millennium Stadium

The construction and opening on schedule, and within budget, of the Millennium Stadium for the International Rugby Board Rugby World Cup in 1999 provided a clear statement of Wales's ability to play a pivotal role in a major global sporting event. At the same time, this development acknowledged that rugby was not the sole sporting pastime of the Welsh. Wales was now branding itself as a nation of sport, not one entirely based on rugby union, with subsequent usage of the stadium by a range of sports including speedway, cricket, football, rugby league and rallying. Without this facility Wales would not have been one of the main hosts of the 1999 tournament and would not have provided the venue for the opening game, six other matches and the final. Much of this hinged on the redevelopment of Cardiff Arms Park and its role in the process of securing funding from the National Lottery. Furthermore, the stadium's location, in the heart of Cardiff's city centre, demonstrated that the venue was an attempt to redefine and re-present the City of Cardiff in addition to the Welsh nation. The marketing video accompanying the opening of the stadium incorporated both traditional Welsh scenes and a strong musical dimension that projected vibrancy.[41] The very nature of the construction was significant with a revolutionary retractable roof as one of its chief characteristics – a post-modern facility in a city geared to increasing revenue on non-match days and the development of a site geared more to consumption and tourism, for the dedicated and casual sport enthusiast.[42] For Cardiff City Council it marked a key step in the effort to regenerate the city, an ideal that lay behind the unsuccessful bid to host the Commonwealth Games in 1986.[43] The purpose-built stadium was deemed to demonstrate a new Wales; although the construction project pre-dates the devolution settlement, much of the preparatory work was being planned and undertaken whilst the political tide was turning. The emergence of the stadium and the broad consensus concerning its value has to be seen in terms of the changing political climate from the late 1980s onwards.

The 1999 Rugby World Cup delivered something very valuable in cultural and sporting terms and marked the start of sports fans' annual pilgrimages to Wales. In many instances this was for the first time, as the stadium managed to capture that most English of institutions the FA Cup competition, whilst the new Wembley stadium was under construction and suffering inordinate delay to its completion. Wales, and Cardiff in particular, were now deemed attractive venues and this was central to the renewal and revitalizing of a nation following a period of economic decline. Furthermore, the projection of the stadium by the international media did much to alert many to the possibilities of greater recognition on the international scene of a small nation. The new stadium represented a symbol of hope, progress and pride.[44] Cardiff's shortlisting as one of the contenders for the European City of Sport Award in 2009 is testament to the changing fortunes of the city.[45] However, as Harris notes, with sport becoming ever more internationalized, the visibility of the capital city will increase, with the possibility that this will lead to Cardiff: 'moving away from its Welsh identity and ... becoming even more of a city beyond the nation'.[46]

Wales and the 2005 Ashes success

Although Wales was unsuccessful in its efforts to win the Rugby World Cup in 1999, thus making any form of celebration redundant, in 2005 there was a significant Welsh contribution to the Ashes victory, yet those involved of Welsh descent did not have the chance to celebrate their success in Cardiff.

Whilst contriving not just to create one culture, sport has given voice to a set of distinct local and regional identities. However, in the case of cricket there has always been a keen interest throughout Wales, yet the history of the development of the game reveals that enthusiasm for the sport was primarily in the south of the country. The game represents the oldest of all modern sports played in Wales with its first recorded game held in Cwmgwilli in 1783. Prior to that point it had existed as an unorganized folk-game.[47]

During the 2005 Ashes series, the Welsh playing representatives, Simon Jones and Geraint Jones, were supplemented by a clutch of coaches and administrators and a support structure with a substantial Welsh flavour. At the apex of this structure was the full-time coach Duncan Fletcher (who coached Glamorgan – in effect a national side – to the County Championship in 1997). He was supported by a Welsh assistant coach Matthew Maynard; David Morgan as Chairperson of the EWCB: the former Glamorgan and England opening batsman Hugh Morris as Deputy Chief Executive of the EWCB and Dean Conway as Team England physiotherapist.

The Welsh dimension was extended with the late appearance of Glamorgan bowler and journeyman Darren Thomas as a fielding substitute in the Fourth Test Match. The decision to call for extra Welsh support came from the assistant coach and former Glamorgan player Matthew Maynard, as he realized that Thomas's athletic fielding would be an asset to England.[48] Even more critical was the discovery of a unique bowling machine conceived by 71-year-old property investor Henry Pryor, and his cricket writer son, Matthew, on the Welsh side of Offa's Dyke.[49] They perfected Merlyn, the first bowling machine to serve up both spin and swerve, and which could be programmed to any particular series of deliveries. This assisted England players in their preparation to counter the twin threats of Shane Warne and Brett Lee. Following successful testing at the National Cricket Centre at the University of Loughborough, Merlyn was fully integrated into England's plans.[50]

Although the contributions of Simon and Geraint Jones are measurable in terms of raw statistics, the exact role of the others named is more difficult to ascertain but should not be underestimated, especially in terms of the stability the coach and key administrators at the EWCB provided. However, the critical issues for this analysis are whether the Ashes victory altered the focus of Welsh sporting interest and why the success was not more strongly celebrated. The success of cricket in Wales had been galvanized by the upturn in fortunes of Glamorgan between 1997 and 2004 and buoyed further by a Welsh victory over England in a one-day international at Sophia Gardens in Cardiff in 2002. The victorious team was in effect a Glamorgan side including players from other counties, in addition to Jacques Kallis, the South African batsman and former Glamorgan player. (This side was also totally separate from that representing Wales in the Minor Counties Championship Western Division.) In seeking to publicize the victory, Plaid Cymru MP Adam Price requested an Early Day Motion in the House of Commons on 24 June 2002. This motion (which was not upheld), supported by MPs from outside Wales, acknowledged the contribution of Wales to cricket and called on Wales to be given national status in the cricketing world. Mohammed Ashgar, the former Plaid Cymru AM, has recently rekindled this issue by suggesting that it is time to establish a full national side for Wales; however, the WAG has responded by remarking that this is an issue for the governing bodies of cricket to resolve.[51]

On the playing front, since the 2005 Ashes series, the combination of injury problems to Simon Jones and the loss of form of Geraint Jones meant that the immediate public reference points were undermined. However, the victory, when set alongside the success of the Welsh Rugby team in securing both the Six Nations Championship and the Grand Slam the previous March, helped to foster a renewed sense of sporting prowess. The level of interest in the Ashes series was strong, particularly in terms of Welsh media, notably in the press and on the radio, with BBC Radio Wales providing regular updates in both English and Welsh. According to Channel 4 viewing figures, the Welsh audience represented up to 12% of the total United Kingdom viewing audience compared with 5% of viewing figures for Test cricket in 2003.[52]

Despite cricket not being on a par with either football or rugby in terms of visibility and mass participation, the game, as a consequence of England's heroics against Australia, was starting to stir interest within Wales. When this was coupled with the campaign to gain test-match status for the Sophia Gardens county venue, with the backing of Cardiff City Council and the WAG, it became evident that by securing international cricket for Wales, more revenue would be generated by Glamorgan and also by the City of Cardiff. Furthermore, this tied in with the WAG's cultural agenda and money was made available to help in bidding for a 2009 Ashes Test Match, much to the chagrin of a number of rival bidders in England.[53]

Although there was a school of thought amongst England-based cricket writers that the securing of the Ashes victory was connected to what Brenkley refers to as the annexation of English cricket by the Welsh (with Lin Tatham, former Head of the Sports Council for Wales, acting as Chair of the EWCB Ground Inspection Team), Brenkley overlooked the fact that the EWCB has a governing board of 12 on which only two Welsh members sit.[54] Yet, as David Hopps notes, the decision to award Sophia Gardens test-match status was based on what the EWCB have described as a balanced scorecard.[55] This gave equal weight to spectator convenience, player facilities and commercial benefits. Thus, what appeared to happen was that the Welsh contribution to the Ashes success generated more interest and controversy beyond Offa's Dyke than on the Welsh side. In Wales, little was made of the victory beyond the adulation heaped on the 'Jones Boys' and the public awareness of the wider role of Welsh personnel was limited as the Welsh sporting media soon returned its attention to rugby and football. Within cricketing circles however, the victory provided the launch pad for the plan to redevelop Sophia Gardens and the WAG was soon part of the process in helping to bring another sporting mega event to Wales.

The Welsh dimension in British cricket was recognized nationally with the creation of the EWCB, though the impact of the 'W' has been limited to the extent that the England players' kit has no semblance of Welshness, such as a dragon or daffodil motif. During the 2005 Ashes Series the team even adopted the hymn 'Jerusalem' as its anthem (which had previously been adopted as the official anthem of the English football team in 2000), much to the chagrin of David Morgan, the EWCB Chairperson.[56] The fact that such a nationalistic piece of music was chosen indicates that Englishness was being heavily promoted and the 'W' was once more being drowned out.

This Ashes series posed a number of difficult questions for long-standing and new cricket fans in terms of whether they supported the whole of the England team, the Welsh personnel, or even Australia, as no affinity existed with England or the EWCB as long as the W was neglected. Most Welshmen would never dream of representing England: in fact, supporting England in football or rugby (inspite of the fact that playing for the British Lions represents the pinnacle of achievement for many rugby players in Wales) may be deemed as traitorous. However, this does not apply to cricket as the game has offered the opportunity to play for one's country) and, according to Robert Croft, the former Test player and ex-Glamorgan captain, the equivalent of the British Lions, as in his eyes, playing for Glamorgan implied representing Wales.[57] This begs the question whether it is because cricket has never really fired the Celtic imagination, even with Ireland's recent success in the 2007 Cricket World Cup, or whether it is because those individuals who want to play at the highest level have no option, as Basini suggests, but to play for England.[58]

Furthermore, Welsh cricket has been content to merge its identity with that of England, (which to a large extent explains the lack of a major public celebration for the Welsh participants) to the extent that Wales is part of the EWCB. The debate as to whether this is appropriate was played out in the *Western Mail* during late August and early September 2005, and the conclusions reached by a range of contributors (utilizing established and new media forms) regarding allegiance were based on pure pragmatism and contrasting notions of Welsh identity. However, for the WAG, the priority was not one of internal naval-gazing, but of utilizing cricketing success for potential lucrative commercial spin-offs which would impact on members of the public that had no interest in cricket in the short-to-medium term. This was one of the key messages being conveyed by the 2005 WAG 'Climbing Higher' strategy.

Welsh baseball

Baseball has a long tradition within Wales but its geographical reach is limited. The game combines elements of American baseball, cricket and rounders, with its origins stretching back in Wales to the early bat-and-ball games of previous centuries. Baseball was formalized in Wales in 1892 with the establishment of the Welsh Baseball Union. In 1908 the first international match between England and Wales was staged with the Welsh team drawing on players from South Wales and Liverpool as these two areas had developed strong supporting local infrastructures of amateur clubs, yet in these localities there was not a sense of uniformity in rules with the American version.[59]

Baseball in Wales represents something of an anomaly. During 2008 the Welsh and English Baseball Unions played a special game to mark the centenary of international contests between the two nations. Yet this contest, and the sport overall, receives little attention today aside from brief match reports in the south-east Wales press, notably the *South Wales Echo* and the *South Wales Argus*. This continues, despite the efforts of Paul Flynn MP (one of Wales's most active politicians) to publicize the sport via his website and his attempt to secure an Early Day Motion in the House of Commons (19 July 2008) to mark the British Baseball Centenary.[60]

The sport was always perceived as the artisan sport in comparison to cricket, which was growing in prominence at the same time as the emergence of baseball, yet it failed to capture the imagination of the nation. The sport lacked the equivalent of a Highland Games and was therefore unable to incorporate itself into the national psyche and the Welsh diaspora. As a consequence the game has suffered and moved into a state of decline with an ageing profile.

Baseball clubs became critical institutions in terms of the development of social hubs, helping to draw communities together, notably in times of severe economic hardship when participation rates were affected by the inability to pay subscriptions, yet the game was associated with the working class and lacked a strong financial underpinning, unlike cricket.

As class consciousness, albeit non-political in nature, developed during the twentieth century, the perception of baseball as a poor-man's cricket served to undermine interest in the game. When coupled with the advent of suburbanization, baseball's position was weakening – yet it remained a constant in its strongholds. However, in parts of Cardiff where the game was strongest there were areas that possessed a strong Irish element which was not well integrated into urban life; this generated some unease, turning some away from the sport as the Irish minority found it difficult to develop sporting bonds with its fellow citizens beyond its ethnic and class barriers. Thus baseball's growth was inhibited by the cleavages of class and ethnicity that permeated city life.[61] With no real hope of successful development in rural Wales, much depended on the efforts to extend the game beyond the confines of the south east of the country. Yet a combination of poor playing standards and scant press attention hindered its development, whilst cricket was also making inroads in the limited proportion of the Welsh population that participated in sport. Public authorities were not well disposed to a sport that required a large playing area and many existing playing fields were just too small.

Despite these obstacles, the game has continued and a certain pride exists in its ability to survive irrespective of its unwillingness to establish the American code, the ageing profile of supporters and, most critically of all, the wider realities of economics and power.[62] The hybrid nature of the game has made the sport harder to sell, yet in a perverse way this represents its strength as a distinctive Welsh pastime. However, despite its community feel, which it has shared with rugby (although this is being eroded through the franchise system that has created four super clubs), and its high female participation rate, the game is disadvantaged by the fact that its season is short and it overlaps increasingly with football and rugby which means that some of its participants are lost when the winter games commence.[63] The lack of a contemporary sporting icon has also hampered the sport's development and made it less attractive to both sponsors and the WAG which does not see a return on possible investment at grass-roots level.

Victory celebrations

Carefully choreographed and formally organized occasions have become something of a phenomenon of the twenty-first century, starting with the 2003 parade for the England rugby team following its victory in the Rugby World Cup; though processions of winning teams through ecstatic city-centre crowds is not a new development. An estimated 100,000 people took to the streets to welcome the Cardiff City team in 1927 after their FA Cup victory. Welsh athletes played their part in the London 'Parade of Heroes' celebration marking the achievement of British participants at the 2008 Olympic and Paralympic Games however, the atmosphere was not as febrile as for the Ashes Parade.[64]

For Wales, public celebrations beyond those marking the success of the national rugby side have been non-existent. There are two possible explanations for this: firstly, a lack of success, particularly in team sports, and secondly the fact that Welsh sporting achievement has often been under the banner of a United Kingdom team. Although the EWCB had indicated a willingness for an Ashes celebration to be staged in Cardiff, this did not transpire. Despite many words of praise from Welsh politicians, there was an underlying contentment to bask in the reflected glory of the Trafalgar Square parade as it was acknowledged that separating Welsh cricket from the EWCB would damage the sport in Wales as the finances would not be available to provide expert coaching and to attract top class players.[65] The distinction between Englishness and Welshness is a particularly sensitive one from the Welsh perspective because of the interrelated histories of the two nations. While both nations are part of the larger British identity (even though Wales is not represented in the Union flag), the power relations between the two regions of Britain have never historically been in favour of the Welsh, except on the rugby field, and not always then. The last three decades have been a sporting drought for the Welsh, on a team, if not on an individual, basis.

However, in 2008, the situation was different despite the fact that Welsh Olympic and Paralympic success was achieved once more under a United Kingdom banner. As both Olympic gold medallist Lyn Davies and Nigel Walker, the former Olympic hurdler and Welsh rugby international noted, the level of Welsh performance attained certainly surpassed all expectations.[66] More importantly, however, the parade marked a longing to celebrate the success a small nation can achieve. Although politicians were again quick to celebrate the athletes' achievements, First Minister Rhodri Morgan missed the Cardiff Bay celebrations marking the homecoming of Welsh athletes, choosing to devote additional time to canvassing support for external investment into Wales on the back of his visit to the 2008 Ryder Cup in Kentucky as part of the preparation for the 2010 event to be staged in

Wales. The celebration did not represent political grandstanding, but rather an expression of a nation climbing out of its years of despondency. Wales supplied 6% of the Paralympics team and contributed 20% of the gold medals.[67] The adulation, however, is tinged with irony, as the Welsh role in the organization of the 2012 Olympics is limited despite the last minute pressure exerted by the WAG, which was rebuffed by Lord Coe.[68] Wales's chief role will be to provide the training facilities for the Australian Paralympics squad.

The outpouring of public emotion needs to be separated from any thorough assessment of the WAG handling of sport; however, it will no doubt inspire many to engage in sport at both a social and professional level. If a public celebration has a wider dimension than merely 'feeling good' as we wave at sporting high achievers on open-topped buses, it does project and document images that inspire, which can lead to concrete progress if adequate funding is available for facilities and high-level coaching. Now that Wales is firmly positioned as a leading sporting venue, with great opportunities availing themselves via cricket and golf in 2009 and 2010, the next stage is for politicians and sport administrators to consolidate progress, move beyond populism and utilize sport even more as a key mechanism for 'joined up government'.[69]

Discussion and concluding remarks

The recent sporting policy examples referred to in previous sections indicate a sense of purpose evident in post-1998 strategy. However, the limitations of devolution coupled with the strength of New Labour at Westminster and the underlying policy consensus, which may only now be changing as a consequence of the April 2009 budget statement, have shown that neo-liberal tendencies have been to the fore. These have reduced the impact of the notion of 'Otherness' which had long scarred Welsh political and social history.

Welsh identity has continued to evolve with sport (not just rugby) and the opening of the Millennium.Stadium not only created a post-modern venue at the heart of Wales's capital city, but revealed a capacity on behalf of the Welsh nation to create a spectacular stadium which opened the city and the nation to outsiders to a far greater degree than previously. The venue has a clear commercial arm and this has shown how neo-liberal thinking could be made more palatable to a society previously glued to the notions of collectivism, radicalism, solidarity and non-conformity. This choice has ruled out the option of placing a heavy emphasis on investing in cultural memories and myths – an elite project of nationalism. Yet the heritage industry is certainly happy to cash on the sporting past when it is deemed relevant, particularly if it boosts tourism or Stead's notion of 'Performance Culture'.[70]

However, the concentration on substantial investment has led some to maintain that the new identity that has emerged is too heavily based on metropolitan Cardiff, thus indicating that the benefits of devolution have not permeated the nation as they should have with Swansea and Newport benefiting far less than Cardiff.[71] In addition, with the capital city as the chief beneficiary, an image of Wales has evolved in which the traditional strength of the public sector has diminished in favour of the constant desire to generate income through the tapping of private-sector sources. Yet, in the case of Newport, the 2010 Ryder Cup will provide a major opportunity for renewal and dynamism. In working towards establishing a competitive advantage for Wales based on a clearer identity, sport has played a key role in placing Wales in the global market. This is a choice in line with the thinking in the policy document *Wales: A Better Country*.[72] In choosing to invest in a commercialized sporting infrastructure, the rationale is that this will create a positive globalized identity.

Small nations require sporting and cultural success to help them gain and sustain self-confidence. Since the 1998 Government of Wales Act, it is possible to trace a growth in Welsh self-belief and pride in sport and cultural spheres as part of the emergence of a post-industrial economy. Although substantial elements of Welsh sport remains rooted in a British context, one can detect a growing assertiveness to claim sporting events. Thus, as the Institute of Welsh Affairs (David, 2005) declares, in terms of attracting major sporting events, Wales now punches above its weight. These successes must also be seen in terms of commercial acumen and the realization of the benefits that can be brought to individuals, communities and local economies, thus helping regeneration and providing employment as well as sporting opportunities. Equally, it is possible to detect how the Welsh nation has grasped the wider link between sport and a range of policy issues and priorities which are at the heart of forging new opportunities for a potentially healthier population; yet positive, identifiable and creative social benefits are needed from 2009 and 2010 as the London Olympics offers far less obvious gains as well as substantial costs for the people of Wales.[73] This constitutes a tough challenge for administrators, the WAG, National Assembly and, in particular, the Heritage Minister who, in each instance, must understand the concepts of collaboration and cooperation as sport remains a key agent in the construction and reshaping of national identity and national well-being.

Although the 1998 legislation has granted an opportunity for more national self-expression, the realities of post-1998 Welsh politics have demonstrated a wider and more rounded understanding of sport. Sport has not been at the forefront of the political struggle for the granting of greater powers to the National Assembly and neither does it represent a sizeable chunk of the WAG budget; but it has seeped into a wide range of WAG policy decisions and it has played an important role in the continuing evolution of national identity. Furthermore, devolution has stimulated discourse in a range of spheres including national identity, citizenship, belonging, ethnicity and inequality; and remains a dynamic and contested process whilst acting as a vehicle for the expression of national sentiment during a period in which Wales has begun to appreciate the vast range of benefits to society that sport can offer, whilst excelling in a range of sports, notably at the individual rather than the team level.

Notes

[1] Polley, *Moving the Goalposts*.

[2] Johnes, *A History of Sport*, 106.

[3] Williams, *Rugby Union in Sport*.

[4] Johnes, *A History of Sport*.

[5] Holt, *Sport and the British,* 237; Jarvie and Reid, 'Scottish Sport'.

[6] Hoberman, 'Sportive Nationalism and Globalization'; see also Anderson, *Imagined Communities*.

[7] Williams, *1905 and All That*.

[8] Cited in Johnes, *A History of Sport*, 31.

[9] Williams, *1905 and All That*, 85.

[10] Bairner, *Sport and the Irish*; Cronin, *Sport and Nationalism;* Jarvie, 'Sport, Nationalism and Cultural Affinity'.

[11] Hoberman, 'Sportive Nationalism and Globalization'.

[12] Andrews, 'Welsh Indigenous!'.

[13] Hoberman, 'Sportive Nationalism and Globalization', 185.

[14] This was manifest in the lyrics of the Welsh rock band The Stereophonics, 'As long as we beat the English we don't care'. This line was used as a trailer by BBC Wales for their coverage of the Six Nations Rugby tournament.

[15] Jarvie, *Sport, Culture and Society*, 115; Jackson and Haigh, 'Between and Beyond Politics'.

[16] Morgan and Pritchard, 'Culture, Identity'.

[17] Rose cited in Morgan and Pritchard, 'Culture, Identity', 10; and, referred to by Colley, *Britons*.

18 Welsh Assembly Government, *Wales: A Vibrant Economy.*
19 Mooney and Williams, 'Forging New "Ways of Life"?'.
20 Harris, 'Match Day in Cardiff'.
21 Johnes, 'Poor Man's Cricket'.
22 Sales data from SA Brains, the Cardiff-based brewers, show that in 2008 sales of Brains beers on a weekend when Wales played in Cardiff increased by an average of 100%.
23 Stead, 'I Was There'.
24 Royles, *Revitalising Democracy.*
25 Redeker, 'Sport as an Opiate'.
26 Bogdanor, *Devolution,* 2.
27 Wyn-Jones, 'In the Shadow of 1979'.
28 Day, 'Chasing the Dragon?'.
29 Grant, 'Cutting Scotland Loose', 252.
30 Bradbury, *Development.*
31 Day, Dunkerley and Thompson, 'Evaluating the "New Politics"', 25.
32 Ibid.
33 Harris, 'Match Day in Cardiff'.
34 Welsh Assembly Government, *Wales: A Vibrant Economy* 5.
35 Welsh Assembly Government, press release, 27 February 2003.
36 Welsh Assembly Government, *Wales: A Vibrant Economy.*
37 Welsh Assembly Government, *Wales: A Better Country.*
38 Holden, 'Labour's Transformation'; Holden, *Making of New Labour's European Policy.*
39 Day, 'Chasing the Dragon?'.
40 Mooney and Williams, 'Forging New "Ways of Life"?'.
41 Johnes, *A History of Sport.*
42 Harris, 'Match Day in Cardiff'.
43 Cardiff Council Leader Russell Goodway, *Western Mail*, 15 May 1996. His sentiments have been echoed by his successors.
44 R. Goodway, 'Western Mail Survey', *Western Mail*, 15 May 1996.
45 R. Houdmont, 'Selling Wales Through Sport Success', *Western Mail*, 14 May 2008.
46 Harris, 'Match Day in Cardiff', 309.
47 Hignell, *A Favourite Game.*
48 BBC Radio Wales, 'Over the Boundary'.
49 Engel, *Wisden Cricketers' Almanack.*
50 The bowling machine was christened Merlyn by its originators as a tribute to the Welsh wizard of the same name.
51 *Wisden Cricket Monthly,* November 2008.
52 S. Burson, 'Ashes Fever Sweeps Wales', *Western Mail*, 25 August 2005. *Western Mail*, 25 August 2005.
53 For further detail see, Welsh Assembly Government, *Strategy for Sport.*
54 S. Brenkley, 'Cricket: Giving Wales an Ashes Test is Not Cricket', *Independent*, 21 April 2006.
55 D. Hopps, 'Why Choose Cardiff?', *Guardian*, 22 April 2006.
56 BBC Wales, 31 December 2005.
57 Johnes, 'Poor Man's Cricket'.
58 M. Basini, 'Why It Is Okay to Shout for Our England', *Western Mail*, 13 August 2005.
59 Johnes, 'Poor Man's Cricket'.
60 Paul Flynn's commitment to baseball is detailed on his personal website, www.paulflynnmp.co.uk.
61 Weltch, 'British Baseball'.
62 Ibid.; Johnes, 'Poor Man's Cricket'.
63 Johnes, 'Poor Man's Cricket'.
64 J. White, 'Britain Salutes the Golden Generation', *Daily Telegraph*, 17 October 2008. *Daily Telegraph*, 17 October 2008.
65 Many senior Welsh politicians based at the National Assembly issued statements congratulating the efforts of the Welsh Olympians.
66 See *Western Mail*, 23 August 2008, for further comment from Nigel Walker, and Lyn Davies comment in more depth on the successful Welsh Olympic campaign.
67 Roberts-Young, 'A Good Haul'.

[68] *South Wales Echo*, 1 July 2008. Lord Coe firmly rebuffed last minute attempts by the WAG to reconsider using more Welsh venues for the 2012 Olympic Games.

[69] The Ryder Cup will be the largest-ever sporting event to be hosted by Wales with respect to international media coverage and the income anticipated from the competition and its associated merchandizing.

[70] Stead, 'I Was There'.

[71] Harris, 'Match Day in Cardiff'.

[72] Welsh Assembly Government, *Wales: A Better Country*.

[73] Welsh Assembly Government, *Strategy for Sport*.

References

Anderson, B. *Imagined Communities: Reflections on the Origin and Spread of Nationalism*. London: Verso, 1983.

Andrews, D.L. 'Welsh Indigenous! and British Imperial? – Welsh Rugby, Culture, and Society 1890–1914'. *Journal of Sport History* 18, no. 3 (1991): 335–49.

Bairner, A.E.S., ed. *Sport and the Irish: Histories, Identities, Issues*. Dublin: University College Dublin Press, 2005.

BBC Radio Wales. 'Over the Boundary: Wales and the 2005 Ashes'. 31 December 2005.

Bradbury, J. *Development: The UK Experience*. London: Routledge, 2008.

Bogdanor, V. *Devolution in the United Kingdom*. Oxford: Oxford University Press, 1999.

Colley, L. *Britons: Forging the Nation, 1707–1837*. London: Pimlico, 1992.

Cronin, M. *Sport and Nationalism in Ireland: Gaelic Games, Soccer and Irish Identity since 1884*. Dublin: Four Courts Press, 1999.

David, R., ed. *Sport and Economic Regeneration: Measuring and Maximising the Benefits for Wales*. Cardiff: Institute of Welsh Affairs, 2005.

Day, G. 'Chasing the Dragon? Devolution and the Ambiguities of Civil Society in Wales'. *Critical Social Policy* 26 (2006): 642–55.

Day, G., D. Dunkerley, and A. Thompson. 'Evaluating the "New Politics": Civil Society and the Welsh Assembly for Wales'. *Public Policy & Administration* 5, no. 2 (2000): 25–45.

Engel, M., ed. *Wisden Cricketers' Almanack*. Alton: John Wisden & Co, 2006.

Grant, W. 'Cutting Scotland Loose: A Southern Briton's Response to Preston'. *British Journal of Politics and International Relations* 11, no. 2 (2009): 352–5.

Harris, J. 'Match Day in Cardiff: (Re) imaging and (Re)imagining the Nation'. *Journal of Sport and Tourism* 13, no. 4 (2008): 297–313.

Hignell, A. *A Favourite Game*. Cardiff: University of Wales Press, 1992.

Hoberman, J. 'Sportive Nationalism and Globalization'. In *Post Olympism? Questioning Sport in the 21st Century*, edited by J. Bale and M. Christiansen, 177–96. Oxford: Berg, 2004.

Holden, R. 'Labour's Transformation: The European Dynamic'. *Politics* 19, no. 2 (1999): 103–8.

Holden, R. *The Making of New Labour's European Policy*. Basingstoke: Palgrave, 2002.

Holt, R. *Sport and the British: A Modern History*. Oxford: Oxford University Press, 1989.

Jackson, S., and S. Haigh. 'Between and Beyond Politics: Sport and Foreign Policy in a Globalizing World'. *Sport in Society* 11, no. 4 (2008): 349–58.

Jarvie, G. *Sport, Culture and Society*. Abingdon: Routledge, 2006.

Jarvie, G. 'Sport, Nationalism and Cultural Affinity'. In *The Changing Politics of Sport*, edited by L. Allison, 58–83. Manchester: Manchester University Press, 1993.

Jarvie, G., and I.A. Reid. 'Scottish Sport, Nationalist Politics and Culture'. *Sport in Society* 2, no. 2 (1999): 22–43.

Johnes, M. *A History of Sport in Wales*. Cardiff: University of Wales, 2005.

Johnes, M. '"Poor Man's Cricket": Baseball, Class and Community in South Wales 1880–1950'. *The International Journal of the History of Sport* 17, no. 4 (2000): 153–66.

Livingstone, T. 'What Happened When Wales Won the Ashes'. *Western Mail*, 22 April 2006.

Mooney, G., and C. Williams. 'Forging New "Ways of Life"? Social Policy and Nation-Building in Devolved Scotland and Wales'. *Critical Social Policy* 26, no. 3 (2006): 608–29.

Morgan, N.J., and A. Pritchard. 'Culture, Identity and Tourism Representation: Marketing Cymru or Wales?'. *Tourism Management* 22 (2001): 167–79.

Polley, M. *Moving the Goalposts: A History of Sport and Society Since 1945*. Abingdon: Routledge, 1998.

Redeker, R. 'Sport as an Opiate of International Relations: The Myth and Illusion of Sport as a Tool of Foreign Diplomacy'. *Sport in Society* 11, no. 4 (2008): 494–500.

Roberts-Young, D. 'A Good Haul'. *Planet* 191 (Aberystwyth) 2008.

Royles, E. *Revitalising Democracy: Devolution and Civil Society in Wales*. Cardiff: University of Wales Press, 2007.

Stead, P. 'I Was There'. *Agenda*, Summer 2008. Cardiff: Institute of Welsh Affairs.

Welsh Assembly Government. *Strategy for Sport and Physical Activity: 'Climbing Higher'*. Cardiff: WAG, 2005.

Welsh Assembly Government. *Wales: A Better Country*. Cardiff: WAG, 2003.

Welsh Assembly Government. *Wales: A Vibrant Economy*. Cardiff: WAG, 2005.

Weltch, A. 'British Baseball: How a Curious Version of the Game Survives in Parts of England and Wales'. *The National Pastime* (2008): 30–4.

Williams, G. *1905 and All That*. Llandysul: Gomer, 1991.

Williams, G. *Rugby Union in Sport in Britain: A Social History*. Cambridge: Cambridge University Press, 1989.

Wyn Jones, R. 'In the Shadow of 1979'. *Planet* Spring (2009): 6–15.

Index